Teaching Phonics & Word Study
in the Intermediate Grades

2nd Edition
Updated & Revised

Wiley Blevins

New York • Toronto • London • Auckland • Sydney
Mexico City • New Delhi • Hong Kong

Dedication

*I dedicate this book to the memory of Jeanne Chall.
She taught me. She guided me. She inspired me.*

Photos ©: cover: Jan Von Holleben/Trunk Archive; 12: racorn/Shutterstock, Inc.; 46: monkeybusinessimages/
iStockphoto; 57: Monashee Frantz/Getty Images; 66: Christopher Futcher/iStockphoto; 220: kali9/iStockphoto;
223: Monkey Business Images/Shutterstock, Inc.; 245: author; 311: Christopher Futcher/iStockphoto;
312: MoMo Productionsz/Getty Images; 315: Steve Debenport/iStockphoto.

Cover Design: Tannaz Fassihi
Interior Design: Maria Lilja

ISBN: 978-1-338-11348-8

Copyright © 2017 by Wiley Blevins. All rights reserved. Printed in the U.S.A.

6 7 8 9 10   40   22 21

Table of Contents

What Is Phonics?

"At one magical instant in your early childhood, the page of a book—that string of confused, alien ciphers—shivered into meaning. Words spoke to you, gave up their secrets; at that moment, whole universes opened. You became, irrevocably, a reader."

—Alberto Manguel

It was almost midnight. The crowd outside the brightly lit building grew restless as the clock inched toward the eagerly awaited hour. Children clutched their parents' hands as the doors to the building slowly opened. As the crowd crammed into the building, onlookers stared in amazement. What awaited this breathless crowd wasn't a television star, a movie premiere, or the release of a new toy; rather, it was a book—the fourth in a series about a little boy named Harry Potter. These children (and adults) illustrate the power of books. For months they had been captivated by the promise of another tale about the adventures of a much-loved character. Indeed, they were so transported into this boy's magical world that they were prepared to tackle a 734-page novel with twists and turns unlike any they had previously read. Oh, the joys of reading!

All children deserve the promise that books hold. Whether they transport us to another world, make us laugh or cry, teach us something new, or introduce us to people we wouldn't otherwise meet, we are thankful for their gifts. In turn, all children deserve the gift of reading. And as educators, we bear the responsibility and honor of delivering that gift.

As teachers of intermediate grade children, your students come to you with a wide range of reading skills and ability levels. Some have mastered most of the skills they'll need to decode and comprehend more complex text; others still struggle with the most basic and critical skills. Your task—and challenge—is to prepare each of these students for the demands of texts filled with new and long words and complex ideas.

All children deserve the gift of reading. And as educators, we bear the responsibility and honor of delivering that gift.

Each year millions of teachers enter classrooms across our nation (and the world) facing this same challenge. They must make key decisions as they wrestle with how best to help their students improve their reading skills and develop a love of books. This guidebook is designed to help you, the intermediate grades teacher, better understand our unique and sometimes complex language and use that knowledge to improve and expand your students' reading skills. Its focus is on **advanced phonics**. Phonics involves the relationship between sounds and their spellings. Advanced phonics builds on the skills taught in the primary grades (e.g., consonants, short vowels, silent *e*) and enables students to read multisyllabic words with often complex vowel and syllabication patterns. It also includes the study of structural analysis (prefixes, suffixes, roots) and fluency. As you explore advanced phonics, your students will gain insights into our fascinating language, get excited about words, and become fluent readers. You'll help them develop a passion for books and an understanding of how books can provide pleasure and information.

The first edition of this book was published over fifteen years ago. Since then I have continued my study and exploration of advanced phonics, how best it's taught, and the common obstacles that stand in the way of teachers delivering the most effective instruction to maximize student learning. I have conducted research on topics such as using decodable text and developing fluency, and written numerous phonics instructional programs (including adaptive technology systems). I have observed countless teachers offering instruction of the sound-spelling system of our language, worked with district administrators to select and monitor instructional delivery, and analyzed almost all curricular materials produced in the last two decades. I've also delved into advances made through current reading studies, including promising brain research. This edition is a reflection of that new learning on advanced phonics, and it is my hope that it will help you fine-tune your instruction for increased student achievement. With the reading demands on our intermediate level students increasing (e.g., exposure to more complex texts, new and challenging assessments), learning how to tackle multisyllabic words to aid in decoding and focusing on word parts to build vocabulary are essential for their success. It is my hope that this resource will provide some of the tools you need to help these students. Enjoy!

Phonics: A Definition

According to a 2014 survey conducted by Scholastic, 71% of parents identified strong reading skills as the most important skill their child needed to have. Teachers have also identified reading as the most important skill for children to learn in national polls conducted by the American Federation of Teachers (AFT); recent polls by the AFT demonstrate the importance teachers place on the new reading standards (2013).

With such agreement on the importance of reading, what should be the primary goals of reading instruction? The following goals are often cited:

1. automatic word recognition (fluency)
2. comprehension of text
3. development of a love of literature and a desire to read

The first of these goals—automatic word recognition— is the primary focus of this book. To become skilled readers, students must be able to identify words quickly and accurately. And to do that, they must be proficient at decoding words. Decoding words involves converting the printed word into spoken language. A reader decodes a word by sounding it out, using structural analysis and syllabication techniques, or recognizing the word by sight. In order to sound out words, a reader must be able to associate a specific spelling with a specific sound. Phonics involves this relationship between sounds and their spellings.

Phonics is not a specific teaching method. In fact, there are many ways to teach phonics. However, what most types of phonics instruction have in common is that they focus on the teaching of sound-spelling relationships so that the reader can come up with an approximate pronunciation of a word and then check it against his or her oral vocabulary.

Approximately 84% of English words are phonetically regular. Therefore, teaching the most common sound-spelling relationships in English is extremely useful to readers. As Anderson, Heibert, Scott, & Wilkinson (1985) write, "English is an alphabetic language in which there are consistent, though not entirely predictable, relationships between letters and sounds. When children learn these relationships well, most of the words in their spoken language become accessible to them when they see them in print. When this happens, children are said to have 'broken the code.'"

One of the arguments against teaching phonics is that the approximately 16% of so-called **irregular** English words appear with the greatest frequency in text (about 80% of the time). As you will discover throughout this book, these words are not as irregular as they may seem. Although they must be taught as **sight words**, the reader has to pay attention to their spelling patterns in order to store them in his or her memory. Some detractors of teaching phonics also contend that reading develops in the same way as speaking—naturally. Foorman (1998) responds by saying "humans are biologically specialized to produce language and have done so for nearly one million years. Such is not the case with reading and writing. If it were, there would not be illiterate children in the world."

Clearly then, most children need instruction in learning to read. One of the critical early hurdles in reading instruction is helping children grasp the alphabetic principle. That is, in order to read, children must understand that this series of symbols we call the alphabet maps out the sounds of our language in roughly predictable ways. This alphabetic principle is a key insight into early reading. And it enables children to get off to a quick start in relating sounds to spellings and thereby decoding words.

Phonics in the Intermediate Grades: What and Why

Once children grasp the alphabetic principle and learn the most common sound-spellings they meet in primary grade texts, their next hurdle involves decoding multisyllabic words. Some older students find it extremely difficult to read these words. They can't recognize common spelling patterns or larger chunks of the words that may help in sounding them out. And many more of the words in the books they're now reading are new to them, are not in their speaking or listening vocabularies. Discovering the meanings of these unfamiliar words is critical to understanding the text. Learning advanced phonics skills helps. For example, one important aid in determining a word's meaning is understanding prefixes and roots, as there are significant differences between "relevant" and "irrelevant," "play" and "playful."

Comprehension is certainly the most important part of reading. But how does the ability to decode words help a reader understand a text? The flow chart on page 10 illustrates that strong decoding ability is necessary for reading comprehension.

However, this is not the only skill a reader needs to make meaning from text. When they read, children need to be able to use three cueing systems. These systems represent signals in text that interact and overlap to help the reader understand what he or she is reading.

1. **Graphophonic cues** involve a reader's knowledge of sound-spelling relationships. Phonics instruction helps children to use these cues.

2. **Syntactic cues** involve a reader's knowledge of the grammar or structure of language. These cues do not help children sound out words. Rather, this knowledge helps the reader predict what type of word might appear in a certain place in a sentence. It might be a naming word (noun), an action word (verb), or a describing word (adjective). This cueing system also involves an understanding of word order and the use

The Connection Between Decoding and Comprehension

Phonics instruction helps the reader to map sounds onto spellings. This ability enables readers to decode words. **Decoding** words aids in the development of and improvement in word recognition. The more words one recognizes, the easier the reading task. Therefore, phonics instruction aids in the development of **word recognition** by providing children with an important and useful way to figure out unfamiliar words while reading.

When children begin to be able to recognize a large amount of words quickly and accurately, **reading fluency** improves. Reading fluency refers to the ease with which children can read a text. As more and more words become firmly stored in a child's memory (that is, the child recognizes more and more words on sight), he or she gains fluency and **automaticity** in word recognition. Having many opportunities to decode words in text is critical to learning words by sight. The more times a child encounters a word in text, the more likely he or she is to recognize it by sight and to avoid making a reading error (Gough, Juel, & Roper-Schneider, 1983).

Reading fluency improves **reading comprehension**. Since children are no longer struggling with decoding words, they can devote their full attention (mental energies) to making meaning from the text. As the vocabulary and concept demands increase in text, children need to be able to devote more of their attention to making meaning from text, and increasingly less attention to decoding. If children have to devote too much time to decoding words, their reading will be slow and labored. This will result in comprehension difficulties.

of function words, such as *the* and *an*. For example, read the following sentence and choose a word to fill in the blank.

We saw the _____ on the road.

All possible words to fill in the blank must be naming words. You determined this from your knowledge of English syntax.

Most children have an understanding of the basic syntactic structures of English when they enter school. However, oral language is different from "book language." Written material might pose difficulties for some children because their oral language patterns differ so much from the more formal language patterns of text. Reading many books aloud will help these children gain an understanding of the more formal syntactic structures used for writing. In particular, children may struggle with the vocabulary and structure of nonfiction texts. Reading numerous informational books aloud and discussing their text structures will be beneficial to students.

3. Semantic cues involve a reader's knowledge of the world. This knowledge helps the reader to use cues in the text to discover the meaning of a word that fits into a specific place in a particular sentence. Readers use their semantic knowledge to determine if a text makes sense.

Ten Important Research Findings About Phonics

Countless research studies have been conducted on phonics instruction. Much of this research has focused on the usefulness of phonics instruction and the best ways to teach children about sound-spelling relationships. Below is a list of ten of the top research findings regarding phonics.

#1 Phonics Instruction Can Help All Children Learn to Read

All children can benefit from instruction in the most common sound-spelling relationships and syllable patterns in English. This instruction helps children decode words that follow these predictable sound-spelling relationships and syllable-spelling patterns.

Phonics instruction can help students become active word detectives.

Phonics instruction is particularly beneficial for children at risk for learning difficulties. This might include children who come to school with limited exposure to books, have had few opportunities to develop their oral languages, are from low socio-economic families, have below-average intelligence, are learning English as a second language, or are suspected of having a learning disability. However, even children from language-rich backgrounds benefit from phonics instruction (Chall, 1967). As Chall states, "By learning phonics, students make faster progress in acquiring literary skills—reading and writing. By the age of six, most children already have about 6,000 words in their listening and speaking vocabularies. With phonics they learn to read and write these and more words at a faster rate than they would without phonics."

Phonics instruction is therefore an essential ingredient in reading instruction, as it teaches children how to read with accuracy, comprehension, fluency, and pleasure. The early ability to sound out words successfully is a strong predictor of future growth in decoding (Lundberg, 1984) and comprehension (Lesgold & Resnick, 1982). Weak decoding skills are characteristic of poor readers (Carnine, Carnine, & Gertsen, 1984; Lesgold & Curtis, 1981; Langenburg, 2000). Readers who are skilled at decoding usually comprehend text better than those who are poor decoders. Why this is so can be gleaned from the work of cognitive psychologists, who contend that we have a set amount of mental energy that we can devote to any task (Kahneman, 1973). Since decoding requires so much of this mental energy, little is left over for higher-level comprehension. As decoding skills improve and more and more words are recognized by sight, less mental energy is required to decode words and more mental energy can be devoted to making meaning from the text (Freedman & Calfee, 1984; LaBerge & Samuels, 1974).

Readers who are skilled at decoding usually comprehend text better than those who are poor decoders.

In addition, successful early decoding ability is related to the number of words a reader encounters. That is, children who are good decoders read many more words than children who are poor decoders (Juel, 1991). This wide reading subsequently results in greater reading growth. Children not only learn more words, but they become more familiar with the common spelling patterns of English, which in turn helps them decode longer words.

Phonics instruction also helps get across the alphabetic principle (that the letters of the alphabet stand for sounds) by teaching the relationship between letters and the sounds they represent. Beginning readers learn better when their teachers emphasize these relationships (Beck & Beck, 2013; Chall, 1996; Hattie, 2012).

#2 Explicit Phonics Instruction Is More Beneficial Than Implicit Instruction

According to Chall (1996), "systematic and early instruction in phonics leads to better reading: better accuracy of word recognition, decoding, spelling, and oral and silent reading comprehension." The most effective type of instruction, especially for children at risk for reading difficulties, is **explicit (direct) instruction** (Adams, 1990; Anderson et al., 1985; Beck & Beck, 2013; Chall, 1996; Evans & Carr, 1985; Hattie, 2012; Honig, 1995; Langenburg, 2000; Stahl & Miller, 1989). **Implicit instruction** relies on readers "discovering" clues about sound-spelling relationships. Good readers can do this; poor readers aren't likely to. Good readers can generalize their knowledge of sound-spelling relationships and syllable patterns to read new words in which these and other sound-spellings and patterns occur. Poor readers must rely on explicit instruction.

Although explicit instruction has proved more effective than implicit instruction, the key element in its success is having many opportunities to read decodable words (words containing previously taught sound-spellings) (Adams, 1990; Juel & Roper-Schneider, 1985; Stahl, Osborn, & Pearson, 1992) and ample modeling of applying these skills to real reading. In fact, students who receive phonics instruction achieve best in both decoding and comprehension if the text they read contains high percentages of decodable words. In addition, by around second or third grade, children who've been taught by explicit phonics instruction generally surpass the reading abilities of their peers who've been taught by implicit phonics instruction (Chall, 1996).

Clearly, explicit phonics instruction and reviewing primary phonics skills needs to occur for many students in the intermediate grades to ensure they have achieved mastery. Short daily lessons with decodable text reading practice can have a significant impact.

#3 Most Poor Readers Have Weak Phonics Skills and a Strategy Imbalance

Most poor readers have a strategy imbalance. They tend to over-rely on one reading strategy, such as the use of context clues, to the exclusion of other strategies that might be more appropriate (Sulzby, 1985). To become skilled, fluent readers, children need to have a repertoire of strategies to figure out unfamiliar words (Cunningham, 1990). These strategies include using a knowledge of sound-spelling relationships, using context clues, and using structural clues and syllabication. Younger and less skilled readers in the primary and intermediate grades rely more on context than other, often more effective, strategies (Stanovich, 1980). This is partly due to their inability to use sound-spelling relationships to decode words. Stronger readers don't need to rely on context clues because they can quickly and accurately decode words by sounding them out.

Unfortunately, children who get off to a slow start in reading rarely catch up to their peers and seldom develop into strong readers (Juel, 1991; Stanovich, 1986). Those who experience difficulties decoding early on tend to read less and thereby grow less in terms of word recognition skills and vocabulary.

A longitudinal study conducted by Juel (1988) revealed an 88% probability that a child who is a poor reader at the end of first grade would still be a poor reader at the end of fourth grade. Stanovich (1986) refers to this as the "Matthew Effect": the "rich get richer" (children who are successful decoders early on read more and therefore improve in reading), and the "poor get poorer" (children who have difficulties decoding become increasingly distanced from the good decoders in terms of reading ability).

#4 Phonics Knowledge Has a Powerful Effect on Decoding Ability

Phonics knowledge affects decoding ability positively (Stanovich and West, 1989; Wong, 2015; Yoncheva, Wise, & McCandliss, 2015). Early attainment of decoding skill is important because this accurately predicts later skill in reading comprehension (Beck & Juel, 1995).

One way to help children achieve the ultimate goal of reading instruction, to make meaning of text, is to help them achieve automaticity in decoding words (Gaskins, Downer, Anderson, Cunningham, Gaskins, Schommer, & Teachers of Benchmark School, 1988). Skilled readers recognize the majority of words they encounter in text quickly and accurately, independent of context (Cunningham, 1975-76; Stanovich, 1984). The use of graphophonic cues (knowledge of sound-spelling relationships) furthers word recognition abilities. In fact, a child's word recognition speed in first grade was found to be a strong predictor of reading comprehension ability in second grade (Beck & Juel, 1995; Lesgold & Resnick, 1982).

However, the inability to automatically recognize frequently encountered words affects reading in the following ways (Royer & Sinatra, 1994):

1. Since words can be stored in working memory for only about 10–15 seconds, slow decoding can result in some words "decaying" before the reader can process a meaningful chunk of text.

> **The whole word method (meaning emphasis) may serve a student adequately up to about second grade. But failure to acquire and use efficient decoding skills will begin to take a toll on reading comprehension by grade 3.**
>
> —Jeanne Chall

2. Devoting large amounts of mental energy to decoding words leaves less mental energy available for higher-level comprehension. This can result in comprehension breakdowns.

#5 Good Decoders Rely Less on Context Clues than Poor Decoders

Good readers don't need to rely as much on context clues because their decoding skills are so strong (Gough & Juel, 1991). It's only when good readers can't use their knowledge of sound-spelling relationships to figure out an unfamiliar word that they rely on context clues. In contrast, poor readers, who often have weak decoding skills, over-rely on context clues to try to make meaning of text (Nicholson, 1992; Stanovich, 1986). Any reader, strong or weak, can use context clues only up to a certain point. It has been estimated that only one out of every four words (25%) can be predicted using context (Gough, Alford, & Holley-Wilcox, 1981). The words that are the easiest to predict are function words such as *the* and *an*. Content words—the words that carry the bulk of the meaning in a text—are the most difficult to predict. Researchers estimate that content words can be predicted only about 10% of the time (Gough et al., 1983). A reader needs to use his or her knowledge of phonics (sound-spelling relationships) to decode these words.

#6 The Reading Process Relies on a Reader's Attention to Each Letter in a Word

Eye-movement studies have revealed that skilled readers attend to almost every word in a sentence and process the letters that compose each word (McConkie & Zola, 1987). Therefore, reading is a "letter-mediated" rather than a "whole-word-mediated" process (Just & Carpenter, 1987). Prior to these findings, it was assumed that readers did not process each letter in a word; rather they recognized the word based on shape, a few letters, and context.

Research has also revealed that poor readers do not fully analyze words; for example, some poor readers tend to rely on initial consonant cues only (Stanovich, 1992;

Vellutino & Scanlon, 1987). Therefore, phonics instruction should help in focusing children's attention on all the letters or spellings that make up words and the sounds each represents by emphasizing full analysis of words. In addition, phonics instruction must teach children strategies to use this information to decode words. The reader has to pay attention to the spelling patterns in words in order to store the words in his or her memory. And by more fully analyzing the common spelling patterns of English, the reader becomes a better speller (Ehri, 1987).

#7 Phonemic Awareness Is Necessary for Phonics Instruction to Be Effective

Before children can use a knowledge of sound-spelling relationships to decode words, they must understand that words are made up of sounds (Adams, 1990). Many children come to school thinking of words as whole units—*cat, dog, run.* Before they can learn to read, children must realize that these words can be broken into smaller units—and sounded out. **Phonemic awareness** is the understanding, or insight, that a word is made up of a series of discrete sounds. Without this insight, phonics instruction will not make sense to children. Some students with weak phonemic awareness skills are able to make it through the first few years of reading instruction by memorizing words. This strategy breaks down when the number of unique words in text increases in grades 3 and up. Therefore, if weak phonemic awareness skills are not detected and corrected, these students may enter the intermediate grades with a very serious reading deficit, and intermediate-grade teachers will need to use an intensive phonemic awareness program to address the issue.

Phonemic awareness is the understanding, or insight, that a word is made up of a series of discrete sounds. Without this insight, phonics instruction will not make sense to children.

#8 Phonics Instruction Improves Spelling Ability

Reading and writing are interrelated and complementary processes (Pinnell, 1994). Whereas phonics is characterized by putting together sounds to form words that are printed, spelling involves breaking down spoken words into sounds in order to write them. To spell, or encode, a word a child must map a spelling onto each sound heard in the word.

Spelling development lags behind reading development. A word can generally be read before it can be spelled. The visual attention a child needs to recognize words is stored in his or her memory. This information—the knowledge of the spelling patterns, also known as **orthographic** knowledge— is used to spell. Spelling, however, requires greater visual recall than reading and places higher demands on memory (Moats, 2010).

Good spellers are generally good readers because spelling and reading share an underlying knowledge base. Poor readers, however, are rarely good spellers. Phonics is a particularly powerful tool in improving spelling because it emphasizes spelling patterns, which become familiar from reading. Studies show that half of all English words can be spelled with phonics rules that relate one letter to one sound. Thirty-seven percent of words can be spelled with phonics rules that relate groups of letters to one sound. The other 13% must be learned by memorization. Good spellers have not memorized the dictionary; they apply the phonics rules they know and have a large store of sight words.

Writing, in turn, supports a child's reading development because it slows the process by focusing the child's attention on how print works. Poor spellers experience difficulties in both writing and reading. Poorly developed spelling ability also hinders vocabulary development (Adams, Treiman, & Pressley, 1996; Read, 1986).

#9 A Teacher's Knowledge of Phonics Affects His or Her Ability to Teach Phonics

A teacher's knowledge of phonics has a strong effect on his or her ability to teach phonics (Blevins, 2016; Carroll, 1990; Moats, 1995b). This understanding of the various sounds and corresponding spellings of the English language enables the teacher to choose the best examples for instruction, provide focused instruction, and better understand and interpret students' reading and writing errors in relationship to their developing language skills. I highly recommend that all teachers take a basic course in phonics or linguistics to gain further insights into our language that can be used in the classroom in productive and purposeful ways.

#10 Knowledge of Common Syllable Patterns and Structural Analysis Improves the Ability to Read, Spell, and Learn the Meanings of Multisyllabic Words

For many children, reading long words is an arduous task. Explicit instruction in the six common spelling patterns, the most common syllable types (e.g., VCe, VCCV), prefixes, suffixes, roots, and word origins helps students recognize larger word chunks, which makes decoding and figuring out meaning easier. For example, it may be efficient for a student to decode text containing simple CVC words such as *cat* and *ran* sound by sound; however, it is not efficient for him or her to decode text containing words such as *transportation* and *unhappy* sound by sound. Rather, it is more efficient for the child to recognize common word parts such as *trans*, *port*, *tion*, *un*, and *happy* and blend these larger chunks to sound out the word.

Stages of Reading Development: Where Phonics Fits In

Before I begin discussing advanced phonics instruction in depth, I want to focus on the big picture. Knowing the stages of reading development can help put phonics in its proper perspective and enable you to make instructional decisions based on where each student fits in the continuum. I've chosen the stages of reading development proposed by Chall (1983) because they provide a clear and useful framework for how children learn to read. The time frames are general. (See page 21.)

As Chall (1983) states, the value of this framework is that it "suggests that different aspects of reading be emphasized at different stages of reading development, and that success at the beginning is essential since it influences not only early reading achievement but also reading at subsequent stages of development." This framework highlights the need for reading programs to provide children with strong instruction in decoding words. It is also a warning that a prolonged stay in any one stage can result in serious reading problems.

As you read this book and assess the reading development of your students, keep in mind the Stages of Reading Development framework. Consider how you can use it to modify instruction. For example, the way you teach a fourth grade child stuck in Stage 2 is different from the way you teach a fourth grade child already in Stage 3.

The greatest gift you can give students is a love of reading.

Aside from providing balanced, strong reading instruction that meets the needs of all your children, the greatest gift you can give them is a love of reading. I am constantly reminded of Mrs. Fry, my fourth grade teacher. Throughout the school year, she read to us the entire *Little House* series by Laura Ingalls Wilder, as well as many other classics. The words seemed to melt off the page as she read. I can still remember the emotion in her voice. When the book was sad, her voice would crack, and we could feel the pain. When the book was happy, her voice sounded like it would burst from within her. She made me want to read everything she picked up. Indeed, many of us purchased our own *Little House* set of books or checked out of the library every book she "blessed" with these memorable readings. She brought books to life for hundreds of children during her career. It is that love of literature we can and must share with our students in order to lead them into a world of adventure, information, comfort, and wonderment.

The Six Stages of Reading Development

Stage 0: Birth to Age Six

Prereading The most notable change is the child's growing control over language. By the time a child enters grade 1 (at around age six), he or she has approximately 6,000 words in his or her listening and speaking vocabularies. During this stage, children also develop some knowledge of print, such as recognizing a few letters, words, and environmental print signs. Many children learn to write their names. It is common to see them "pretend" read a book that has been repeatedly read to them. At this stage, children bring more to the printed page than they take out.

Stage 1: Grades 1 Through 2

Initial Reading or Decoding During this time, children develop an understanding of the alphabetic principle and begin to use their knowledge of sound-spelling relationships to decode words.

Stage 2: Grades 2 Through 3

Confirmation, Fluency, and Ungluing from Print Children further develop and solidify their decoding skills. They also develop additional strategies to decode words and make meaning from text. As this stage ends, children have developed fluency; that is, they can recognize many words quickly and accurately by sight and are skilled at sounding out the words they don't recognize by sight. They are also skilled at using context clues.

Stage 3: Grades 4 Through 8

Learning the New During this stage, reading demands change. Children begin to use reading more as a way to obtain information and learn about the values, attitudes, and insights of others. Texts contain many words not already in a child's speaking and listening vocabularies. These texts, frequently drawn from a wide variety of genres, also extend beyond the background experiences of the children.

Stage 4: Throughout High School (Grades 9–12)

Multiple Viewpoints During this stage, readers encounter more complex language and vocabulary as they read texts in more advanced content areas. Thus the language and cognitive demands required increase. Students are also reading texts containing varying viewpoints and must analyze them critically.

Stage 5: Throughout College and Beyond

Construction and Reconstruction This stage is characterized by a "world view." Readers use the information in books and articles as needed; that is, they know which books (and articles) will provide the information they need and can locate that information without having to read the entire book. At this stage, reading is considered constructive; that is, readers take in a wide range of information and construct their own understanding for their individual uses based on their analysis and synthesis of the information. Not all readers progress to this stage.

From *The Stages of Reading Development* by Jeanne Chall ©1983, ©1996.

Meeting Rigorous Standards

Current state and national literacy standards provide strong guidelines for what phonics and word study skills need to be taught and at which grade level. On the following pages are the relevant Common Core State Standards for Grades 2-8. Standards associated with phonics are grouped in the Foundational Skills section of the standards. However, no foundational skills exist beyond Grade 5. By this grade the basic phonics skills need to have been mastered by students. However, word study, which begins as early as kindergarten and is taught in tandem with phonics skills, extends beyond the scope of the foundational skills and continues to be a focus of instruction beyond Grade 5. In most standard documents word study skills, such as using affixes and Greek and Latin roots, can be found in the Language section of the standards (specifically the Vocabulary Acquisition and Use section in the Common Core State Standards). In the intermediate grades, phonics and vocabulary begin to overlap in powerful ways; using word parts to read unknown words as well as determine word meanings should be the focus of most phonics/word study lessons.

NOTE: There is great consistency in foundational skill standards across the United States and published reading curriculum reflects this. The states that have not adopted the Common Core State Standards have either used the CCSS Foundational Skills in their entirety or closely based their state standards on these well-established ones.

Reading Standards Foundational Skills

Grade 2 students:

Phonics and Word Recognition
3. Know and apply grade-level phonics and word analysis skills in decoding words.

  a. Distinguish long and short vowels when reading regularly spelled one-syllable words.

  b. Know spelling-sound correspondences for additional common vowel teams.

  c. Decode regularly spelled two-syllable words with long vowels.

  d. Decode words with common prefixes and suffixes.

  e. Identify words with inconsistent but common spelling-sound correspondences.

  f. Recognize and read grade-appropriate irregularly spelled words.

Fluency
4. Read with sufficient accuracy and fluency to support comprehension.

  a. Read grade-level text with purpose and understanding.

  b. Read grade-level text orally with accuracy, appropriate rate, and expression on successive readings.

  c. Use context to confirm or self-correct word recognition and understanding, rereading as necessary

Grade 3 students:

Phonics and Word Recognition
3. Know and apply grade-level phonics and word analysis skills in decoding words.

  a. Identify and know the meaning of the most common prefixes and derivational suffixes.

  b. Decode words with common Latin suffixes.

  c. Decode multisyllable words.

  d. Read grade-appropriate irregularly spelled words.

Fluency
4. Read with sufficient accuracy and fluency to support comprehension.

  a. Read grade-level text with purpose and understanding.

  b. Read grade-level prose and poetry orally with accuracy, appropriate rate, and expression on successive readings

  c. Use context to confirm or self-correct word recognition and understanding, rereading as necessary.

Language Skills

Grade 2 students:

Vocabulary Acquisition and Use
4b. Determine the meaning of the new word formed when a known prefix is added to a known word (e.g., happy/unhappy, tell/retell).

  c. Use a known root word as a clue to the meaning of an unknown word with the same root (e.g., addition, additional).

  d. Use knowledge of the meaning of individual words to predict the meaning of compound words (e.g., birdhouse, lighthouse, housefly; bookshelf, notebook, bookmark).

Grade 3 students:

Vocabulary Acquisition and Use
4b. Determine the meaning of the new word formed when a known affix is added to a known word (e.g., agreeable/disagreeable, comfortable/uncomfortable, care/careless, heat/preheat).

  c. Use a known root word as a clue to the meaning of an unknown word with the same root (e.g., company, companion).

Reading Standards Foundational Skills

Grade 4 students:

Phonics and Word Recognition
3. Know and apply grade-level phonics and word analysis skills in decoding words.
   a. Use combined knowledge of all letter-sound correspondences, syllabication patterns, and morphology (e.g., roots and affixes) to read accurately unfamiliar multisyllabic words in context and out of context.

Fluency
4. Read with sufficient accuracy and fluency to support comprehension.
   a. Read grade-level text with purpose and understanding.
   b. Read grade-level prose and poetry orally with accuracy, appropriate rate, and expression on successive readings.
   c. Use context to confirm or self-correct word recognition and understanding, rereading as necessary.

Grade 5 students:

Phonics and Word Recognition
3. Know and apply grade-level phonics and word analysis skills in decoding words.
   a. Use combined knowledge of all letter-sound correspondences, syllabication patterns, and morphology (e.g., roots and affixes) to read accurately unfamiliar multisyllabic words in context and out of context.

Fluency
4. Read with sufficient accuracy and fluency to support comprehension.
   a. Read grade-level text with purpose and understanding.
   b. Read grade-level prose and poetry orally with accuracy, appropriate rate, and expression on successive readings.
   c. Use context to confirm or self-correct word recognition and understanding, rereading as necessary.

Language Skills

Grade 4 students:

Vocabulary Acquisition and Use
4b. Use common, grade-appropriate Greek and Latin affixes and roots as clues to the meaning of a word (e.g., telegraph, photograph, autograph).

Grade 5 students:

Vocabulary Acquisition and Use
4b. Use common, grade-appropriate Greek and Latin affixes and roots as clues to the meaning of a word (e.g., photograph, photosynthesis).

Grade 6 students:

Vocabulary Acquisition and Use
4b. Use common, grade-appropriate Greek or Latin affixes and roots as clues to the meaning of a word (e.g., audience, auditory, audible).

Grade 7 students:

Vocabulary Acquisition and Use
4b. Use common, grade-appropriate Greek or Latin affixes and roots as clues to the meaning of a word (e.g., belligerent, bellicose, rebel).

Grade 8 Students

Vocabulary Acquisition and Use
4b. Use common, grade-appropriate Greek or Latin affixes and roots as clues to the meaning of a word (e.g., precede, recede, secede).

Learning About Sounds & Letters

"Knowledge is power. The teacher with some knowledge of linguistics can be a far better kidwatcher, as well as be able to participate more learnedly in conversations and debates about teaching methodology."

—Sandra Wilde

Why is the most common vowel sound in English the colorless murmur we refer to as the schwa (/ə/) sound? Why do the vowels *e, i, o,* and *u* act as consonants in words such as *azalea, onion, one,* and *quick;* and the consonants *w* and *y* act as vowels in words such as *snow* and *fly?* Why don't the word pairs *five/give, low/how, paid/said,* and *break/speak* rhyme?

These and other questions might cause you to reconsider the teaching of reading and writing because of the seemingly irregular and unpredictable nature of the English language. However, 84% of English words do conform to regular spelling patterns. Of the remaining 16%, only 3% are highly unpredictable, such as *colonel* and *Ouija* (Bryson, 1990). Given the high degree of *regularity* of spelling, it's easy to see why teaching children the most common sound-spelling relationships in English and helping them to attend to common spelling patterns in words will help them with reading. It is important, therefore, for teachers to have a working knowledge of the many sounds in our language and the even greater number of spellings that can represent them.

Why Should I Know About Linguistics?

In 1995, Louisa Moats examined teacher preparation in the areas of reading and learning disabilities and surveyed teachers' background knowledge of language. Five of the fifteen questions she asked are listed here (answers provided).

---

1. How many speech sounds are in the following words?

ox (3) **boil** (3)
king (3) **thank** (4)
straight (5) **shout** (3)
though (2) **precious** (6)

2. Underline the consonant blends:
doubt, known, fir<u>st</u>, pu<u>mp</u>kin, <u>squ</u>awk, <u>scr</u>atch

3. What letters signal that a *g* is pronounced /j/? (*e, i, y*)

4. List all the ways you can think of to spell "long *a*"? (*a, ai, a-e, ey, ay, eigh*)

5. Account for the double *m* in *comment* or *commitment*. (The first *m* closes the syllable to make it short; *com* is a Latin morpheme—the smallest unit of meaning in language—as are *ment* and *mit*.)

The results of Moats' survey showed that the majority of teachers could benefit from additional training in linguistics. Only about half of the teachers surveyed could successfully answer most of the questions. Knowledge of phonics was particularly weak. Only about 10–20% of the teachers could identify consonant blends; almost none could consistently identify digraphs; less than half could identify the schwa sound in words; and only 30% knew the conditions in which the letters *ck* were used to stand for the /k/ sound. Moats contends that some of her survey results can be attributed to:

1. a lack of teacher training in phonics and linguistics.
2. the fact that most adult readers think of words in terms of spellings instead of sounds. Their knowledge of print may stand in the way of attending to individual sounds

in words—a skill they no longer need to be conscious of because they have already acquired automaticity.

3. the fact that some adults have underdeveloped metalinguistic skills. That is, the skills they have acquired are sufficient for reading, but not sufficient for explicitly teaching reading and spelling.

During my years as a teacher, I've improved my ability to assess students' reading and writing skills because I've increased my understanding of the English language. The more I learn about English, the more regular its spelling seems. For example, at one time I thought of words such as *love* and *come* as being "irregular" since they didn't follow the typical *o-e* spelling for the long *o* sound. But when I realized how many words follow a similar spelling pattern (*shove, glove, above, some*, etc.), a regularity began to emerge. The *o-e* spelling pattern is not random; rather, it can represent either the /ō/ sound or the /u/ sound in words. Now, these are the two sounds I try out when confronted with this spelling pattern in an unfamiliar word. In addition, the more I learn about English and its spelling patterns, the more my students' reading and writing errors make sense. This knowledge has helped me to target specific difficulties students have had and to design appropriate instruction. If you have a basic knowledge of phonics and linguistics, you'll be able to help your students by (Moats, 1995b):

- **interpreting and responding to student errors.** You can use student errors to modify instruction. For example, when a student substitutes *k* for *g* in a word, knowing that the sounds these two letters represent are formed in almost the same manner helps to explain the student's error. You can instruct students in the major difference between these two sounds (voicing).
- **choosing the best examples for teaching decoding and spelling.** You can help children distinguish auditorily confusing sounds such as /e/ and /i/, and use words for instruction that provide the clearest, simplest examples.
- **organizing and sequencing information for instruction.** You'll be able to separate the introduction

of auditorily confusing sounds such as /e/ and /i/ and teach easier concepts before more complex ones (such as teaching consonants before consonant clusters).

- **using your knowledge of morphology to explain spellings.** Morphology is the study of units of meaning, or morphemes, such as root words (Latin, Greek). Use these to explain spelling patterns and guide children to figure out word meanings.
- **integrating the components of language instruction.** You'll be able to take better advantage of the "teachable moment" and more completely integrate the language arts.

Linguistics is the formal study of language and how it works. You don't have to be a linguist to be an effective teacher of reading and writing. However, a deeper understanding of our language can enhance any teacher's abilities. This chapter begins by defining a few basic terms associated with linguistics and another related area of study—**phonetics** (the study of speech sounds). It concludes by providing brief information on the sound-spellings covered in most intermediate-grade reading curriculums and word lists for instruction.

The 44 Sounds of English

A **phoneme** is a speech sound. It's the smallest unit of sound that distinguishes one word from another. The word *phoneme* is derived from the Greek root *phon* (as in the word *telephone*), which refers to *voice* or *sound*. The following pairs of words differ by only one phoneme, the first—*cat/hat, men/pen*.

Since sounds cannot be written, we use letters to represent or stand for the sounds. A **grapheme** is the written representation (a letter or cluster of letters) of one sound. For example, the /b/ sound can be represented by the letter *b*; the /sh/ sound can be represented by the letters *sh*. The word *sat* has three phonemes (/s/ /a/ /t/) and three graphemes (*s, a, t*). The word *chop* also has three phonemes (/ch/ /o/ /p/) and three graphemes (*ch, o, p*).

Linguists disagree on the actual number of sounds in the English language. The number varies according to dialect, individual speech patterns, changes in stress, and other variables. However, for the sake of our study, we will deal with the 44 phonemes commonly covered in elementary school reading programs.

The 44 Sounds of English

Consonant Sounds

1. /b/ (bat)	10. /n/ (nest)	19. /ch/ (cheese)
2. /d/ (dog)	11. /p/ (pig)	20. /sh/ (shark)
3. /f/ (fan)	12. /r/ (rock)	21. /th/ (thumb)
4. /g/ (gate)	13. /s/ (sun)	22. /th̸/ (the)
5. /h/ (hat)	14. /t/ (top)	23. /hw/ (wheel)
6. /j/ (jump)	15. /v/ (vase)	24. /zh/ (treasure)
7. /k/ (kite)	16. /w/ (wagon)	25. /ng/ (ring)
8. /l/ (leaf)	17. /y/ (yo-yo)	
9. /m/ (mop)	18. /z/ (zebra)	

Vowel Sounds

26. /a/ (cat)	33. /ī/ (bike)	40. /oi/ (boy)
27. /e/ (bed)	34. /ō/ (boat)	41. /ô/ (ball)
28. /i/ (fish)	35. /yo͞o/ (cube)	42. /û/ (bird)
29. /o/ (lock)	36. /ə/ (alarm*)	43. /â/ (chair)
30. /u/ (duck)	37. /o͞o/ (moon)	44. /ä/ (car)
31. /ā/ (cake)	38. /o͝o/ (book)	
32. /ē/ (feet)	39. /ou/ (house)	

*The target vowel sound occurs in the first syllable of *alarm*.

The 44 English phonemes are represented by the 26 letters of the alphabet individually and in combination. Therefore, a letter can sometimes represent more than one sound. For example, the letter *a* can stand for the sounds heard in words such as *at, ate, all, any, was,* and *father.* Likewise, a phoneme can sometimes be represented by more than one grapheme. For example, the /f/ sound can be represented by *f* (*fan*), *ph* (*phone*), or *gh* (*laugh*).

Adding to the complexity, some letters do not represent any sound in a word. For example, the letter *k* in the word *knot* is silent. In addition, some letters do not represent a unique or distinctive sound. The letter *c*, for instance, stands for either the /s/ sound (usually represented by the letter *s*), or the /k/ sound (usually represented by the letter *k*). The letters *q* and *x* also represent no distinctive sound.

To distinguish between a letter and a sound in writing, sounds are placed between **virgules**, or slashes. For example, to indicate the sound that the letter *s* stands for, we would write /s/. Other markings aid us in representing sounds in written form. These markings are called **diacritical marks**. The chart below shows some of the most common diacritical marks. The two most common are the macron and the breve. The **macron** (⁻) is used to represent long-vowel sounds, such as the /ā/ sound in *gate*. The **breve** (˘) is used to represent short-vowel sounds such as the /ă/ sound in *hat*. Short-vowel sounds can also be written using only the letter between virgules, such as /a/. The International Phonetic Alphabet has conventionalized the symbols for every sound of every language in the world. These differ somewhat from the symbols commonly found in dictionaries. For the sake of consistency, this book deals with only those markings and symbols commonly found in children's dictionaries and taught in elementary reading programs.

Diacritical Marks		
Markings	**Symbol**	**Example**
macron	⁻	/ā/ as in *cake*
breve	˘	/ă/ as in *cat*
tilde	~	/ñ/ as in *piñon*
dieresis	¨	/ä/ as in *car*
circumflex	^	/ô / as in *ball*

Phonics instruction involves teaching the relationship between sounds and the spellings used to represent them. There are hundreds of spellings that can be used to represent the 44 English phonemes. Only the most common need to be taught explicitly. Throughout this book, when I refer to the most common sound-spelling relationships, I choose the term "sound-spelling" instead of the more common term "sound-symbol" because it is more accurate. Many sound-spelling relationships are represented by more than one symbol or letter. For example, the /ch/ sound is represented by the letters, or spelling, *ch*; the long /ē/ sound can be represented by the spellings *e*, *ea*, or *ee*. When teaching phonics, we want children to attend to these spelling patterns to develop their understanding of English **orthography**—the spelling system of our language.

The 44 English sounds can be divided into two major categories—consonants and vowels. A **consonant** sound is one in which the air flow is cut off either partially or completely when the sound is produced. In contrast, a **vowel** sound is one in which the air flow is unobstructed when the sound is made. The vowel sounds are the music, or movement, of our language.

Consonants

Of the 26 letters in the English alphabet, 21 are generally considered consonants. These are *b, c, d, f, g, h, j, k, l, m, n, p, q, r, s, t, v, w, x, y*, and *z*. The letters *w* and *y* sometimes act as vowels, as in the words *my, happy*, and *show*. Of the 44 English phonemes, 25 are consonant phonemes. (See the chart on page 29.) Eighteen of these phonemes are represented by a single letter, such as /b/ and /m/; seven are identified by a digraph, such as /sh/ and /ch/. A **digraph** is a letter cluster that stands for one sound. The letters *c, q*, and *x* do not have a unique phoneme assigned to them; the sounds that they stand for are more commonly represented by other letters or spellings.

Consonants can be further categorized according to (1) how they are produced, (2) where they are produced in the mouth, and (3) whether they are voiced. The five major categories of consonants based on their **manner of articulation** are:

1. **plosives (stops):** formed by closing or blocking off the air flow and then exploding a puff of air (examples: /b/, /p/, /d/, /t/, /g/, /k/). Place your hand in front of your mouth when producing these sounds. Do you feel a burst of air?

2. **fricatives:** formed by narrowing the air channel and then forcing air through it—this creates friction in the mouth (examples: /f/, /v/, /th/, /tḦ/, /z/, /s/, /zh/, /sh/). A subgroup of this category is the **affricative**, which is a sound produced by the sequence of a stop followed by a fricative (examples: /ch/, /j/).

3. **nasals:** formed when the mouth is closed, forcing the air through the nose (examples: /n/, /m/, /ng/). These sounds are also referred to as nasal stops.

4. **liquids:** formed by interrupting the airflow slightly, but no friction results (examples: /l/, /r/).

5. **glides:** sometimes called semivowels because they are formed in similar ways as vowels (examples: /w/, /y/, /h/).

In addition to how sounds are produced, where they are produced in the mouth distinguishes one sound from another. For example, the fricative /v/ is formed using the lips and teeth. Therefore, it is referred to as a **labiodental** (labio = lips; dental = teeth). The fricative /z/ is formed using the front of the mouth. Therefore, it is referred to as an **alveolar**; the alveolar ridge is the name of the front of the mouth where the teeth arise. Similarly, the fricative /sh/ is formed using the roof of the mouth. Therefore, it is referred to as a **palatal**; the hard palate is the name of the roof of the mouth. Other labels you might encounter include **velar** (the velum, or soft palate, is the back of the mouth) and **bilabial** (both lips).

The chart that follows shows most of the consonant sounds according to where they are articulated. It also divides sounds according to those that are **voiced** and those that are **unvoiced**. When producing a voiced sound, the vocal cords vibrate. When producing an unvoiced sound, there's no vibration. To test this, place your hand on your throat. Then make the /b/ sound. You'll feel a vibration because this is a voiced sound. Now make the /p/ sound, the voiceless counterpart of the /b/ sound, and you won't feel vibration.

Where Consonant Sounds Are Voiced

Place of Articulation	Voiced	Unvoiced	Nasal
lips (bilabial)	/b/ (plosive)	/p/ (plosive)	/m/
front of mouth (alveolar)	/d/ (plosive) /z/ (fricative)	/t/ (plosive) /s/ (fricative)	/n/
back of mouth (velar)	/g/ (plosive)	/k/ (plosive) /ä/ as in car	/ng/
lips and teeth (labiodental)	/v/ (fricative)	/f/ (fricative)	
teeth (dental)	/th/ (fricative)	/th/ (fricative)	
roof of mouth (palatal)	/zh/ (fricative) /j/ (affricative)	/sh/ (fricative) /ch/ (affricative)	

One aspect of consonant sounds that affects how we assess students' spelling is the issue of allophones. An **allophone** is a slightly different version of each phoneme. It generally results from the ease (or lack of ease) in articulating a sound in relation to its surrounding sounds. For example, pronounce the words *late* and *later*. The *t* in the word *later* sounds more like /d/. Pronounce the words *like* and *pill*. The *l* in *like* is pronounced with greater force and clarity than the *l* in *pill*. Therefore, when sounds are coarticulated, the surrounding sounds and the ease with which the mouth must move to form each sound affect the resulting sound. These slight sound variations don't bother us when we read, but children's invented spellings often reflect this.

Most of the consonant phonemes are highly reliable, or dependable. That is, when we see the most common letter or spelling for each consonant sound it generally stands for that sound. These regularities result in several generalizations that are helpful for the teacher of reading. The list on page 35 shows several of the most reliable consonant generalizations (Groff, 1977; Henderson, 1967; Mazurkiewicz, 1976). It's not necessary to teach these generalizations to students. It's better to point them out at appropriate moments to help students clarify and organize their understanding of English spelling patterns.

Consonants can appear by themselves or in combination with other consonants. Two consonants that appear together can be a cluster or a digraph. A **cluster** refers to two or more consonants that appear together in a word, each consonant retaining its own sound. For example, the cluster *sn* in *snail* represents the /sn/ sounds. The combination of sounds that the cluster stands for is called a **blend**. In contrast, sometimes when two consonants appear together in a word, they stand for one sound that is different from either sound of each individual consonant. This is called a **digraph**. The digraph *sh* stands for the /sh/ sound. This sound is not a combination of the /s/ and /h/ sounds, rather it is a new and unique sound. There are both consonant and vowel digraphs. An example of a vowel digraph is *oa*, which stands for the /ō/ sound.

Notable Consonants

Notable sound-spellings from the list of "The 44 Sounds of English" (see page 29) that need special attention are the consonants *c*, *q*, and *x*, and the digraphs *gh* and *ph*. These consonants and digraphs do not represent distinctive sounds.

The Letter *c*

The letter *c* can stand for many sounds:

- It can stand for the /k/ sound as in *cat*. The letter *c* generally stands for the /k/ sound when it comes before the letter *a, o,* or *u* in a word (*cat, cot, cut*). This is sometimes referred to as the "hard" sound of *c*.
- It can stand for the /s/ sound as in *city*. The letter *c* generally stands for the /s/ sound when it comes before the letter *e, i,* or *y* in a word (*cent, cinder, cycle*). This is sometimes referred to as the "soft" sound of *c*.

Consonant Generalizations

1. Some letters represent no sound in words.

2. Some sounds are almost always represented by the same spelling, such as *th, v,* and *h*.

3. Some spellings appear to be purely arbitrary, such *igh* in *night* and *eau* in *beau*.

4. The English spelling system often uses doubled letters, especially in the middle of words. However, only one sound is produced unless the sounds cross morpheme boundaries, such as in *bookcase* or *unknown*.

5. Certain letters are almost never doubled: *j, k, q, w, x,* and *v*.

6. English spellings have been influenced by other languages, such as *qu* and *th* from Latin-French, *ou* and *ch* from French, and *ps* from Greek.

7. When the letter c comes before *e, i,* or *y* in a word, it usually represents the /s/ sound (examples: *cent, city, cycle*).

8. When double *c* comes before *e* or *i* in a word, it usually represents two sounds /ks/ (example: *success*).

9. When the letter g comes before *e, i,* or *y* in a word, it usually represents the /j/ sound.

10. When the letters *c* and *g* are followed by *e* at the end of words, they are usually pronounced /s/ and /j/, respectively (examples: *race, cage*).

11. When the letter *h* appears after *c* in a word, the letter pair can be pronounced /ch/, /k/, or /sh/. Try /ch/ first. Note that *ch* before another consonant is usually pronounced /k/ (example: *chlorine*).

12. The letters *sh* and *ph* almost always represent one sound—/sh/ and /f/, respectively.

13. The letters *gh* represent /g/ at the beginning of words and /f/ at the end of words. However, *gh* is often silent, as in *night*.

14. The digraph *th* has two pronunciations—/th/ and /t͟h/.

15. The digraph *wh* is pronounced /hw/. However, when it appears before the letter *o*, only the *h* is pronounced (example: *whole*).

16. The letters *se* indicate that the *s* may be pronounced /s/ or /z/. Try /z/ first, as in *these*.

17. When the letter *s* is followed by *y, i,* or *u* in the middle of words, it may be pronounced /zh/ or /sh/. Try /zh/ first (examples: *measure, fission*).

18. When the letter *i* follows *c, s, ss, sc,* or *t* in the last part of a word, it is usually silent and indicates that these graphemes represent /sh/ (example: *nation*).

19. When the letter *e* follows *v* and *z* at the end of words, it is silent and indicates that *v* and *z* rarely come at the end of words.

20. When the letter *e* follows *ng* at the end of words, it indicates that *ng* stands for /nj/ (example: *strange*).

21. When the letters *le* appear at the end of a word, the *l* is pronounced /ul/ (example: *table*).

22. When a word ends in *dure, ture, sure,* or *zure*, the first letter in each ending is pronounced /j/, /ch/, /sh/, /zh/, respectively (examples: *procedure, denture, ensure, azure*).

- The word *cello* is an exception. In this word, the letter *c* stands for the /ch/ sound.
- The letter *c* usually stands for the /k/ sound when it is followed by a consonant as in *cliff* and *cry*. The consonant digraph *ck* also stands for the /k/ sound. Many consider the *c* silent in this digraph. The most notable exception to this is when the letter *c* is followed by the letter *h*. The letters *ch* can stand for the /k/ sound as in *chemistry* and *school* or the /ch/ sound as in *cheese*.
- When the letter *c* follows the letter *s* the two letters combined can stand for the /sk/ sounds as in *scold* and *scream*; or the *c* can be silent as in *science* and *scene*.
- When the letter *c* is doubled in a word, one of the *c*'s is usually silent. When they come before the letters *u* or *o*, the double *c*'s usually stand for the /k/ sound as in *occupy* and *tobacco*. When they come before the letters *e* or *i*, they usually stand for the /ks/ sounds as in *success*, *accident*, *access*, and *accept*. The *c* before *i* and *e* in these words stands for the /sh/ sound: *conscious*, *special*, *ocean*, *official*, *social*, *delicious*, *racial*. Note that the letter *i* is silent in these words.

The Letter *q*

- The letter *q* could be deleted from our alphabet and replaced with the letter *k*. The letter *q* almost always represents the /k/ sound and is usually followed by the letter *u*. In some words the letter *u* is silent (*antique*, *bouquet*, *croquet*). In most words the *u* stands for the /w/ sound (*quack*, *quail*, *quake*, *quart*, *quarter*, *queen*, *question*, *quick*, *quiet*, *quill*, *quilt*, *quirk*, *quit*, *quite*, *quiz*, *require*, *request*, *square*, and *squash*).

The Letter *x*

- The letter *x* frequently stands for the /ks/ sounds as in *ax*, *box*, *fix*, *flax*, *fox*, *lox*, *mix*, *ox*, *sax*, *six*, *tax*, and *wax*.
- It also stands for the /gz/ sounds as in *exact*, *exit*, *exist*, *exam*, *auxiliary*, *exhaust*, and *exhibit*. We generally use /gz/ when the letter *x* appears between two vowels.
- The letter *x* can also stand for the /z/ sound as in *xylophone*, *anxiety*, *xylem*, and *Xerox*.

- There are words in which we use *x* as a letter (/eks/), as in *x-ray* and *x-ograph*.
- Other sounds that the letter *x* represents include the following: /ksh/ *anxious, anxiously*; /k/ *excite, exceed, excellent, except, excuse*; and /kzh/ *luxury*.
- The letter *x* is silent in the word *Sioux*.

The Digraphs *gh* and *ph*
- The digraphs *gh* and *ph* can stand for the /f/ sound (*tough, phone*).
- The digraph *gh* can be silent as in *light*.
- The digraph *ph* almost always stands for the /f/ sound as in *phone* and *graph*. However, in the word *diphthong*, the *p* stands for the /p/ sound and the letter *h* is silent.

If you have students struggling with more basic letter-sound correspondences, see *Phonics From A to Z*, 3rd Edition (Blevins, 2017).

Vowels

Nineteen of the 44 English phonemes are vowel phonemes. (See the chart on page 29.) The letters *a, e, i, o,* and *u* are classified as vowels. These five letters are used to represent many different sounds. Therefore, each vowel is used for a variety of purposes. The letter *o*, for instance, has at least ten distinct sounds assigned to it (*on, old, son, corn, room, look, word, lemon, out, oil*) and is used in more than 30 different ways (*oasis, old, road, though, shoulder, snow, on, gone, thought, soldier, one, son, enough, does, other, look, could, room, through, to, two, buoy, oil, boy, buoyant, out, how, drought, lemon, word, colonel, Ouija, board*).

In addition, the consonants *w* and *y* often act as vowels, as in the words *show, fly,* and *happy*. The letter *y* acts as a vowel when it appears at the end of a word or syllable. The letter *w* acts as a vowel when it is used in combination with another vowel, as in the words *few, how, slow, thaw,* and *threw*. As vowels, the letters *w* and *y* do not represent distinctive sounds.

The most important distinguishing characteristic of a vowel is its place of articulation. Depending on the approximate place in the mouth in which part of the tongue is raised, vowels can be produced in the front, central, or back part of the mouth. In addition, the degree to which the tongue is raised distinguishes sounds. The sounds can be produced with the tongue raised to a high, mid, or low degree. The following chart illustrates this.

Vowel Sounds			
	Front	**Central**	**Back**
HIGH	/ē/		/o͞o/
MID	/ī/ /e/	/ə/(shwa) /ər/(shwar)	/ō/ /ô/
LOW	/a/	/u/	/o/

Missing from this chart are the diphthongs. A **diphthong** is a sound in which the position of the mouth changes from one place to another as the sound is produced. The sounds /oi/ and /ou/ are commonly classified as diphthongs. In addition, two so-called long-vowel sounds—long *i* (/ī/) and long *u* (/yo͞o/)—are often classified as diphthongs. The long *u* sound is actually a combination of a consonant and vowel sound. To note the difference between a diphthong and other vowel sounds, say aloud the /ā/ sound as in *gate*. Notice how the mouth, tongue, and lips remain in the same position while the sound is produced. Now try the /oi/ sound as in *boy*. Note how the mouth, particularly the lips, changes position while the sound is being produced. This is characteristic of a diphthong. Interestingly, Southern dialects generally produce most of their vowels as diphthongs. This helps to explain the beautiful singsong, rhythmic nature of Southern speech.

In basal reading programs, vowels are generally classified into the following categories:

1 Long-vowel sounds The macron (ˉ) is the diacritical mark used to represent long-vowel sounds. The word *macro* means *long* or *great*. Long-vowel sounds are also referred to as **glided sounds**. The long-vowel sounds covered in most basal reading programs include /ā/, /ē/, /ī/, /ō/, and /yo͞o/, although long *i* and long *u* are generally classified as diphthongs by linguists. Common long-vowel spelling patterns include CVCe (*race*) and VCe (*age*). Long-vowel sounds are often represented by vowel digraphs such as *ai, ay, ee, ea, oa, ow, ey, igh,* and *ie*. The vowel sound in an **open syllable**, a syllable that ends in a vowel, is generally a long-vowel sound (*ti/ger, a/pron*).

2 Short-vowel sounds The breve (˘) is the diacritical mark used to represent short-vowel sounds. Often no mark is used. The short-vowel sounds include /a/, /e/, /i/, /o/, and /u/. Short-vowel sounds are also referred to as **unglided sounds**. The most common short-vowel spelling pattern is CVC (*cat*). Short-vowel sounds are usually represented by the single vowels *a, e, i, o,* and *u*. The vowel sound in a **closed syllable**, a syllable that ends in a consonant, is often a short-vowel sound (*bas/ket*).

3 Other vowel sounds The other vowel sounds include diphthongs (/oi/, /ou/), variant vowels (/o͞o/, /o͝o/, /ô/, /ä/), schwa (/ə/), and *r*-controlled vowels (/ôr/, /ûr/, /âr/). In addition to the letter *r*, the letters *l* and *w* also affect the vowel sound that precedes or follows.

Many vowel generalizations are unreliable. For example, the commonly taught generalization, "When two vowels go walking, the first does the talking" has been found to be only about 45% reliable. However, if you limit the generalization to the vowel digraphs *ai, ay, ee,* and *oa,* it becomes a highly useful generalization. The list that follows shows several of the most reliable vowel generalizations (Groff, 1977; Henderson, 1967; Mazurkiewicz, 1976). It's not necessary to teach these to students. Point them out at appropriate moments to help students clarify and organize their understanding of English spelling patterns.

Vowel Generalizations

1. A single vowel followed by one or two consonants usually stands for a short sound. However, it may be a long sound. Try the short sound first.

2. The letter *e* following a vowel and a consonant (other than *c, g, l, ng, s, th, v, z,* and *ur*) usually indicates that the vowel represents a long sound.

3. The letter *a* before *l* in a word, and in the spellings *au* and *aw,* usually represents the /ô/ sound.

4. When the vowel digraphs *ai, ay, ee,* and *oa* appear together in a word, the first vowel usually represents its long sound.

5. The letter *y* usually represents the long-*i* sound at the end of short words (example: *fly*), but the letters *y* and *ey* usually stand for the long-*e* sound in longer words (examples: *happy, monkey*).

6. Some vowel spellings are used in reading to distinguish word meanings (examples: *meat/meet*), but cause problems in spelling.

7. The final *e* (silent *e,* e-marker) accounts for many of the sound distinctions in words.

All the vowels, except *a*, can also act as consonants.

1. The letter *e* stands for the /y/ sound in the word *azalea.*

2. The letter *i* when it follows *c, s, ss, sc, t,* and *x* stands for the /sh/ sound (example: *nation*). The letter *i* can also stand for the /y/ sound as in *union, opinion, senior, brilliant, civilian, junior, onion, million, spaniel,* and *stallion.*

3. The letter *o* stands for the /w/ sound as in *one* and *once.*

4. The letter *u* when it follows *s* and *ss* stands for the /zh/ sound (example: *measure*). The letter *u* also stands for the /w/ sound as in *liquid, quiet, quick, queen, quill, quilt, suite, suave, language,* and *penguin.*

How Phonics Is Taught

- -

"Teach to mastery rather than just exposure."

—John Shefelbine

- -

Many years ago, Flintstone lunch box in hand, I entered a small, rural classroom in a school building I had occasionally passed by and frequently wondered about. The large, brick building was old and run-down, but memories of the brightly illustrated books and seemingly fun activities my older sister brought home piqued my interest. On my first day of grade 1, my teacher, Mrs. Wershaw, distributed to each of us eager, neatly dressed six-year-olds a basal reader and introduced us to three characters we would grow to love—Dick, Jane, and Sally. In addition, she gave us a phonics workbook whose plaid cover had the same design as the girls' skirts at the Catholic school in a neighboring town. Mrs. Wershaw's combined approach to teaching us how to read (sight-word and phonics methods) was the key that unlocked the mysteries of print for me. And, even though some argue about the lack of engaging text in these early readers, I was enthralled by the ability to take those strange looking lines and squiggles on the page and turn them into something that made sense.

My strongest memory of the impact of these stories came one Friday afternoon. Mrs. Wershaw had a strict rule that we could not read ahead in our basals. So, on Friday when Sally fell headfirst into a clothes hamper, and I couldn't turn the page to discover the outcome, I had a weekend of tremendous anxiety. On Monday I raced into school to see if Sally was okay. She was! It was my first taste of suspense in books, and I was forever hooked.

You may be asking yourself, "Why is he telling me about early phonics instruction? I teach the intermediate grades!" Well, many of the instructional principles critical to early phonics instruction also apply to advanced phonics instruction. In addition, some of your students may be at a lower stage of reading development, and the instruction you give them will mirror that of the primary grades.

Two Ways to Teach Phonics

Generally speaking, phonics instruction falls into two camps, or approaches. The first is the **synthetic approach**. This method is also known as **direct** or **explicit phonics**. It follows a bottom-up model of learning to read. That is, children begin by learning to recognize letters, then blend words, and finally read connected text. Instruction roughly follows this sequence:

1. The letter names are taught.
2. The sound that each letter stands for is taught and reviewed. Some rules or generalizations might be discussed.
3. The principle of blending sounds to form words is taught.
4. Opportunities to blend unknown words in context are provided.

The following model illustrates the introduction of the /sh/ sound using this approach:

The Synthetic Approach: A Model

Write the letters *sh* on the board. Explain to students that the letters *sh* stand for the /sh/ sound, such as the first sound heard in the word *shop*. Write the letters *sh* on the board as students chorally say the /sh/ sound. Then write the word *shop* on the board, and have a volunteer circle the letters *sh*. Slowly blend the word as you run your finger under each letter/spelling. Then ask students for other words that begin with the /sh/ sound. List these words on the board. Have volunteers circle the letters *sh* in each word. Continue by providing students with words containing the /sh/ sound to blend. Make sure these words can be decoded based on the sound-spelling relationships previously taught.

The second is the **analytic approach**. This method is also known as **indirect** or **implicit phonics**. It is sometimes referred to as the "discovery method." With this approach, children begin with words and are asked to deduce the sound-spelling relationship that is the focus of the lesson. Instruction roughly follows this sequence:

1. A list of words with a common phonic element is shown. For example, the words *shop*, *shut*, and *shell* might be written on the board.
2. The children are asked to examine the words and discover what they have in common, focusing on finding a similar sound in each.
3. Once the common sound is discovered, the spelling that stands for the sound might be discussed.
4. The children are asked to verbalize a generalization about the sound and spelling, such as "the letters *sh* stand for the /sh/ sound."

The analytic approach gained popularity with teachers who believed that if children discovered these principles for themselves, they would better internalize them. However, one of the drawbacks of the analytic approach is that it relies on a child's ability to orally segment words. It isn't effective for children who can't break off the first sound in a given word, or who don't understand what is meant by the word *sound*. These children lack the **phonemic awareness** (the understanding that a word is made up of a series of discrete sounds) skills they need for the analytic approach to have meaning. And the method has proved least effective with students at risk for reading disorders.

Current research supports a combined approach to teaching phonics, with a heavy emphasis on synthetic (explicit) instruction (Adams, 1990; Anderson et al., 1985; Beck & Beck, 2013; Langenburg, 2000). Before I share my other recommendations for phonics instruction, it will be helpful for us to take a brief look at how children's decoding abilities develop. This will help to form the "big picture" within which instructional decisions can be made.

How Readers Develop

In order to understand the decoding issues of some intermediate grade students, it's helpful to review the stages early readers go through as they develop their skills and where and when issues might arise. For some intermediate students, it will be necessary to revisit these early skills as they are stuck in an earlier stage of reading development. During the primary grades, most children are at a stage of reading development referred to as the Initial Reading, or Decoding, Stage (Chall, 1983). It is at this stage that children are taught sound-spelling relationships and how to blend sounds to form words. (For more information on reading development stages, see page 21.) Within each stage of reading development, children progress in roughly predictable ways. Several researchers, including Biemiller (1970a, 1970b) and Juel (1991), have looked at how children progress through the Initial Reading, or Decoding, Stage. Juel has outlined three stages, or levels of progression, within the Initial Reading Stage. She calls these stages the **Stages of Decoding**.

When you think about the stages of decoding, it's important to ask yourself, "What do children need instructionally to progress effectively through each stage?" Each stage has instructional implications, and an emphasis on any one without consideration of the others can result in problems. Well-designed instruction is the key to moving children through the three stages efficiently and effectively.

For example, one of the instructional problems I see frequently is that children can't connect the sound-spelling relationships they've been taught to the text they are given to practice decoding. That is, few words in these stories contain the sound-spelling relationship taught or are decodable based on the sound-spelling relationships learned. Therefore, having few opportunities to use their growing knowledge of sound-spelling relationships, the children are likely to undervalue the importance of the phonics they're learning. Why should they pay attention during phonics lessons when they rarely use what they learn? As a result, these children don't gain fluency, are forced to rely on meaning cues such as context and pictures, and lose out on important blending practice. Many researchers have found that most poor readers over-rely on meaning cues. They're likely stuck in an earlier stage of decoding, unable to progress because of flawed instruction (Stanovich, 1980).

The Stages of Decoding

1. **Selective-cue stage:** Readers learn about print and its purposes. Activities to help children gain this insight include labeling classroom objects, reading aloud Big Books, group-writing exercises such as shared and interactive writing, and reading patterned/predictable books. To read words, children rely on three possible cues: (1) **random cues**, which include almost any visual clue that will help the child to remember the word. It can be something as abstract as a thumbprint or smudge next to the word (Gough & Juel, 1991); (2) **environmental cues**, such as where the word is located on the page; and (3) **distinctive letters**, such as the *y* in *pony* or the two *ll*'s in *yellow*.

2. **Spelling-sound stage:** Readers focus on graphophonic (phonics) cues to learn sound-spelling relationships and the importance of attending to each letter in a word. They learn how to blend words and make full use of their growing knowledge of sound-spelling relationships. Phonics instruction plays a crucial role at this stage.

3. **Automatic stage:** Readers use both contextual (meaning) and graphophonic (phonics) cues. It's at this point that readers develop fluency (accuracy and speed in decoding). Fluency is critical and comes with "over-learning"—constant review and repetition using sound-spelling knowledge to blend words in context. Automaticity, or fluency, is the result. This acquired automaticity enables readers to focus on the meaning of increasingly complex passages instead of the mechanics of reading. It is critical for students in grade 3 and above.

Another frequently encountered problem is the trailing off of phonics instruction in grades 2 and beyond. In order to develop fluency and read multisyllabic words, students still need explicit instruction in more complex sound-spellings, syllabication patterns, and structural analysis, as well as information on word origins. They also need ample modeling and practice reading longer words. This instruction is more commonly referred to as "word study" and combines both vocabulary and phonics development. Research has found some very efficient ways to provide this instruction and practice. I'll expand on these techniques later in the book.

Characteristics of Strong Phonics Instruction

Active. Social. Reflective. These three words best express the phonics instruction to strive for in your classroom. Look to design a program that makes students aware of what they're doing, why they're doing it, and how they're progressing. This type of phonics instruction can be described as "metaphonics"—phonics combined with metacognition. As you develop an advanced phonics program, never lose sight of these goals: to provide students with (1) sufficient skills for breaking apart longer words to decode them and determine their meanings, and (2) ways to use these skills to read for pleasure and information. "The purpose of phonics instruction is not that children learn to sound out words. The purpose is that they learn to recognize words, quickly and automatically, so that they can turn their attention to comprehension of text" (Stahl, 1992).

Based on my work with teachers, school districts, and publishers, these big ideas can be grouped into seven characteristics that all strong phonics programs or systems must have in place. Absence or weakness in any one or more of these characteristics can have negative effects on student learning gains. While not all of these are applicable to the intermediate grades (I'll focus on those that do in the pages that follow), it is helpful to consider them all.

1 **Readiness Skills** The two best predictors of early reading success are phonemic awareness and alphabet recognition. Phonemic awareness is the understanding that words are made up of discrete sounds. A range of subskills is taught to develop phonemic awareness, with oral blending and oral segmentation having the most positive impact on reading and writing development. I refer to these skills as the power skills. Alphabet recognition involves learning the names, shapes, and sounds of the letters of the alphabet with fluency. Phonemic awareness and alphabet recognition are focused on primarily in kindergarten and Grade 1.

2 **Scope and Sequence** A strong scope and sequence that builds from the simple to the complex in a way that works best for student learning is critical to student achievement at all stages of learning. While there is no one "right" scope and sequence, programs that strive to connect concepts and move through a series of skills in a small stair-step way offer the best chance at student success.

3 **Blending** This is the main strategy for teaching students how to sound out words and must be frequently modeled and applied. It is the focus of early phonics instruction, but still plays a role when transitioning students from reading one-syllable words to multisyllabic words.

4 **Dictation** To best transition students' growing reading skills to writing, dictation (guided spelling) is critical and should begin as early as kindergarten. While not a spelling test, this activity can accelerate students' spelling abilities and understanding of common English spelling patterns.

5 **Word Awareness** While the introduction to phonics skills is best when explicit and systematic, students need opportunities to play with words and experiment with how word parts combine to solidify and consolidate their understanding of how English words work. Word sorts and word building are two key activities to increase students' word awareness.

6 **High-Frequency Words** Those high-utility words that are irregular based on common sound-spelling patterns or need to be taught before students have all the phonics skills to access them through sounding out must be addressed instructionally in a different way. Past Grade 2, when the majority of the key high-frequency words have been introduced, students need to be continually assessed on their mastery of these words as a lack of fluency can impede comprehension.

7 **Reading Connected Text** The types of text we use in early reading instruction has a powerful effect on the word reading strategies students develop (Juel & Roper-Schneider, 1985) and can affect student motivation to read. While no longer an issue at the intermediate grades, struggling readers will benefit from a stronger connection between the text they read and the phonics skills they have mastered and/or are practicing for mastery.

And most important of all is you, the teacher. The power and impact of the above characteristics depend on them being implemented by a skilled, informed teacher. Teachers with stronger backgrounds in linguistics and research-based phonics instructional routines are better equipped at noticing and addressing student errors, have improved language of instruction, and can more easily differentiate their teaching to meet student needs. Differentiated professional development can assist schools and districts in building teacher capacity when it comes to phonics and word study instruction at the intermediate grades.

You can use the checklist on page 50 to evaluate your phonics instruction; it's also available online as Resource 3.1 (see page 367 for details on how to access). It's based on guidelines established by research and practice over the past several decades (Beck & Beck, 2013; Beck & McCaslin, 1978; Chall, 1996; Stahl, 1992; Vacca, Vacca, & Gove, 1995).

Evaluation Checklist

My Phonics Instruction...

❑ builds on a foundation of phonemic awareness and knowledge of how language works.

❑ is clear, direct, and explicit.

❑ contains instruction in blending and ample modeling of applying phonics skills.

❑ is integrated into a total reading program. Reading instruction must include these goals: decoding accuracy and fluency, increased word knowledge, experience with various linguistic structures, knowledge of the world, and experience in thinking about texts. Phonics is one important element.

❑ focuses on reading words and connected text, not learning rules.

❑ develops independent word recognition strategies, focusing attention on the internal structure of words, such as affixes, roots, and common spelling patterns.

❑ develops automatic word recognition skills (fluency) so that students can devote their attention to comprehension.

❑ contains repeated opportunities to apply learned sound-spelling relationships to reading and writing.

My Phonics Instruction Avoids...

Some phonics instructional strands fail because (Beck & McCaslin, 1978; Chall, 1996):

❑ instruction is hit-or-miss, instead of systematic.

❑ instruction is too abstract.

❑ students are not taught how to blend words.

❑ instruction is not connected to actual reading.

❑ there is not enough review and application.

❑ too many rules and sound-spelling relationships are taught.

❑ the pace of instruction is too fast.

❑ phonics is taught as the only way to figure out unfamiliar words.

❑ too much time is spent on tasks that have little relationship to authentic reading and writing application (Blevins, 2016).

What About Scope and Sequence?

One of the most difficult decisions to make when developing any phonics program is the order, or **sequence**, in which the sound-spelling relationships are taught. Educators have considerable debates about this issue. One of the key areas of dissent is how to teach vowel sounds. Some argue that long-vowel sounds should be taught first since these sounds are easier to auditorily discriminate than short-vowel sounds. In addition, the long vowels "say their names." One drawback to this approach is that there are many long-vowel spellings and introducing children to such complexities before they have gained key insights into how the "system" works might create serious problems. Others argue that short-vowel sounds and their one key spelling should be taught first because many simple CVC (consonant-vowel-consonant) words (such as *cat, sun, hit*) can be generated. Many of these "high utility" words appear in early reading materials, and it is thought that introducing them first makes it easier to teach the "system."

I offer the following recommendations regarding sequence:

- **Teach short-vowel sounds before long-vowel sounds.** Efficiency and ease of learning is critical. The simplicity of using short-vowel spellings and CVC words is beneficial to struggling readers.
- **Teach consonants and short vowels in combination so that words can be generated as early as possible.** Phonics is useless if it can't be applied, and what is not applied is not learned. By teaching short vowels and consonants in combination, you can create decodable connected text so children can apply their knowledge of learned sound-spelling relationships.
- **Make sure the majority of the consonants you teach early on are continuous consonants,** such as *f, l, m, n, r,* and *s*. This makes it easier to model blending because these consonant sounds can be sustained without distortion.

- **Use a sequence in which the most words can be generated.** For example, many words can be generated using the letter *t*; however, few can be generated using the letter *x*. Therefore, higher-frequency sound-spelling relationships should precede less-frequent ones.
- **Progress from simple to more complex sound-spellings.** For example, consonant sounds should be taught before digraphs (*sh*, *ch*, *th*, *wh*, *ph*, *gh*, *ng*) and blends (*br*, *cl*, *st*, etc.). Likewise, short vowel sound-spellings should be taught before long vowel sound-spellings, variant vowels, and diphthongs.
- **Once complex sound-spellings have been taught, focus on larger spelling patterns,** common syllable types and patterns, and useful word parts such as prefixes, suffixes, and roots.

Another major decision in teaching phonics is the **scope** of instruction: deciding which sound-spelling relationships are important enough to warrant instruction and which, because of their lower frequency in words, can be learned on an as-needed basis. The chart on page 53 shows the most frequent spellings of the 44 sounds covered in this book. These are the sounds and spellings covered in most basal reading programs.

The percentages provided in parentheses are based on the number of each sound-spelling that appeared in the 17,000 most frequently used words (Hanna, Hodges, Hanna & Rudolph, 1966). These included multisyllabic words. (See page 202 for information on the most important syllable patterns and types to teach.)

The Most Frequent Spellings of the 44 Sounds of English

Sound	Common Spellings	Sound	Common Spellings
1. /b/	b (97%), bb	23. /hw/	wh (100%)
2. /d/	d (98%), dd, ed	24. /zh/	si (49%), s (33%), ss, z
3. /f/	f (78%), ff, ph, lf	25. /ng/	n (41%), ng (59%)
4. /g/	g (88%), gg, gh	26. /a/	a (96%)
5. /h/	h (98%), wh	27. /e/	e (91%), ea, e_e (5%)
6. /j/	g (66%), j (22%), dg	28. /i/	i (66%), y (23%)
7. /k/	c (73%), cc, k (13%), ck, lk, q	29. /o/	o (79%)
8. /l/	l (91%), ll	30. /u/	u (86%), o, ou
9. /m/	m (94%), mm	31. /ā/	a (45%), a_e (35%), ai, ay, ea
10. /n/	n (97%), nn, kn, gn	32. /ē/	e (70%), y, ea (10%), ee (10%), ie, e_e, ey, i, ei
11. /p/	p (96%), pp	33. /ī/	i-e (37%), i (37%), igh, y (14%), ie, y_e
12. /r/	r (97%), rr, wr	34. /ō/	o (73%), o_e (14%), ow, oa, oe
13. /s/	s (73%), c (17%), ss	35. /yoo/	u (69%), u_e (22%), ew, ue
14. /t/	t (97%), tt, ed	36. /ə/	a (24%), e (13%), i (22%), o (27%), u
15. /v/	v (99.5%), f (of)	37. /yoo/	oo (38%), u (21%), o, ou, u_e, ew, ue
16. /w/	w (92%)	38. /oo/	oo (31%), u (54%), ou, o (8%), ould
17. /y/	y (44%), i (55%)	39. /ou/	ou (56%), ow (29%)
18. /z/	z (23%), zz, s (64%)	40. /oi/	oi (62%), oy (32%)
19. /ch/	ch (55%), t (31%)	41. /ô/	o, a, au, aw, ough, augh
20. /sh/	sh (26%), ti (53%), ssi, s, si sci	42. /û/	er (40%), ir (13%), ur (26%)
21. /th/	th (100%)	43. /â/	a (29%), are (23%), air (21%)
22. /th/	th (100%)	44. /ä/	a (89%) (as in *car*)

In addition to sound-spelling relationships, it's important to cover other aspects of phonics knowledge such as structural analysis and syllabication. Below is a recommended scope of skills for each grade (Blevins, 2017; Chall, 1996).

Kindergarten

- concepts of print
- alphabet recognition
- phonemic awareness
- blending
- sense of story
- building word knowledge
- short vowels (*a, e, i, o, u*—CVC pattern)

Grade 1

- phonemic awareness
- blending and word building
- short vowels (*a, e, i, o, u*—CVC pattern)
- consonants
- final *e* (*a_e, e_e, i_e, o_e, u_e*—CVCe pattern)
- long-vowel digraphs (*ai, ay, ea, ee, oa, ow*, etc.)
- consonant clusters (*br, cl, st*, etc.)
- digraphs (*sh, ch, th, wh*, etc.)
- some other vowels such as *oo, ou, ow, oi, oy*
- early structural analysis: verb endings (*-ing, -ed*), plurals, contractions, compound words
- connected text reading
- vocabulary development/word knowledge

Grades 2–3

- grade 1 skills review
- more complex vowel spellings
- more structural analysis (compound words, affixes, etc.)
- multisyllabic words
- syllabication strategies (common syllable spelling patterns)
- connected text reading
- vocabulary development/word knowledge

Grades 4–8

- more complex vowel spellings
- more structural analysis (compound words, affixes, etc.)
- multisyllabic words
- syllabication strategies (common syllable spelling patterns and types)
- word origins (Greek and Latin roots)
- connected text reading
- vocabulary development/word knowledge

Beyond decisions about scope and sequence, I recommend that you make your instruction systematic. What do I mean by this? Systematic instruction follows a sequence that progresses from easy to more difficult. Systematic instruction includes constant review and repetition of sound-spelling relationships, application to reading and writing, and a focus on developing fluency through work with reading rate and decoding accuracy. Just because a program has a scope and sequence doesn't mean it's systematic. The instruction must be cumulative. The students' growing knowledge of sound-spellings must be reflected in the texts they're given to practice using these sound-spellings to decode words. In addition, the instruction must help students understand how words "work"—how to use knowledge of sound-spellings to blend the sounds in words. In essence, the system should not only be in the reading program, it should be in the students. They should be able to internalize how the "system" works through the type of instruction they are given.

Blending: Teaching Children How Words Work

Blending is a primary phonics strategy (Resnick & Beck, 1976). It is simply stringing together the sounds that each spelling stands for in a word in order to say the word. Some children seem to develop the ability to blend sounds in words naturally (Whaley & Kirby, 1980), whereas others need explicit teaching of this skill. It is critical to teach these children how to generalize sound-spelling relationships with new words (Golinkoff, 1978). Until a child can blend the sounds in words, phonics instruction will be of limited value. Research has revealed that students of teachers who spend more than average instructional time on modeling and reinforcing blending procedures achieve greater than average gains on first- and second-grade reading achievement tests (Haddock, 1976; Rosenshine & Stevens, 1984).

Two blending procedures have the greatest reading pay-off: **final blending** and **successive blending** (Resnick & Beck, 1976).

Final blending. With this strategy, the sound of each spelling is stated and stored. The whole word isn't blended until all the sounds in the word have been identified and pronounced. For example, for the word *sat*:

1. Point to the letter *s* and say /s/.
2. Point to the letter *a* and say /a/.
3. Slowly slide your finger under the letters *sa* and say /sa/ slowly.
4. Then, quickly slide your finger under the letters *sa* and say /sa/ quickly.
5. Next, point to the letter *t* and say /t/.
6. Slowly slide your finger under *sat* and say /sat/ slowly.
7. Circle the word with your finger and say, "The word is *sat*."

The main advantage of this procedure is that you can determine where a student is having difficulty as he or she attempts to blend an unfamiliar word. For example, if the student doesn't provide the correct sound for the spelling *s*, you know how to target further instruction. You also know if the student can't orally string together sounds. If a child correctly identifies /s/ for the letter *s* and /a/ for the letter *a*, but pronounces these two sounds in combination as "suh-aa," the student is not blending the sounds.

Successive blending. With this strategy, the sound that each spelling stands for is produced in sequence, without pauses. For example, for the word *sat*:

1. Point to the beginning of the word *sat*.
2. Run your finger under each letter as you extend the sound that each letter stands for. For example, you would say *ssssaaaat*. Do not pause between sounds. For example, don't say /s/ (pause) /a/ (pause) /t/. If the first sound is not a continuous consonant sound, quickly blend the first sound with the vowel sound that follows. For example, say *baaaat*.
3. Slowly compress the extended word. Therefore, go from *ssssaaaat* to *ssaat* to *sat*.
4. Circle the word with your finger and say, "The word is *sat*."

Blending Multisyllabic Words: A Model

How do these techniques apply to multisyllabic words? When working with longer words, it's important for students to see larger word chunks and be able blend those chunks successively instead of sound by sound. For example, for the word *unhappy*:

1. Tell students that you first look for larger word parts within this long word.
2. Point to the prefix *un* and say its sounds—/un/. Then point to the word *happy*.
3. Slowly put together these two word parts—*un* and *happy*—to say the word *unhappy*.
4. Circle the word with your finger and say, "The word is *unhappy*."
5. Explain to students how the word parts also help you determine the meaning of the word. "I know that *un* often means 'not.' Therefore, *unhappy* must mean 'not happy.'"

If students don't readily recognize larger word parts, have them look for syllable chunks and use their knowledge of syllabication spelling patterns and sound-spellings to decode each chunk. More information on syllable spelling patterns can be found on page 202.

Word Awareness Activities

While the initial introduction of phonics skills is best using an explicit approach that does not mean there shouldn't be a time during the instructional cycle in which students play with and explore letter-sounds. In fact, I think this exploration is *critical* for students to consolidate and solidify their learning of how words work. Yes, the initial introduction begins this learning efficiently, but it takes time and loads of experiences reading and writing words for that knowledge to be mastered. These types of "exploratory" activities provide essential "thinking" time for students as they incorporate new learning into already established learning. When phonics instruction fails, it often does so because it is rote, unthinking, and not applied to real reading and writing experiences.

Word Building and Word Sorts

The two best types of exploration exercises that increase a student's word awareness are *word building* and *word sorts*.

Both should be an important part of the phonics instructional cycle for each skill introduced.

In **word building**, students are given a set of letter cards and asked to create a series of words in a specified sequence. This can occur during both whole- and small-group lessons. Generally each new word varies by only one sound-spelling from the previous word (can be more variance as students progress in skills). For example, students might be asked to build, or make with letter cards, these words in sequence: *sat*, *mat*, *map*, *mop*. Notice how each word varies from the preceding word by only one sound-spelling. As students move up the grades, word building should continue with students using syllables instead of individual letters to build increasingly more complex words.

There are two types of word building, each with a clearly defined instructional purpose.

1 Word Building: Blending Focus

In this type of word building, students are asked to make a word, such as *sat*. They are then told to change the letter *s* to the letter *m* and read the new word formed. Thus, the primary goal is for them to blend, or sound out, the new word formed. This is the type of blending you might want to start out with at the beginning of an instructional cycle. It allows students time to decode many words with the new target phonics skills, while also reviewing previously taught skills.

2 Word Building: Word Awareness Focus

In this type of building, students are asked to make a word, such as *sat*. They are then told to change *sat* to *mat*. This is cognitively more demanding than the blending-focused word building. Why? Students have to consider how the words *sat* and *mat* vary (i.e., which sound is different), which letter must be removed from *sat*, which added to form *mat*, and in which position in the word. That's a lot of thinking about how words work! This is why word building is so beneficial. Students gain flexibility in how to use sound-spellings in words. This type of word building is one you can do later in the week after students have had more exposure to the skill. And, by repeating the word building sequences multiple times throughout the week with different instructional focuses, you only need to create one set of words and one set of letter cards—saving you valuable planning time.

Word sorts also allow students time to think about how words work by drawing their attention to important and common spelling patterns. Generally, in word sorts students are given a set of words that have something in common (e.g., all contain the same vowel sound, but with different spellings as in -*oat* and -*oad* words for long *o*). Students are asked to sort the words by their common feature.

There are many types of word sorts, each with a distinct instructional purpose. Below are three of the most common types.

1 **Open Sort** In these sorts, students are not told how to sort the words. That is, students are given a set of words and allowed to sort them in any way they want. This is a good first sort with a set of words because it tells you a lot about how students are thinking about words and what aspects of words they notice. So for example, if you gave the students these words—*boat, road, throw, grow, soap, show*—and they sorted them by first letter-sound, that would indicate the students are noticing very simplistic aspects of words (initial letter-sounds) and not noticing what is truly common among these words (they all contain the long *o* sound spelled *oa* or *ow*).

2 **Closed Sort** In these sorts, students are told how to sort the words. So for the preceding long *o* sort, students are told to sort the words into two piles, each representing a different spelling for the long *o* sound (*oa* or *ow*). These are fairly simple and direct sorts since students are visually scanning each word for a specified spelling pattern. The value in this type of sort is the conversation you have with students *following* the sort. For example, you should

ask students questions like: *What do you notice about these words? What do you notice about these spellings for long o? Do you know other words with these spellings?* Then you guide students (if they don't notice on their own) that the *oa* spelling for long *o* rarely appears at the end of the word. This is really valuable information about how words work that will have positive benefits on students' future reading and writing. That is, when a student encounters a new word when writing (e.g., the word *snow*), what do they do? They think about each sound and the associated spelling. When they get to the long *o* sound at the end of the word *snow*, they know they have two options that they've learned—*oa* or *ow*. Which is a better option? Well, if you've had the discussion during the sort, the student will know that the *ow* spelling is the only option since *oa* cannot appear at the end of a word. This is the kind of thinking and knowledge building we want to have happen as a result of word sorts. Word sorts are far more than a quick, visual, sorting task.

3 Timed Sorts In these sorts, students are told how to sort a set of words, but are given a limited amount of time to do so. This is an ideal type of sort to do with a set of words students have been working with all week (having already completed open and closed sorts). Adding the element of time creates a game-like feel to the task that students enjoy. However, even more, it provides an important benefit. Getting students to readily notice larger word chunks in words, such as these common spelling patterns, is essential to reading longer, multisyllabic words. As students progress up the grades, the words they encounter will increase in length. Instead of reading new words like *cat*, *soap*, and *barn*, they begin to encounter words like *unexpected*, *predetermined*, and *unhappily*. It becomes inefficient for students to attack these words letter-by-letter. Instead, larger chunks of these words need to visually "pop" out so the reader has fewer word parts to tackle, making the reading easier. Doing timed sorts helps to train the eye to see quickly these larger word chunks in new, unfamiliar words. Plus, it's a great way to extend the practice with the word card sets you have created for the week—giving you more bang for your time in creating and organizing the materials for these sorts. You can also set up these timed sorts on a whiteboard using simple word cards and a timer for students to practice during independent work time alone or with a partner.

Other common sorts include sound sorts, pattern sorts, meaning sorts, buddy sorts, blind sorts, and writing sorts. For more information about these other types of sorts I recommend *Words Their Way* (Bear, Templeton, Invernizzi & Johnston, 2016).

Word Sort and Word Building Routines

Word building and word sorts should be a key component of each instructional cycle for every new phonics skill. On the following pages are instructional routines for each. You know word building and word sorts are having a positive effect on students' word awareness when you see an increase in students' ability to comment on how words work and evidence that they are fully analyzing similar words and thereby avoiding common reading issues that result when only portions of a word are looked at in order to read it (e.g., using the beginning and perhaps ending letters, then guessing from those clues and the picture). Also, as students have regular weekly practice analyzing words in this way, you will start to see them noticing common spelling patterns and other aspects of words before you teach them. For example, I've had students point out sound-spellings that we will study in upcoming weeks *before* I formally teach them because they have seen several words with this sound-spelling in books we read together or I read aloud (e.g., the digraph *sh* in *she*, *should*, and *fish*).

These types of word awareness activities create students who become *word detectives*—curious about words and always on the lookout for what is common among words. This improved word awareness has generative effects as students progress through the grades and encounter words with prefixes, suffixes, spelling changes, and Greek and Latin roots.

Word Sort Routine

Step 1: Introduce Name the task and explain its purpose. Distribute the word cards and read each with students to make sure they know all the words. If you are doing a closed sort, introduce the categories in which students will be sorting the words.

Step 2: Sort Have students sort the words. If a closed sort, model sorting one of two of the words. Then have students sort the remaining words. Circulate and ask students questions about why they are putting specific words into each category.

Step 3: Check and Discuss Review the words in each sort category. Ask students what they learned about these words from doing the sort. Guide students to the word awareness aspect of each sort that will assist them in reading and writing. Have students store the word cards for future sorts (e.g., a timed sort using these words).

Too often word sorts are treated as a simple task of rearranging word cards and the follow-up discussion to better understand how words work never occurs. Every word sort should end with a question such as, "What did you notice about these words?" or "What did you learn about these spelling patterns?" Students need to verbalize their thinking about words. Use follow-up questions to guide students if they don't readily recognize important features of the spellings and patterns. For example, "Where does this spelling appear in all the words? How is it different from the other spellings for this sound?" You might include a couple "outlier" words in a sort to highlight a concept. For example, if you are sorting words with final *e* like *hope*, *rope*, *home*, *joke*, and *note* you might want to add the words *come* and *some* and point out common words that break the rule or pattern.

Word Building Routine

Step 1: Introduce Name the task and explain its purpose to students. Say: *Today we will be building, or making, words using the letters and spellings we have learned.*

Step 2: Model Place letter cards in a pocket chart (or use letter cards on a whiteboard) to form the first word you are building. Model sounding out the word. Remember to (a) build words using the new, target sound-spelling, (b) add words with review sound-spellings as appropriate to extend the review and application of these skills to achieve mastery, and (c) use minimal contrasts to require students to fully analyze words and notice their unique differences (e.g., *sat/mat, pan/pen, rip/trip, hat/hate, cot/coat, happy/unhappy/happily/happiness*).

Step 3: Guided Practice/Practice Continue by changing one (or more) letters in the word. Have students chorally blend the new word formed. Do a set of 8-10 words. Say: *Change the letter* s *in* sat *to* m. *What is the new word?* Or, if students are more advanced in their understanding, say, *Change the first sound in* sat *to /m/.*

If the focus on the word building is word awareness (instead of blending like the above example), then tell students what the next word in the sequence is and give them time to form the new word. Circulate and provide assistance and corrective feedback (e.g., modeling your thinking process, modeling how to blend the word, etc). Then build the new word in the pocket chart (or on the whiteboard), modeling aloud your thinking.

Upgrade your work with word building by creating an additional activity each week called Word Ladders (created by Dr. Timothy Rasinski). What distinguishes word ladders from the typical word building exercise is the added element of vocabulary. Instead of asking students to build a word like *top* then change it to make the word *mop*, you ask the students to change "one letter in the word *top* to name something you use to clean a wet floor." This is a fun activity to do at the end of the week when students have had multiple exposures to the words and know their meanings. Students love figuring out the clues, then determining how to make the new word.

Here's an example of a word ladder I helped create with teachers from a large, urban school district. They were simple and fun to create. Published versions of word ladders also exist, most notably those created by Tim Rasinski (e.g., *Daily Word Ladders*, 2005). I love his work and these books are a great resource. I've also included a blank template online for your reference; see page 367 for details on how to access.

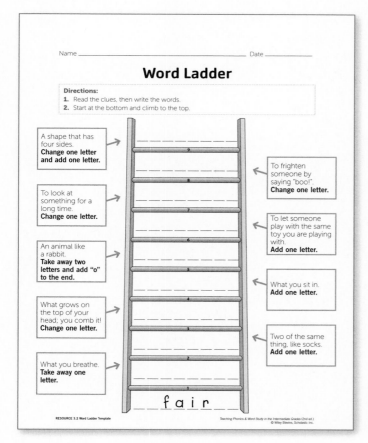

A blank template can be found online as Resource 3.2; see page 367 for details on how to access.

High-Frequency Words

High-frequency words play an important role in reading fluency. What are they, and how should they be taught? Of the approximately 600,000-plus words in English, a relatively small number appear frequently in print. Only 13 words (*a*, *and*, *for*, *he*, *is*, *in*, *it*, *of*, *that*, *the*, *to*, *was*, *you*) account for over 25% of the words in print (Johns, 1980), and 100 words account for approximately 50% (Adams, 1990; Carroll, Davies, & Richman, 1971; Fry, Fountoukidis, & Polk, 1985). About 250 words make up 70–75% of all the words students use in their writing (Rinsland, 1945). Of these about 20% are function words such as *a*, *the*, and *and*.

Although high-frequency word lists disagree on the rank order of words, and many lists contain different words, there is general agreement on the majority of them. Many of the word lists are based on textbooks used in grades 1–8 (Harris & Jacobson, 1972). The Dolch Basic Sight Vocabulary (see page 70) contains 220 words (no nouns). Although this list was generated over 40 years ago, these words account for over 50% of the words found in textbooks today. In addition to this list, I've provided a list of the 150 most frequent words (in order of frequency) in printed school

English according to the *American Heritage Word Frequency Book* (Carroll et al., 1971; see page 69). These are the words most children should have mastered by grade 3. If they have not, concentrated review is in order.

Knowledge of high-frequency words is necessary for fluent reading. Although many of them carry little meaning, they affect the flow and coherence of text. Many of these words are considered "irregular" because they stray from the commonly taught sound-spelling relationships. Research shows that readers store these "irregular" words in their lexical memory in the same way they store so-called "regular" words (Gough & Walsh, 1991; Lovett, 1987; Treiman & Baron, 1981). That is, readers must pay attention to each letter and the pattern of letters in a word and associate them with the sounds that they represent (Ehri, 1992). Therefore, instruction should focus attention on each letter and/or letter pattern.

However, children don't learn "irregular" words as easily or quickly as "regular" ones. Early readers commonly confuse the high-frequency words *of, for,* and *from;* the reversible words *on/no* and *was/saw;* and words with *th* and *w* such as *there, them, their, then, what, were, where, this, these, went, will, that, this, when,* and *with* (Cunningham, 1995). Therefore, children need to be taught "irregular," high-frequency words with explicit instruction. I suggest the following sequence:

1. State aloud the word and use it in a sentence.
2. Write the sentence on the board. Underline the high-frequency word and read it aloud.
3. Discuss the word and mention any special features it contains.
4. Have the children spell aloud the word as you point to each letter.
5. Have the children write the word.
6. Have the children spell aloud the word again as they write it on a piece of paper.
7. Finally, write the word on a note card and display the card on the wall for future reference when reading or writing. Organize the words according to common spelling patterns. Periodically review the note card and any other high-frequency cards you've displayed.

You can provide additional practice using individually given, timed speed drills and daily review; see sample below. Select ten words you want to test students on, write them in random order on a sheet, and then have students read as many words as they can in one minute. Mark on a copy of the drill sheet the words they mispronounce. Have each student count the number of words he or she read correctly and mark this on a progress chart. Students find it highly motivating to track their own progress. Allow students additional opportunities to improve their speed drill times.

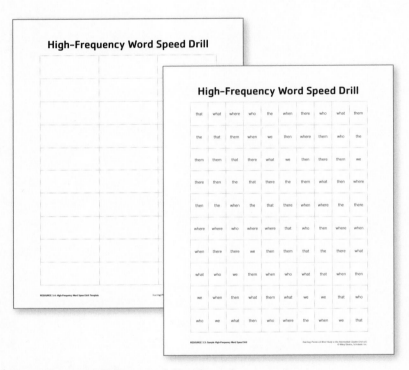

A sample speed drill (Resource 3.3) and speed drill template (Resource 3.4) can be downloaded from www.scholastic.com/phonicsintermediate. See page 367 for details on how to access.

The Most Frequent Words

This chart contains the 150 most frequent words (in order of frequency) in printed school English according to the *American Heritage Word Frequency Book*.

the	can	been	three	had	made	right
of	an	long	word	not	over	look
and	your	little	must	will	did	think
a	which	very	because	each	down	such
to	their	after	does	about	only	here
in	said	words	part	how	way	take
is	if	called	even	up	find	why
you	do	just	place	out	use	things
that	into	where	well	them	may	help
it	has	most	as	then	water	put
he	more	know	with	she	go	years
for	her	get	his	many	good	different
was	two	through	they	some	new	away
on	like	back	at	so	write	again
are	him	much	be	these	our	off
but	see	before	this	would	used	went
what	time	also	from	other	me	old
all	could	around	I	its	man	number
were	no	another	have	who	too	
when	make	came	or	now	any	
we	than	come	by	people	day	
there	first	work	one	my	same	

Note: These words are available as word cards in Resource 3.5, which you can download from www.scholastic.com/phonicsintermediate. See page 367 for details on how to access.

Dolch Basic Sight Vocabulary 220

a	call	funny	just	only	small	use
about	came	gave	keep	open	so	very
after	can	get	kind	or	some	walk
again	carry	give	know	our	soon	want
all	clean	go	laugh	out	start	warm
always	cold	goes	let	over	stop	was
am	come	going	light	own	take	wash
an	could	good	like	pick	tell	we
and	cut	got	little	play	ten	well
any	did	green	live	please	thank	went
are	do	grow	long	pretty	that	were
around	does	had	look	pull	the	what
as	done	has	made	put	their	when
ask	don't	have	make	ran	them	where
at	down	he	many	read	then	which
ate	draw	help	may	red	there	white
away	drink	her	me	ride	these	who
be	eat	here	much	right	they	why
because	eight	him	must	round	think	will
been	every	his	my	run	this	wish
before	fall	hold	myself	said	those	with
best	far	hot	never	saw	three	work
better	fast	how	new	say	to	would
big	find	hurt	no	see	today	write
black	first	I	not	seven	together	yellow
blue	five	if	now	shall	too	yes
both	fly	in	of	she	try	you
bring	for	into	off	show	two	your
brown	found	is	old	sing	under	
but	four	it	on	sit	up	
buy	from	its	once	six	upon	
by	full	jump	one	sleep	us	

Creating Lessons for Success

"Patterns and morphological relationships are the keys to unlocking pronunciation, spelling, and meaning. All students should be issued these master keys."

—Patricia Cunningham

As I've visited classrooms across the country, I've seen a wide range of activities and instructional methods used to teach phonics. Many of these activities and methods have fallen under the umbrella of "explicit" phonics instruction. I have chosen those that are the most effective to help you develop guidelines for writing phonics lessons. Here are a few general do's and don'ts of phonics instruction (Blevins, 2017; Groff, 1977).

Phonics Lessons Do's

- **Use a logical sequence.** Explicitly teach the sound-spelling relationship, syllabication spelling pattern, or structural analysis skill. Progress to guided blending practice, then conclude with reading and writing opportunities.
- **Provide frequent, daily lessons.**
- **Keep the lessons relatively brief and fast-paced.**
- **Keep the lessons focused.** Cover only a small segment at a time.

- **Begin lessons with what students know.**
- **Create a classroom environment in which students become active word watchers** or word detectives—an environment in which there is a curiosity about words.
- **Provide a built-in review** of previously taught sound-spellings or spelling patterns in each lesson (through blending exercises, repeated readings, etc.).
- **Adjust pace or scope according to students' needs.** Don't set absolute deadlines for how much should be covered in a given time.
- **Regroup students according to their needs.**
- **Link phonics instruction to spelling** through dictation and free-writing activities.
- **Make learning public.** Create word walls, make letter charts, and share student writing.
- **Provide instruction that is reflective.** Gaskins, Ehri, Cress, O'Hara, & Donnelly (1996–1997), for example, use the "Talk-To-Yourself Chart" with students to engage them in thinking about words. Here is a completed chart for the word *high*.

  1. The word is *high*.
  2. Stretch the word. I hear _2_ sounds.
  3. I see _4_ letters because *igh* stands for one sound.
  4. The spelling pattern is *igh*.
  5. This is what I know about the vowel: *It is the long* i *sound—/ī/*.
  6. Another word on the Word Wall with the same vowel sound is *light*.

Phonics Lessons Don'ts

Here are five things to avoid in phonics instruction.

- **Avoid having students continually wait for turns.** Instead, use choral response techniques or every-pupil response cards.
- **Avoid instruction in which students are not directly told** what they are being asked to understand and how they should respond.

- **Avoid immediately correcting students' errors.** Provide feedback only after allowing students an opportunity to self-monitor and self-correct.
- **Avoid inadequately addressing exceptions to the generalizations being learned.**
- **Avoid using incorrect language or terminology:**

  1. Instead of saying, "You can hear the *f* sound," say, "You can hear the /f/ sound." *f* is a letter, not a sound.
  2. Rather than saying, "What sounds do you see at the end of *mint*?" say, "What sounds do you hear at the end of the word *mint*?" You see letters; you hear sounds.
  3. Instead of saying, "The letter *t* makes the /t/ sound," say, "The letter *t* stands for or represents the /t/ sound." Letters are inanimate objects; they do not make sounds.
  4. Instead of saying, "The blend *st* stands for the /st/ sound," say, "The letters (cluster) *st* stand for the /st/ sounds." *Cluster* refers to a group of letters; *blend* refers to a group of sounds.
  5. Instead of saying, "The following letters are diphthongs," say, "The following vowel pair (digraph) stands for the /oi/ sound." A diphthong is a sound; a vowel pair, or digraph, is a group of letters.

Sample Lessons and Word Lists

The following sample lessons are set up as templates for you to use when writing your phonics lessons. The lessons are brief and follow a simple 5-step procedure:

- **Step 1—Review and Warm-Up:** repeated reading and warm-up
- **Step 2—Introduce New Skill:** explicit instruction of sound-spelling relationship, spelling pattern, or word analysis skill

- **Step 3—Guided Practice:** blending and word-building exercises
- **Step 4—Apply to Text:** reading connected text
- **Step 5—Apply to Writing:** dictation and writing

Some components of the lessons, such as the warm-up exercises and reading of connected text, will be determined by the materials you have available.

Ways to Use Word Lists

You can use the words in the word lists throughout this section during phonics and spelling instruction in the following ways:

- to create word lists for blending practice
- to create connected text for reading practice
- to create word lists for word sorts
- to create word lists to be sent home for reading practice
- to create word lists to add to a word wall
- to create word lists for dictation (spelling)
- to create activity pages

Consonant Digraphs

Consonant digraphs are two consonants that appear together in a word and stand for one sound. The consonant digraphs include *sh*, *ch*, *th*, *wh*, *ph*, *gh*, and *ng*.

Teaching Guidelines

- Teach the consonant digraphs after students have learned the single consonants.
- Help your students become aware of these unique letter pairs by challenging them to be on the lookout for the digraphs in words.

Consonant Digraphs

Phonic Principle: The cluster *sh* stands for the /sh/ sound.

Step 1: Review and Warm-Up. Begin by displaying index cards with the sound-spellings or spelling patterns previously taught. Flip through the cards rapidly as students chorally say the sound(s) each represents. Then have students reread a story or passage containing previously taught sound-spelling relationships.

Step 2: Introduce New Skill. Explain to students that when we encounter the letters *s* and *h* together in words, they often stand for a new sound. Point out that the letters *sh* stand for the /sh/ sound, as in the words *ship* and *dish*. Write the words *ship* and *dish* on the board as you display a picture of each. Make sure the pictures are labeled. Then blend each word aloud as you run your finger under each letter. Have a volunteer underline the letters *sh*. Point to the letters *sh* and ask students to state the sound that the letters stand for. Continue by having students generate a list of words containing the /sh/ sound in the initial and final position. List these words on the board in separate columns.

Step 3: Guided Practice. Write the following words and sentences on the board. Note that all the words are decodable based on the sound-spelling relationships previously taught. (This should always be the case.) The first line focuses on words with the /sh/ sound in the initial position. A contrast is provided to focus students' attention on the importance of each letter in a word. The second line focuses on words with the /sh/ sound in the final position. The third line

contains multisyllabic words with /sh/. The sentences contain some high-frequency words previously taught.

- sack, shack, hop, shop
- dish, fish, mash, rush
- wishing, shoestring, shuffle, shadow
- The shopkeeper shut the door at nine.
- I should've bought those red dishes for Shirley.

Now distribute the following spelling-card set to each child: *ash, ish, ush, m, f, w, r, st, sp, ll, ing, ed*. Have students build as many words as possible. Ask them to write the words on a sheet of paper. Circulate around the room and model blending when necessary.

Step 4: Apply to Text. Provide students with connected reading practice.

Step 5: Apply to Writing. Dictate the following words and sentence; have students write the words and sentence on a sheet of paper.

- shot, shopkeeper, shared
- She was shopping for shoes.

For students having difficulty segmenting the sounds or syllables in each word, extend the word (you might wish to clap on each sound or syllable to provide another clue). Next, write the words and sentence on the board. Have students self-correct their papers. Don't grade this dictation practice. It's designed to help students segment words and associate sounds with spellings.

Consonant–Digraph Words for Instruction

/ch/ as in cheese

/ch/ Initial Position

chain	chart	cheep	chew	chin	chow
chair	chase	cheerful	chick	chip	chuckle
chalk	chat	cheese	chicken	chipmunk	chug
change	cheap	cheeseburger	child	chirp	chum
chap	cheat	cherry	children	chocolate	chunk
chapter	check	chess	chilly	choose	churn
charge	check-up	chest	chime	chop	
charm	checker	chestnut	chimney	chose	

/ch/ Final Position

beach	hunch	quench	trench	itch	stitch
bench	inch	ranch	batch	latch	stretch
branch	lunch	reach	catch	match	switch
bunch	much	rich	clutch	notch	watch
church	munch	sandwich	crutch	patch	witch
clinch	peach	search	ditch	pitch	
couch	perch	such	fetch	scratch	
crunch	pinch	teach	hitch	sketch	
each	punch	touch	hutch	snatch	

More Multisyllabic /ch/ Words

chairman	charitable	chickadee	chosen	cockroach
challenge	charter	childhood	approach	duchess
chamber	chatter	chimpanzee	attach	enchantment
champion	checkbook	chisel	beseech	hatchet
charcoal	cheesecake	chopstick	bleachers	hopscotch
chariot	cherish	chortle	catcher	launching

leeches	parchment	reattach	speechless
lunchroom	patchwork	research	spinach
merchandise	preacher	richness	stagecoach

Note: The /ch/ sound is frequently represented by the digraph *ch* as in *cheese* or *lunch*. The digraph *ch* is not reliably constant. It can also stand for the /k/ sound in words of Greek origin such as *chemical, character, chorus, orchestra, stomach*, and *school* (the word *ache* is of Anglo-Saxon origin); or the /sh/ sound in words of French origin as in *Chicago, chiffon*, and *machine*.

/sh/ as in shark

/sh/ Initial Position

shack	shampoo	she	sherbet	shock	shorts	show
shade	shape	shear	shield	shoe	shot	shower
shadow	share	shed	shift	shoelace	should	shuck
shake	shark	sheep	shin	shoot	shoulder	shut
shall	sharp	sheet	shine	shop	shout	shy
shallow	shave	shelf	ship	shore	shove	
shame	shawl	shell	shirt	short	shovel	

/sh/ Final Position

ash	cash	dash	fresh	leash	push	splash
blush	clash	dish	gash	mash	rash	trash
brush	crash	fish	gush	mesh	rush	wash
bush	crush	flash	lash	mush	smash	wish

Other /sh/ Spellings

action	attention	fraction	patient	station	vacation
addition	delicious	nation	social	suspicion	vicious

More Multisyllabic /sh/ Words

shabby	shimmer	shortstop	boyish	furnish	rubbish
shaggy	shingle	shrubbery	bushel	garish	selfish
shaken	shipment	shuffle	dishrag	harshly	snapshot
shameful	shipwreck	shuttle	dishwasher	marshal	starfish
shamrock	shoestring	shyness	eggshell	mushroom	tarnish
sharpen	shopkeeper	accomplish	establish	polish	vanish
sheepish	shoreline	anguish	fashion	publish	washboard
shellfish	shortage	banish	fishnet	punish	washcloth
shepherd	shortcut	barbershop	foolish	radish	whiplash
sheriff	shorthand	bloodshot	freshman	rosebush	workshop

Note: The /sh/ sound is frequently represented by the digraph *sh* as in *shark* and *fish*. The digraph *sh* is a very reliable spelling for this sound. Whenever we see the letters *sh* together in a word they stand for the /sh/ sound unless they appear in separate syllables, such as in *mishap* or *dishonor*. The /sh/ sound can be represented by many other spellings such as *s* (*sure, sugar*), *ti* (*nation*), *ch* (*machine*), and *ci* (*special*). The *ch* spelling for the /sh/ sound occurs mostly in words of French origin such as *chalet, chamois, chef, machine, parachute, sachet, cliché, chic, Chevrolet, Michigan*, and *Chicago*.

/zh/ as in *treasure*

/zh/ Medial Position

Asia	casual	exposure	measure	rouge	television	vision
azure	decision	garage	occasion	sabotage	treasure	
bonjour	equation	luxurious	pleasure	seizure	usual	

Note: The /zh/ sound is never represented by the letters *zh*. This letter combination doesn't appear in English words. The /zh/ sound is, instead, represented by a wide range of spellings including the following: *si* (*vision, occasion*), *s* (*pleasure, measure*), *g* (*rouge, garage*), *z* (*azure*), *zi* (*brazier*), *ssi* (*scission*), *ti* (*equation*), *x* (*luxurious*).

/th/ as in *thumb*

/th/ (voiceless) Initial Position

thank	thermos	think	thistle	through
Thanksgiving	thick	third	thorn	throw
thaw	thief	thirst	thought	thumb
theater	thimble	thirsty	thousand	thump
theme	thin	thirteen	three	thunder
thermometer	thing	thirty	thread	

/th/ (voiceless) Final Position

bath	both	fifth	math	oath	south	worth
Beth	broth	fourth	moth	path	teeth	wreath
birth	cloth	growth	mouth	Ruth	tooth	
booth	death	length	north	sixth	with	

More Multisyllabic /th/ Words

thankful	thresh	author	henceforth	pathway
therapist	throbbing	birthplace	hither	plaything
thicken	throughout	blacksmith	method	ruthless
thirtieth	thumbnail	eighteenth	methodical	sympathy
thirteenth	thunderbolt	eleventh	mother	tablecloth
thorough	thunderous	faithful	otherwise	tollbooth
thoughtful	afterthought	father	overthrow	washcloth
thoughtless	another	fifteenth	parentheses	wither
thousandth	anthem	gather	pathetic	within

Note: This /th/ sound is most frequently spelled by the digraph *th* as in *thin* or *bath*. The digraph *th* represents two sounds—the voiceless /th/ sound as in *thin* and the voiced /t͟h/ sound as in *the*. The letters *th* are fairly reliable for these two sounds. However, sometimes the letters *th* stand for the /t/ sound as in *Thomas* and *thyme*, and sometimes they are silent as in *isthmus*. When the letters *th* appear together in a word, but are in separate syllables (example: *boathouse*) the *t* stands for /t/ and the *h* stands for /h/.

/t͟h/ as in *the*

/t͟h/ (voiced) Initial Position

than	the	them	there	they	those	thus
that	their	then	these	this	though	

/t͟h/ Medial/Final Position

bathe	gather	smooth	together	whether

More Multisyllabic /t͟h/ Words

themselves	thereby	therefore	therein

Note: This /t͟h/ sound is most frequently spelled by the digraph *th* as in *the* or *that*. Most of the words containing the /t͟h/ sound are of higher-frequency in English than those containing the /th/ sound. The digraph *th* represents two sounds—the voiceless /th/ sound as in *thin* and the voiced /t͟h/ sound as in *the*. The letters *th* are fairly reliable for these two sounds. However, sometimes the letters *th* stand for the /t/ sound as in *Thomas* and *thyme*, and sometimes they are silent as in *isthmus*. When the letters *th* appear together in a word, but are in separate syllables (example: *boathouse*), the *t* stands for /t/ and the *h* for /h/.

/hw/ as in *wheel*

/hw/ Initial Position

whack	wheelbarrow	whey	whinny	whistle
whale	wheelchair	which	whip	white
wham	when	whiff	whir	whittled
what	whenever	while	whirl	whiz
whatever	where	whim	whisk	whoops
wheat	wherever	whimper	whisker	whopper
wheel	whew	whine	whisper	why

More Multisyllabic /hw/ Words

whereabouts	whichever	whippoorwill	whirlwind	whitewash

Note: The /hw/ sound is rapidly disappearing from the English language. Many dialects do not distinguish the /hw/ sound in *whether* from the /w/ sound in *weather*. Listen carefully as you say aloud these words. Do you pronounce the beginning sound differently? When making the /hw/ sound, /h/ (just a puff of air) is vocalized before /w/. The jaws are apart to produce /h/, then close as the lips come closer together to produce /w/. You should be able to feel a slight vibration of the lips. The /hw/ sound is represented by the digraph *wh*. This spelling appears only at the beginning of a word or syllable. The digraph *wh* can also represent /h/ as in *who, whom, whose,* and *whole*.

/ng/ as in *ring*

/ng/ Medial/Final Position

angry	hang	rang	strangler	young	junk	sink
bang	hung	ring	strong	bank	link	sunk
clang	hunger	rung	strength	brink	mink	tank
clung	king	sang	thing	drink	pink	thank
finger	linger	sing	wing	drunk	rank	wink
gang	long	song	wrangler	honk	sank	
gong	longer	sprung	wringer	ink	shrunk	

More Multisyllabic /ng/ Words

accusingly	anything	clippings	daring	earring
adjoining	banging	convincingly	drawing	evaluating
admiringly	being	crossing	dwelling	exhilarating
amazing	belong	cunning	earning	finger

glancing	lightning	overdoing	springtime	uninteresting
good-looking	linger	pleasing	sterling	unknowing
greeting	longing	pudding	surprisingly	warning
hangar	making	rasping	sweet-smelling	
helpings	meaning	recording	tantalizing	
increasing	misleading	seemingly	trimmings	
knowingly	occurring	springboard	unceasing	

Note: The /ng/ sound is frequently represented by the letters *ng* as in *ring*. This sound never occurs at the beginning of a word or syllable and always follows a vowel sound. The letters *ng* are only moderately reliable for this sound. At the end of words, the letters *ng* always stand for the /ng/ sound. However, within words the two letters *n* and *g* can cause confusion. For example, the letter *n* alone may stand for the /ng/ sound and the *g* for /g/ as in *finger*; or the letter *n* may stand for the /n/ sound and the *g* for the /g/ sound as in *ungrateful, ongoing,* or *engulf*. The letters *ng* can also stand for the /n/ and /j/ sounds as in *angel, change, plunge,* and *ranger*. The letter *n* alone can represent the /ng/ sound when followed by *k* as in *pink, rank, think,* and *sink*. In the words *linger* and *mango* you also hear the /g/ sound after /ng/

Consonant Clusters

Consonant clusters are two consonants that appear together in a word, with each retaining its sound when blended. The sounds that each cluster stands for is called a blend. Therefore, the term **cluster** refers to the written form and the term **blend** refers to the spoken form.

The clusters are highly reliable; that is, when we see these letter combinations in words, they almost always stand for the blended sounds of each consonant. The one major exception is *sc*, which can stand for the /sk/ sounds as in *scare* or the *c* can be silent as in *science*. In addition, the consonant cluster *ck* stands for one sound, the /k/ sound.

There are three major categories of consonant clusters:

- *r*-blends (*br, cr, dr, fr, gr, pr, tr*)
- *s*-blends (*sc, sk, sl, sm, sn, sp, st, sw*)
- *l*-blends (*bl, cl, fl, gl, pl, sl*)
- In addition, a few other consonant clusters can be formed, such as *tw* and *qu*. There are also three-letter consonant clusters such as *str, spr, spl, scr, squ, thr, chr, phr,* and *shr*. The clusters *thr, phr,* and *shr* are comprised of a digraph and a consonant. The cluster *ngth* as in *strength* is made up of two digraphs—*ng* and *th*.

Teaching Guidelines

- Teach the consonant clusters after students have learned the single consonant sound-spellings.
- Teach beginning clusters before ending clusters.

Consonant Clusters

Phonic Principle: *s*-blends

Step 1: Review and Warm-Up. Begin by displaying index cards with the sound-spellings or spelling patterns previously taught. Flip through the cards rapidly as students chorally say the sound(s) each represents. Then have students reread a story or passage containing previously taught sound-spelling relationships.

Step 2: Introduce New Skill. Write the words *snake, stone,* and *spot* on the board. Underline the letters *sn, st,* and *sp* in each word. Explain that these letters stand for the /sn/, /st/, and /sp/ sounds, respectively. Point out that often when *s* and another consonant appear together in a word, the sounds that both letters stand for are blended together. Blend each word aloud as you run your finger under each letter. Have a volunteer underline the letters *sn, st,* and *sp*. Point to each of these clusters and ask students to state the sounds the letters stand for. Continue by having students generate a list of words containing these sounds. List the words on the board.

Step 3: Guided Practice. Write the following words and sentences on the board. Note that all the words are decodable based on the sound-spelling relationships previously taught. The first line contains contrasts to focus students' attention on the importance of each letter in a word. The sentences contain some high-frequency words previously taught.

- sell, spell, sack, stack
- sneak, speak, stop, spot
- snapshot, snowflake, spaceship, stampede
- The rainstorm caused water to flood the streets.
- The spider slipped out of its snug web.

Now distribute the following spelling-card set to each child: *a, o, e, s, t, n, ll, m, p, s, sh*. Have students build as many words as possible. Ask them to write the words on a sheet of paper. Circulate around the room and model blending when necessary.

Step 4: Apply to Text. Provide students with connected reading practice.

Step 5: Apply to Writing. Dictate the following words and sentence; have students write the words and sentence on a sheet of paper.

- snack, stoplight, sparkle
- The snowfall was spectacular!

For students having difficulty segmenting the sounds in each word, extend the word or segment syllable by syllable. Then, write the words and sentence on the board. Have the students self-correct their papers. Don't grade this dictation practice. It's designed to help students segment words and associate sounds with spellings.

Consonant-Cluster Words for Instruction

r-blends

br				
brace	bray	brisk	brush	broadcast
Brad	bread	broad	bracelet	bronco
braid	break	broil	bracket	brontosaurus
brain	breath	broke	brambles	broomstick
braise	breathe	bronze	brandish	brother
brake	breeze	brood	bravery	brotherhood
bran	brew	brook	breakdown	
branch	brick	broom	breakfast	
brand	bride	broth	breathless	
brass	bridge	brought	briefcase	
brat	bright	brown	brighten	
brave	brim	browse	brilliant	
brawl	bring	bruise	brittle	

cr				
crab	cried	crunch	crazy	critical
crack	croak	crust	creation	criticize
craft	crook	cry	creativity	crocodile
crane	crop	cracker	creature	crossroad
crash	cross	crackle	cricket	crossword
crawl	crow	cradle	criminal	cruelty
creek	crowd	cranberry	crinkle	crumble
creep	crown	crawfish	cripple	crusade
crib	crumb	crayon	crisscross	crystallized

dr

drab	dread	drive	dragonfly	driftwood
draft	dream	droop	dramatic	driveway
drag	dress	drop	draperies	drizzle
drain	drew	drove	drastic	droplets
drake	drift	drug	drawback	drugstore
drank	drill	drum	dreadful	drummer
drape	drink	dry	dreamlike	
draw	drip	dragon	dribble	

fr

frail	freeze	fringe	fruit	frantic	freshmen	frustration
frame	freight	frizz	fry	freckles	Friday	frying
France	fresh	frog	fraction	freeway	friendliness	
frank	friend	from	fragile	freezer	frighten	
freak	fright	front	fragment	frenzy	frostbite	
free	frill	frost	framework	frequency	frozen	

gr

grab	grate	grill	grow	graduation	gratitude	groceries
grace	grave	grim	growl	grammar	gravity	grotesque
grade	gravy	grime	grown	grandchild	greasy	grounder
graft	gray	grin	grub	grandeur	greatness	gruesome
grain	graze	grind	grudge	grandfather	greenery	
gram	grease	grip	gruff	grandmother	greenhouse	
grand	great	grit	grump	grandstand	greetings	
grant	greed	groan	graceful	granite	griddle	
grape	green	groom	gracias	grapefruit	grievance	
graph	greet	grouch	gracious	grasshopper	grimace	
grasp	grew	ground	gradual	grassland	gritty	
grass	grid	group	graduate	grateful	grizzly	

pr

praise	proof	prediction	presumably	probably	pronounce
prance	prop	prefer	pretty	problem	propeller
pray	proud	prejudice	pretzel	procedure	prophet
press	prove	preliminary	prevention	proclamation	prosperous
price	prowl	preoccupied	priceless	produce	protect
pride	prune	preparation	prickly	product	protective
priest	pry	prepare	primarily	profession	protein
prince	practical	prescription	primitive	professor	protest
print	practice	present	princess	profit	provide
prison	prayer	president	principal	program	province
prize	precaution	pressure	priority	project	provoke
probe	precious	presto	prisoner	promise	
prod	predict	prestigious	privilege	pronoun	

tr

trace	trim	trademark	transportation	trimmings
track	trip	tradition	trapeze	triumphant
trade	troll	traditional	travel	trivial
trail	tromp	traffic	traveler	trophy
train	troop	tragedy	treacherous	tropical
tramp	trot	trailer	treasurer	trouble
trap	trough	traitor	treatment	trouser
trash	trout	trample	tremble	truckload
tray	truck	tranquil	tremendous	truly
tread	true	transfer	trespasser	trumpet
treat	trunk	transformation	tribune	truthful
tree	trust	transition	tribute	tryout
trek	truth	translator	triceratops	
tribe	try	transplant	trickery	
trick	tractor	transport	trillion	

l-blends

bl					
blab	bleat	blip	blow	blackout	blizzard
black	bleed	blob	blue	bladder	bloodhound
blade	bleep	block	bluff	blanket	blossom
blame	blend	blonde	blunt	bleachers	blubber
blank	bless	blood	blush	blessings	blueberry
blast	blew	bloom	blackberry	blindfold	bluebird
blaze	blind	blot	blackbird	blissful	blueprint
bleach	blink	blouse	blackboard	blister	blunder

cl						
clack	class	cling	cloth	clamber	cleanup	closet
clad	claw	clink	clothes	clamor	clergyman	clothesline
claim	clay	clip	cloud	clarify	cleverness	clothing
clam	clean	cloak	clove	clarinet	client	clubhouse
clamp	clear	clock	clown	classic	climate	clumsy
clan	cleat	clod	club	classical	climber	cluster
clang	clerk	clog	cluck	classmate	clinical	
clap	click	clomp	clue	classroom	clipboard	
clash	cliff	close	clump	clatter	clockwise	
clasp	climb	closet	clutch	cleanliness	closeness	

fl						
flag	flaw	flick	flood	fluff	flabbergasted	flatten
flake	flea	flight	floor	fluid	flagpole	flatter
flame	fleck	fling	flop	fluke	flagship	flavor
flap	fleet	flint	floss	flunk	flashback	fledgling
flare	flesh	flip	flour	flush	flashbulb	flexible
flash	flew	float	flow	flute	flashlight	flicker
flat	flex	flock	flu	fly	flatland	flimsy

flipper	flounder	flower	fluorescent	fluster	flutter	flyer
floppy	flourish					

gl

glad	gleam	gloat	gloss	glacial	gleeful	glorious
glance	glee	glob	glove	glacier	glimmer	glossary
glare	glide	globe	glow	gladness	glisten	glossy
glass	glitch	gloom	glue	glamorous	glitter	

pl

place	plate	plod	placid	plastic	pleasure	plunder
plaid	play	plot	plaintive	plateau	plentiful	
plain	plead	plow	planet	platform	plenty	
plan	please	plug	plankton	player	pliers	
plane	pleat	plum	planner	playground	plumage	
plank	pledge	plump	plantation	plaza	plumber	
plant	plink	placement	plaster	pleasant	plummet	

sl

slab	sleep	slight	slow	slaughter	slippery
slack	sleet	slim	slug	sleazy	slither
slam	sleeve	slime	slump	sleepless	slobber
slant	slept	sling	slush	sleepy	sloppy
slap	slice	slip	sly	slender	slouchy
slate	slick	slit	slacker	slightly	slowly
sled	slid	slope	slander	slingshot	slugger
sleek	slide	slot	slapstick	slipper	

s-blends

sc

scab	scar	scoop	scout	scandal	scornful
scald	scarce	scoot	scuff	scarecrow	scorpion
scale	scare	scope	scallion	scarlet	scoundrel
scalp	scarf	scorch	scallop	scatter	sculpture
scamp	scat	score	scaly	scooter	scurry
scan	scold	scour	scamper	scoreboard	scuttle

sk

skate	skin	skunk	skeptical	skimmer	skyrocket
sketch	skip	sky	sketchy	skinny	
ski	skirt	skateboard	skidproof	skipper	
skid	skit	skedaddle	skillet	skirmish	
skill	skull	skeleton	skillful	skyline	

sm

smack	smear	smog	smallpox	smolder
small	smell	smoke	smelling	smoothest
smart	smile	smooth	smitten	smother
smash	smock	smudge	smoky	smuggle

sn

snack	snarl	snob	snakebite	snowball
snag	snatch	snoop	snappy	snowdrift
snail	sneak	snore	snapshot	snowfall
snake	sneeze	snout	sneaker	snowman
snap	sniff	snow	sniffle	snowmobile
snare	snip	snug	snorkel	snuggle

sp					
space	spell	sponge	spaghetti	spectacular	spiral
span	spend	spoon	spaniel	spectator	spirit
spare	spent	sport	sparkle	speculate	spiritual
spark	spike	spot	sparrow	speculation	spontaneous
spat	spill	spout	spasm	speechless	spoonful
speak	spin	spur	spatter	spellbound	spotless
spear	spine	spy	special	spellings	spotlight
speck	spire	spacecraft	specialize	spider	
speech	spoil	spaceship	specific	spinach	
speed	spoke	spacious	specimen	spindle	

st					
stack	state	stink	stagger	station	stirrup
staff	stay	stir	staircase	stationery	stocking
stage	steak	stitch	stallion	statue	stomach
stain	steal	stock	stamina	steadfast	stomachache
stair	steam	stone	stammer	steadily	stopwatch
stake	steel	stool	stampede	steady	storage
stale	steep	stoop	standard	steamboat	storekeeper
stalk	steer	stop	standstill	steeple	storybook
stall	stem	store	stanza	stegosaurus	stovepipe
stamp	step	storm	staple	stepfather	stubborn
stand	stew	story	stapler	stepmother	student
star	stick	stove	starfish	stereo	sturdy
starch	stiff	style	starlight	sticky	stutter
stare	still	stable	starter	stiffness	
start	stilt	stadium	starvation	stimulate	
starve	sting	stagecoach	statement	stingy	

sw					
swam	swatch	sweet	swim	swoop	sweatshirt
swamp	swarm	swell	swine	swagger	sweeper
swan	sway	swept	swing	swallow	sweeten
swap	sweat	swerve	swish	swampland	swiftness
swat	sweep	swift	switch	sweater	swollen

Three Letter Consonant Clusters

scr				
scram	scrawl	screw	scrabble	screwdriver
scrap	scream	script	scramble	scribble
scrape	screech	scroll	scrapbook	scrimmage
scratch	screen	scrub	scraper	scrutiny

squ				
square	squeak	squid	squirm	squirt
squash	squeal	squint	squirrel	squish
squat	squeeze			

str					
straight	stray	strict	stroke	straighten	stricken
strain	streak	stride	stroll	strainer	stronger
strand	stream	strike	strong	stranger	structure
strange	street	string	struck	strawberry	struggle
strap	strength	strip	strum	streetcar	
straw	stretch	stripe	straddle	stretcher	

spr				
sprain	spray	spring	spruce	sprinkle
sprang	spread	sprint	springboard	sprinkler
sprawl	sprig	sprout	springtime	sprinter

spl					
splash	splint	split	splashdown	splendid	splinter

thr				
thrash	throat	through	threadbare	throttle
thread	throb	thrush	threshold	throughout
thrill	throne	thrashing		

Other Consonant Clusters

tw						
tweed	twelve	twig	twine	twist	twentieth	twilight
tweet	twice	twin	twirl	tweezers	twenty	twinkle

qu						
quack	quart	quench	quiet	quirk	quote	quarter
quail	quartz	quest	quill	quit	quality	question
quake	queen	quick	quilt	quiz	quarrel	

Ending Consonant Clusters

ct						
act	fact	district	exact	impact	impact	overreact
duct	pact	enact	extract	interact	interact	subtract

ft					
cleft	graft	rift	swift	makeshift	witchcraft
craft	left	shaft	thrift	snowdrift	
draft	lift	shift	tuft	spacecraft	
drift	loft	sift	aircraft	spendthrift	
gift	raft	soft	airlift	uplift	

ld					
bald	gold	scold	behold	stepchild	withheld
bold	held	shield	billfold	stronghold	withhold
build	hold	sold	blindfold	threshold	
child	mild	told	brainchild	unfold	
cold	mold	weld	foothold	untold	
field	old	wild	household	upheld	
fold	scald	beheld	retold	windshield	

lp			
help	gulp	scalp	yelp

lt					
belt	fault	kilt	salt	deadbolt	somersault
bolt	felt	knelt	tilt	default	
built	guilt	melt	welt	exalt	
colt	halt	pelt	asphalt	heartfelt	
dealt	jolt	quilt	assault	revolt	

mp					
blimp	clamp	shrimp	hump	pump	tramp
bump	clump	skimp	jump	stamp	tromp
camp	cramp	slump	lamp	stomp	trump
champ	crimp	damp	limp	stump	trumpet
chimp	ramp	dump	lump	swamp	
chomp	romp	grump	plump	thump	

nd					
and	bland	bond	extend	grand	hind
band	blend	bound	find	grind	hound
bend	blind	brand	found	ground	husband
bind	blonde	end	friend	hand	intend

kind	send	wound	beyond	offend	respond
land	sound	abound	command	offhand	surround
lend	spend	apprehend	compound	pretend	suspend
mend	stand	armband	correspond	profound	understand
mind	strand	around	demand	quicksand	unkind
mound	tend	attend	extend	rebound	unwind
pound	trend	bandstand	firsthand	recommend	
round	wand	beforehand	greyhound	remind	
sand	wind	behind	mastermind	reprimand	

nk

bank	drink	junk	plunk	stink	wink
blank	dunk	link	rank	stunk	chipmunk
blink	frank	mink	rink	sunk	kerplunk
bunk	honk	wink	sank	tank	outrank
chunk	hunk	pink	sink	think	rethink
drank	ink	plank	skunk	trunk	

nt

absent	invent	scent	ballpoint	evident	peppermint
ant	lent	sent	blueprint	experiment	pinpoint
bent	lint	spent	cement	fingerprint	prevent
bunt	meant	splint	checkpoint	frequent	represent
cent	mint	tent	compliment	implant	torment
dent	paint	tint	consent	invent	transplant
faint	pint	want	content	lament	underwent
front	plant	went	disenchant	manhunt	viewpoint
grant	print	account	eggplant	misrepresent	
hint	rent	amount	enchant	newsprint	
hunt	runt	appoint	event	paramount	

pt

apt	slept	accept	except	intercept	rainswept
kept	wept	concept	inept	overslept	windswept

rd

bird	herd	afford	boulevard	landlord	record
board	lard	backyard	discard	leotard	safeguard
cord	sword	barnyard	discord	lifeguard	scorecard
guard	toward	blackbird	disregard	lovebird	shipyard
hard	word	bodyguard	hummingbird	mockingbird	smorgasbord
heard	yard	bombard	jailbird	postcard	songbird

rk

ark	fork	mark	work	birthmark	landmark	trademark
bark	hark	park	aardvark	bookmark	pitchfork	
clerk	jerk	perk	ballpark	disembark	postmark	
dark	lark	stork	berserk	earmark	remark	

sk

ask	desk	dusk	risk	task
asterisk	disk	mask		

sp

clasp	crisp	gasp	rasp	wasp

st

best	contest	fest	least	nest	rust	adjust
blast	cost	fist	list	past	test	aghast
boast	crust	ghost	lost	pest	toast	almost
bust	dentist	gust	mast	post	trust	arrest
cast	dust	jest	mist	quest	twist	assist
chest	east	just	most	rest	west	bedpost
coast	fast	last	must	roast	wrist	bombast

broadcast	contrast	enlist	innermost	outlast	robust	telecast
checklist	defrost	enthusiast	insist	overcast	sawdust	unjust
coexist	detest	exist	invest	persist	signpost	utmost
combust	disgust	forecast	manifest	protest	stardust	
conquest	distrust	goalpost	mistrust	request	steadfast	
consist	downcast	headfirst	newscast	resist	suggest	

Double Consonants

ss						
bass	class	gloss	kiss	miss	toss	message
bless	dress	grass	less	moss	dresser	messy
brass	fuss	guess	mass	pass	fussy	passage
chess	glass	hiss	mess	press	lesson	session

ll						
ball	drill	hall	sell	still	belly	session
bell	dull	hill	shell	swell	cellar	shallow
bill	dwell	hull	sill	tall	collect	silly
bull	fall	ill	skill	tell	dollar	smaller
call	fell	jell	skull	till	follow	smelly
cell	fill	kill	small	toll	football	taller
chill	frill	mall	smell	wall	hello	valley
dell	gill	mill	spell	well	holler	village
dill	grill	pill	spill	will	hollow	willow
doll	gull	roll	stall	yell	pillow	yellow

tt						
attic	bitter	cottage	flutter	kitten	rattle
batter	bottle	critter	glitter	letter	sitter
battle	butter	fatter	gutter	little	smitten
better	cattle	fitter	hotter	matter	tattered
bitten	chatter	flatter	kettle	mitten	

ff				
bluff	cuff	huff	sniff	stuff
buff	fluff	puff	staff	buffet
cliff	gruff	scuff	stiff	coffee

bb				
blubber	cubby	hobble	rabbit	wobble
bubble	dabble	lobby	rubble	
chubby	gobble	pebble	stubble	

dd				
bidding	hidden	meddle	puddle	saddle
bladder	huddle	muddle	redder	sudden
fiddle	ladder	muddy	riddle	waddle
haddock	madder	paddle	rudder	

pp			
apple	happen	preppy	stopper
dapple	happy	puppy	supper
grapple	pepper	sipping	zipper

zz				
buzz	fuzz	buzzer	dizzy	nuzzle
fizz	jazz	dazzle	guzzle	puzzle

gg				
egg	buggy	goggle	mugger	soggy
baggy	digger	jiggle	rugged	suggest
bigger	foggy	juggle	saggy	wiggle
biggest	giggle	logger	slugger	

Silent Letters

Most of the letters in our alphabet are silent in words at one time or another. Frequently consonants are silent because the pronunciation of a particular word has changed over time, but the spelling has remained constant. Silent consonants also occur in words borrowed from other languages. Our inner speech seems to ignore silent letters when we read.

The following list, based on Hanna's 17,000 most frequent words (Burmeister, 1971), shows the 15 most frequent silent letters and their corresponding sounds.

1. tch /ch/ (hatch)
2. dg /j/ (lodge)
3. wr /r/ (write)
4. kn /n/ (know)
5. gn /n/ (gnaw, sign)
6. mb /m/ (lamb)
7. ps /s/ (psychology)
8. lk /k/ (talk)
9. lm /m/ (calm)
10. rh /r/ (rhino)
11. dj /j/ (adjust)
12. wh /h/ (who)
13. bt /t/ (debt)
14. gh /g/ (ghost)
15. mn /m/ (hymn)

The chart below shows the conditions under which each letter is silent and provides some sample words for instruction.

Letters That Are Sometimes Silent

Letter(s)	Condition	Sample Words
b	• silent before *t* and after *m* unless this letter and the *b* are in separate syllables (example: *timber*)	debt, doubt, subtle, lamb, climb, comb, crumb, dumb, thumb, plumb, tomb, numb
c	• silent in the cluster *ck*	back, pick, sack, lick
	• silent occasionally after *s*	science, scene, scenery, scenic, scent, scientific, scientist, scissors, sciatic, scintillate
	• silent in a few other words	Connecticut, indict
ch	• rarely silent	yacht

Letters That Are Sometimes Silent

Letter(s)	Condition	Sample Words
d	• rarely silent (sometimes a result of lazy pronunciation)	handkerchief, Wednesday, grandmother
g	• silent when it comes before *n* or *m*	gnat, gnaw, gnarl, gnu, gnarled, gnash, gneiss, gnocchi, gnome, Gnostic, sign, design, assign, resign, phlegm
h	• silent when it follows *r* or *k*	rhyme, rhapsody, rhatany, rhea, rhebok, rheumatic, rhesus, rhetoric, rheumatic, rhexis, rhinestone, rhino, rhinoceros, rhizome, Rhode Island, rhodium, rhombus, rhubarb, rhythmic, rhythm, rhyton, khaki, khaddar, khamsin, khan, Khartoum, Khmer
	• sometimes silent when it follows *x*	exhaust
	• often silent between a consonant and the unstressed vowel	shepherd
	• silent after vowels at the end of a word	oh, hurrah
	• sometimes silent at the beginning of a word	honor, honesty, honorary, hors d'oeuvre, hour, heir, heiress, heirloom
k	• silent before *n* at the beginning of a word or syllable	know, knife, knew, knapsack, knack, knee, kneel, knob, knit, knight, knock, knot, knowledge, knave, knead, knickers, knotty, knoll, known, knuckle
l	• silent usually before *f, k, m,* or *v*	calf, talk, calm, salve
	• silent in the *-ould* spelling pattern	would, could, should
m	• rarely silent	mnemonic
n	• silent after *m* (this is considered to be morphophonemic because the *m* is maintained in all derivatives of the word and pronounced in many other forms of the word such as *hymnal*)	autumn, hymn

Letters That Are Sometimes Silent

Letter(s)	Condition	Sample Words
p	• silent before *n, s,* or *t*	pneumonia, psychology, ptomaine, pneumatic, psalm, psaltery, pseudo, pseudonym, psoriasis, psyche, psychotic, psyche, psychic, psyllium, ptarmigan, pterodactyl, Ptolemy, ptosis
s	• silent sometimes when it follows *i* • silent in the word *Arkansas*	island, debris, aisle
t	• silent in words with *-sten* and *-stle* • silent in words borrowed from French that end in *-et, -ot,* or *-ut*	fasten, listen, castle, whistle, bristle, bustle, gristle, hustle, rustle, thistle bouquet, ballet, depot, debut
th	• rarely silent	asthma, isthmus
u	• silent sometimes when it follows *g* or *q*	guard, opaque
w	• silent before *r* at the beginning of a word or syllable • silent in a few other words • silent in words beginning with *who-*	wrong, write, wrap, wrapper, wrath, wreath, wreck, wreckage, wren, wrench, wrestle, wrestler, wriggle, wring, wrinkle, wrist, wristwatch, write, writer, writhe, writings, wrote, wrought, wring, wry two, answer, sword who, whose, whole
x	• rarely silent	Sioux
z	• rarely silent	rendezvous

Silent Letters

Phonic Principle: silent letter spelling *wr*

Step 1: Review and Warm-Up. Begin by displaying index cards with the sound-spellings or spelling patterns previously taught. Flip through the cards rapidly as students chorally say the sound(s) each represents. Then have students reread a story or passage containing previously taught sound-spelling relationships.

Step 2: Introduce New Skill. Explain to students that sometimes a letter stands for no sound in a word; it is silent. Point out that when the letters *wr* appear together at the beginning of a word such as *write*, the letter *w* is silent. Put the word *write* on the board, then blend the word aloud as you run your finger under each letter. Have a volunteer underline the letters *wr*. Point to the letters *wr* and ask students to state the sound that the letters stand for. Continue by having students suggest words that begin with *wr*. Encourage them to become "word explorers" and search through classroom books for these words. List these words on the board.

Step 3: Guided Practice. Write the following words and sentences on the board. Note that all the words are decodable based on the sound-spelling relationships previously taught. The sentences contain some high-frequency words previously taught.

- rap, wrap, wing, wring
- wreckage, wrongdoing, wristwatch, wrinkled
- I have written two books.
- The worm wriggled out of the soil.

Now distribute the following letter-card set to each child: *wr, a, e, i, s, t, p, ck*. Have students build as many words as possible. Ask them to write the words on a sheet of paper. Circulate around the room and model blending when necessary.

Step 4: Apply to Text. Provide students with connected reading practice.

Step 5: Apply to Writing. Dictate the following words and sentence; have students write the words and sentence on a sheet of paper.

- write, wrinkle, wrecking
- Are those your writings?

For students having difficulty segmenting the sounds in each word, extend the word or segment it syllable by syllable. Have students write one syllable at a time. Then, write the words and sentence on the board and have students self-correct their papers. Don't grade this dictation practice. It's designed to help students segment words and associate sounds with spellings.

Long Vowels

Teaching Guidelines

- Begin instruction with simple, one-syllable words. Start with CVCe (consonant-vowel-consonant-e) words, since this pattern is an extremely useful and unencumbered long-vowel pattern. Word lists are provided on pages 105–106. The silent e (also known as final e or the e-marker) acts as a diacritical mark, alerting the reader that the preceding vowel probably stands for a long vowel sound. There are four basic, one-syllable patterns in the English language, including the CVCe pattern (Eldredge, 1995).

  1. The **closed syllable** pattern is the most common. There's one vowel in the syllable and the syllable ends with a consonant. Most of the words using this pattern contain short-vowel sounds. There are 13 variations: CVC (*cup*), CVCC (*hand*), CCVCC (*fresh*), CCVC (*trip*), CVCCC (*match*), CVCCe (*judge*), CCVCCC (*crutch*), CCVCCe (*grudge*), CCCVCC (*script*), VCC (*add*), VC (*in*), CCCVC (*scrap*), VCCC (*inch*)

  2. The **vowel team (vowel digraph) pattern** is the second most common. There are 12 variations: CVVC (*heat*), CCVVC (*treat*), CVVCC (*reach*), CVV (*pay*), CCVV (*play*), CVVCe (*leave*), CCVVCC (*bleach*), CCVVCe (*freeze*), CCCVVC (*sprain*), VVC (*oat*), VVCC (*each*), CCCVV (*three*)

  3. The **vowel-consonant–silent e pattern** is the third most common. There are 4 variations: CVCe (*race*), CCVCe (*shave*), CCCVCe (*strike*), VCe (*ate*)

  4. The **open syllable** pattern is the fourth most common. There is only one vowel letter in the syllable and the syllable ends with the vowel's sound. There are two variations: CCV (*she*), CV (*we*)

- Use contrasts in instruction (*rat/rate*, *hat/hate*) so that students can see how one letter can make all the difference in a word's vowel sound. Following is a list of contrasts for CVC and CVCe words. Contrasts can also be made for words with vowel digraphs (*pan/pain*, *cot/coat*, *red/read*).

A Note About Silent *e*

The silent *e* is important in English spelling (Moats, 1995a). For example, the silent *e* helps to keep some words from looking like plurals (*please*, not *pleas*; and *moose*, not *moos*). Since the letter *v* doesn't appear at the end of words, the silent *e* in words such as *dove*, *love*, *shove*, and *above* gives them orthographic regularity. Although this silent *e* doesn't indicate that the preceding *o* stands for the long *o* sound, it does indicate that the preceding *o* is **not** a short *o* sound. In essence, the silent *e* helps to create a spelling pattern that is consistent and far from random. The final *e* also indicates when the letter *g* or *c* stands for its "soft" sound (*page*, *race*).

Short–Vowel/Long–Vowel Contrasts

bit/bite	grad/grade	past/paste	slid/slide
can/cane	hat/hate	pin/pine	slim/slime
cap/cape	hid/hide	plan/plane	slop/slope
cod/code	hop/hope	rag/rage	spin/spine
cub/cube	kit/kite	rat/rate	strip/stripe
cut/cute	mad/made	rid/ride	tap/tape
dim/dime	man/mane	rip/ripe	twin/twine
fad/fade	mat/mate	rob/robe	us/use
fat/fate	not/note	rod/rode	van/vane
fin/fine	pal/pale	scrap/scrape	wag/wage
glob/globe	pan/pane	shin/shine	

- Teach vowel digraphs. In addition to silent *e*, many vowel spellings are formed by vowel digraphs, also known as vowel pairs or vowel teams. These include *ea, ee, oa, ai, ay,* and others. The following chart shows the predictability of various vowel digraphs, many of which are long-vowel digraphs (Burmeister, 1968b).

The Predictability of Common Vowel Digraphs

Vowel Digraph	Predictability	Vowel Digraph	Predictability
ai	/ā/ (pain) 74%, air (chair) 15%	**ou**	/ə/ (trouble) 41%, /ou/ (house) 35%
ay	/ā/ (say) 96%	**au**	/ô/ (haul) 94%
ea	/ē/ (seat) 51%, /e/ (head) 26%	**aw**	/ô/ (hawk) 100%
ee	/ē/ (feet) 86%, eer (steer) 12%	**oo**	/o͞o/ (food) 59%, /o͝o/ (foot) 36%
ey	/ē/ (key) 58%, /ā/ (convey) 20%, /ī/ (geyser) 12%	**ei**	/ā/ (reign) 40%, /ē/ (deceit) 26%, /i/ (foreign) 13%, /ī/ (seismic) 11%
oa	/ō/ (boat) 94%	**ie**	/ē/ (chief) 51%, /ī/ (lie) 17%, /ə/ (patient) 15%
ow	/ō/ (snow) 50%, /ou/ (how) 48%	**ew**	/yo͞o/ (few) 95%
oi	/oi/ (soil) 98%	**ui**	/o͞o/ (fruit) 53%, /i/ (build) 47%
oy	/oi/ (boy) 98%		

Long Vowels

Phonic Principle: The letters *ea* and *ee* stand for the /ē/ sound.

Step 1: Review and Warm-Up. Begin by displaying index cards with the sound-spellings or spelling patterns previously taught. Flip through the cards rapidly as students chorally say the sound(s) each represents. Then have students reread a story or passage containing previously taught sound-spelling relationships.

Step 2: Introduce New Skill. Explain to students that the letters *ee* and *ea* can stand for the /ē/ sound as in *feet* and *seat*. Write the words *feet* and *seat* on the board. Then blend the words aloud as you run your finger under each letter. Have a volunteer underline the letters *ee* or *ea*. Point to the letters and ask students to state the sound that the letters stand for. Continue by having students generate a list of words containing the /ē/ sound. List these words on the board. Have volunteers circle the letters *ee* or *ea* in all the words containing these spellings for the /ē/ sound.

Step 3: Guided Practice. Write the following words and sentences on the board. Note that all the words are decodable based on the sound-spelling relationships previously taught. The first line focuses on short-vowel/long-vowel contrasts. The sentences contain some high-frequency words previously taught.

- bet, beat, fed, feed
- leaflet, needed, beanbag, deepen
- My teammate is the best!
- Keeping the seeds in the bag is important.

Distribute the following spelling-card set to each student: *eat, eed, eep, eak, eam, b, t, cr, p, bl, s, tr, sp, f, n, br*. Have the students build as many words as possible. Ask them to write the words on a sheet of paper. Circulate around the room and model blending when necessary.

Step 4: Apply to Text. Provide students with connected reading practice.

Step 5: Apply to Writing. Dictate the following words and sentence; have students write the words and sentence on a sheet of paper.

- reading, feed, heater
- We are eating green beans and peas.

For students having difficulty segmenting the sounds in each word, extend the word or segment it syllable by syllable. Have the students write one syllable at a time. Write the words and the sentence on the board, then have the students self-correct their papers. Don't grade this dictation. It's designed to help children segment words and associate sounds with spellings.

One-Syllable CVCe Words for Instruction

a_e (long a)						
ace	cave	gave	late	quake	shape	trace
age	chase	gaze	made	race	shave	trade
bake	crane	glaze	make	rage	skate	vane
base	crate	grace	male	rake	slate	vase
blade	date	grade	mane	rate	snake	wade
blame	daze	grape	mate	rave	space	wage
blaze	drape	grate	name	safe	spade	wake
brace	face	grave	pace	sake	stage	waste
brake	fade	haste	page	sale	stake	wave
brave	fake	hate	pale	same	stale	whale
cage	fame	haze	pane	save	state	
cake	flake	jade	paste	scale	take	
came	flame	lace	pave	scrape	tale	
cane	frame	lake	place	shade	tame	
cape	game	lame	plane	shake	tape	
case	gate	lane	plate	shame	taste	

EXCEPTIONS: advantage, are, average, breakage, cabbage, climate, courage, delicate, furnace, have, manage, message, palace, passage, private, purchase, senate, separate, surface, village

i_e (long i)						
bike	file	like	pine	slice	swine	wife
bite	fine	lime	pipe	slide	tide	wipe
bride	five	line	price	slime	tile	wise
chime	glide	live	pride	smile	time	write
crime	hide	mice	rice	spice	twice	
dice	hike	mile	ride	spike	twine	
dime	hive	mine	ripe	spine	vine	
dine	kite	nice	rise	stride	while	
dive	lice	nine	shine	strike	white	
drive	life	pile	side	stripe	wide	

EXCEPTIONS: active, aggressive, automobile, determine, engine, examine, expressive, favorite, figurine, give, justice, live, machine, magazine, massive, native, notice, office, opposite, police, practice, promise, representative, routine, service

o_e (long o)							
bone	code	hole	lone	pole	slope	stove	whole
broke	cone	home	mole	robe	smoke	stroke	woke
choke	dome	hope	nose	rode	spoke	those	zone
chose	drove	hose	note	rope	stole	tone	
close	globe	joke	poke	rose	stone	vote	

EXCEPTIONS: above, become, come, done, glove, gone, improve, lose, love, lovely, move, movement, none, purpose, remove, shove, some, something, welcome, whose

u_e (long u)				
cube	cute	fuse	mule	use

EXCEPTIONS: assure, conclude, include, measure, pleasure, rule, sure, treasure, crude, duke, dune, flute, June, prune, rude, rule, tube, tune

Multisyllabic CVCe Words for Instruction

aflame	candidate	drainpipe	gateway	lemonade	pancake
alpine	capsize	eliminate	handmade	lifeboat	parade
animate	celebrate	enclose	handshake	maypole	persuade
anyplace	cheesecake	engage	headline	mealtime	pipeline
appetite	classmate	episode	hesitate	microscope	porcupine
arcade	coincide	escape	homemade	microwave	profane
awake	contemplate	estate	humane	mistake	provide
backbone	crusade	estimate	illustrate	nickname	rattlesnake
bathrobe	cupcake	evaluate	inhale	nightingale	reptile
bedtime	daytime	exchange	inside	nineteen	sacrifice
birthplace	demonstrate	excite	intimidate	offstage	senile
blockade	dictate	exhale	keepsake	outrage	separate
bookcase	disgrace	explode	landscape	overcame	shapeless
calculate	dislike	fireplace	lateness	overtake	shipmate

Multisyllabic CVCe Words for Instruction *continued*					
shoelace	statement	summertime	tailgate	telephone	upscale
sideways	stockpile	sunrise	tailpipe	tightrope	wasteland
snowflake	subscribe	sunshine	teammate	tradewind	whaleboat
staircase	suitcase	sunstroke	teenage	upgrade	wildlife

Long-Vowel Words for Instruction

/ā/ as in *cake*					
bake	grade	shape	chain	raid	hay
blade	grape	skate	claim	rain	jay
brace	grapes	space	drain	rail	lay
brake	lake	stage	fail	raise	may
brave	late	take	faint	sail	maybe
cage	made	tale	faith	snail	pay
cake	make	tape	frail	Spain	play
came	male	trace	grain	stain	player
case	maze	trade	jail	strain	pray
cave	name	vase	laid	tail	ray
chase	page	wade	maid	trail	say
date	place	wake	mail	train	spray
face	plate	wave	main	vain	stay
fade	race	whale	nail	waist	stray
flake	rake	aid	paid	wait	sway
flame	sale	aim	pail	bay	today
game	same	bait	pain	clay	tray
gate	save	braid	paint	day	way
gave	shade	Braille	plain	gay	
grace	shake	brain	praise	gray	

More Multisyllabic /ā/ Words

abstain	explain	overpaid	subway
afraid	faraway	paintbrush	throwaway
away	hallway	paycheck	unchain
birthday	holiday	payday	unpaid
complain	mailbox	pigtail	waistband
contain	mainland	railway	waitress
crayon	maintain	raindrop	yesterday
decay	mermaid	refrain	
entertain	midday	runway	

/ē/ as in *feet*

be	easy	pea	team	feel	see
me	eat	peach	treat	feet	seed
we	feast	peak	weak	flee	seek
beach	flea	plead	wheat	free	seem
bead	gleam	pleat	yeast	greed	seen
beak	heal	reach	zeal	green	seep
beam	heap	read	bee	greet	sheep
bean	heat	real	beech	heed	sheet
beat	jeans	scream	beef	jeep	sleep
bleach	lead	sea	beep	keep	sleet
bleak	leaf	seal	beet	knee	speech
cheap	leak	seam	cheek	meet	speed
cheat	lean	seat	cheep	need	steel
clean	leap	sneak	cheese	peek	steep
cream	leash	speak	creep	peel	street
deal	least	steal	deed	peep	sweep
dear	meal	steam	deep	queen	sweet
dream	mean	stream	deer	reef	teen
each	meat	tea	fee	screech	teeth
east	neat	teach	feed	screen	three

tree	field	beauty	family	muddy	sixty
weed	fierce	bunny	fifty	navy	sleepy
week	grief	candy	forty	ninety	slowly
weep	niece	carry	funny	only	smoothly
wheel	parties	chilly	fuzzy	party	sticky
babies	pennies	city	gravy	penny	story
belief	pierce	county	happy	plenty	strawberry
believe	relief	daddy	jelly	pony	sunny
berries	shield	daisy	kitty	pretty	thirsty
brief	shriek	dirty	lady	puppy	thirty
brownie	siege	dizzy	lately	quickly	tiny
Charlie	thief	dusty	lobby	sandy	tricky
chief	yield	duty	lucky	seventy	ugly
cities	any	easy	many	shiny	windy
cookies	baby	eighty	mommy	silly	

More Multisyllabic /ē/ Words

absentee	cartwheel	esteem	mainstream	proofread	succeed
agreed	decease	freedom	mislead	reason	sunbeam
antifreeze	decrease	freeway	nosebleed	seashell	teapot
asleep	defeat	guarantee	outreach	seasick	treetop
beneath	degree	heartbeat	overeat	seaweed	upbeat
between	disagree	impeach	peanut	sixteen	
bloodstream	eighteen	indeed	pedigree	sleepless	
bumblebee	employee	indiscreet	proceed	steamship	

/ī/ as in *bike*

bike	chive	drive	grime	ice	line
bite	dime	fine	hide	kite	lime
bride	dine	fire	hike	life	live
chime	dive	five	hive	like	mice

mile	slice	wife	bind	died	knight
mine	slide	wise	blind	dries	light
nice	spice	by	child	flies	might
nine	spike	cry	climb	fries	night
pike	splice	dry	find	lie	right
pine	stride	fly	grind	pie	sigh
pipe	strive	fry	hind	skies	sight
price	tide	my	kind	spies	slight
rice	time	pry	mild	tie	thigh
ride	tire	shy	mind	tries	tight
ripe	twice	sky	rind	bright	
rise	twine	sly	wild	fight	
shine	whine	spy	wind	flight	
side	white	try	cries	fright	
size	wide	why	die	high	

More Multisyllabic /ī/ Words

airtight	exemplify	gratify	midnight	overnight	simplify
amplify	falsify	headlight	modify	oversight	stoplight
brightness	flashlight	highlight	moonlight	playwright	starlight
bullfight	foresight	highway	multiply	reply	sunlight
daylight	frighten	imply	nightfall	satisfy	tonight
delight	gaslight	insight	occupy	sightless	upright

/ō/ as in *boat*

ago	hold	scold	volt	clove	drove
bold	jolt	scroll	alone	code	froze
bolt	mold	so	bone	cone	globe
cold	no	sold	broke	cope	grove
colt	old	stroll	choke	cove	hole
fold	poll	told	chose	dome	home
go	pro	toll	close	dose	hope
gold	roll	troll	clothes	doze	hose

joke	stove	coat	road	flown	swallow
lone	stroke	croak	roam	glow	throw
nose	those	float	roast	grow	thrown
note	throne	foam	soak	grown	tow
phone	tone	goal	soap	know	willow
poke	vote	goat	throat	known	window
pole	whole	groan	toad	low	yellow
pose	woke	Joan	toast	mellow	doe
robe	wrote	load	whoa	mow	foe
rode	yoke	loaf	below	row	goes
rope	zone	loan	blow	show	hoe
rose	boat	moan	blown	shown	Joe
slope	cloak	moat	bow	slow	toe
smoke	coach	oak	bowl	snow	woe
spoke	coal	oats	crow	sparrow	
stone	coast	roach	flow	stow	

More Multisyllabic /ō/ Words

boatload	follow	rainbow	sailboat	snowman
coatrack	oatmeal	roadbed	seacoast	trainload
elbow	pillow	roadway	shadow	
fellow	railroad	rowboat	snowdrift	

/yōō/ as in *cube*

cube	puke	January	unit	mew	fuel
cute	use	menu	united	pew	hue
fume	bugle	museum	university	preview	rescue
fuse	community	music	unusual	review	value
huge	future	pupil	usual	view	beautiful
mule	human	regular	Utah	argue	beauty
muse	humid	uniform	few	continue	
mute	humor	union	hew	cue	

Other Vowel Sounds

Some vowel digraphs stand for sounds that are not commonly classified as long or short vowels. These include the following, which I've classified according to the way they are grouped in most basal reading programs:

Variant Vowels

/o͞o/ (f**oo**d), /o͝o/ (f**oo**t), /ô/ (b**a**ll, c**au**se, cl**aw**, f**o**r)
Note that the *o* in *for* can also be classified as an *r*-controlled vowel (see next page). The vowel digraph *oo* has a long and a short sound assigned to it. The long sound is more frequent in words than the short sound. Therefore, when students encounter this vowel digraph in a word, they should try the long sound first. The only way for students to know which sound is correct is to try both sounds and see which forms a word that is in their speaking or listening vocabularies (assuming they have heard the word before).

Diphthongs

/oi/ (b**oi**l, b**oy**), /ou/ (h**ou**se, c**ow**)
Diphthongs are vowel sounds formed by a gliding action in the mouth. That is, unlike other vowel sounds, the tongue and lip positions often change as the sound is formed. For example, say and extend the /a/ sound. Notice the position of the lips and tongue. Do they change while forming the sound? No. Now say the /oi/ sound. Notice how the lips are thrust forward and close together as the sound begins, but quickly retract and open slightly as the sound is concluded. This gliding action is characteristic of diphthongs. Many linguists also consider the long-*i* and long-*u* sounds diphthongs. As mentioned earlier, people speaking in a Southern dialect form many vowel sounds in this manner, which accounts for much of the liveliness, beauty, and sing-song nature of Southern speech.

r–Controlled Vowels

/âr/ (ch**air**), /ûr/(f**er**n, b**ir**d, h**ur**t), /är/ (p**ar**k, fath**er**)
The letter *r* affects the sound of the vowel that precedes it in many ways. The following suggested sequence for teaching *r*-controlled vowels is based on frequency and predictability of spellings (Blevins, 1997; Groff, 1977):

1. /ûr/ (ir, er, ur)   **2.** /ôr/ (or, ore, oar)
3. /âr/ (ar)   **4.** /är/ (are, air, eir, ear)

In addition to the letter *r*, the letters *l* and *w* have effects on the vowels that precede or follow them (i.e., **wa**ter, f**all**, t**alk**). Instead of trying to explain to students the intricacies of how the vowel sound is affected by these consonants, the sounds are best taught as spelling patterns such as *ar, er, ir, or, ur, air, ear, are, all, alk,* and *wa*.

Schwa

/ ə/ (**a**lone, happ**e**n, d**i**rect, gall**o**p, circ**u**s)
Some linguists don't consider the schwa a separate sound; rather they think of it as an allophone—a variant of a particular sound caused by a reduction in stress on that sound in a word. The schwa is also known as a murmur or neutral sound. Up to 22 different spellings of the schwa sound have been identified (Hanna et al., 1966). It is difficult to teach rules for identifying this sound in words. Some educators suggest telling students to try the short sound of a questionable vowel when decoding multisyllabic words (Chall & Popp, 1996); others have suggested telling students to say "uh" for every vowel sound in a word they are unsure of. They believe that this approximation will be close enough for the student to identify the word if it is in the student's speaking or listening vocabulary.

Other Vowel Sounds

Phonic Principle: The letters *oi* and *oy* stand for the /oi/ sound.

Step 1: Review and Warm-Up. Begin by displaying index cards with the sound-spellings or spelling patterns previously taught. Flip through the cards rapidly as students chorally say the sound(s) each represents. Then have students reread a story or passage containing previously taught sound-spelling relationships.

Step 2: Introduce New Skill. Explain to the students that the letters *oi* and *oy* stand for the /oi/ sound as in *boil* and *boy*. Write the words *boil* and *boy* on the board. Then blend the words aloud as you run your finger under each letter. Have a volunteer underline the letters *oi* or *oy*. Point to the letters and ask students to state the sound that the letters stand for. Continue by having students generate a list of words containing the /oi/ sound. List these words on the board.

Step 3: Guided Practice. Write the following words and sentences on the board. Note that all the words are decodable based on the sound-spelling relationships previously taught. Contrasts are given in the first line.

The sentences contain some high-frequency words previously taught.

- box, boy, pint, point
- coin, joyful, toys, noisily
- The boy is enjoying the game.
- I found five coins.

Then distribute the following spelling-card set to each student: *oi, oy, b, l, c, n, j*. Have students build as many words as possible. Ask them to write the words on a sheet of paper. Circulate around the room and model blending when necessary.

Step 4: Apply to Text. Provide students with connected reading practice.

Step 5: Apply to Writing. Dictate the following words and sentence; have students write the words and sentence on a sheet of paper.

- boyish, pointing, coiled
- We gave her the royal treatment.

Then write the words and sentence on the board. Have the students self-correct their papers. Don't grade this dictation. It's designed to help students segment words and associate sounds with spellings.

Words for Instruction for Other Vowel Sounds

schwa /ə/ as in *alarm*

about	afraid	alarm	anew	ashamed	awake
above	again	alas	annoy	ashore	aware
account	ago	alone	another	aside	away
adult	agree	along	apart	asleep	awhile
afloat	ahead	America	appear	avoid	awoke
afoot	ajar	among	applause	await	

Note: The /ə/ sound is referred to as the schwa sound or murmur sound. It is graphically represented by an upside-down *e*. Some linguists don't consider it a sound, rather a phonetic variant or allophone. The /ə/ sound can be spelled with any vowel: *a* (*alone*), *e* (*happen*), *i* (*direct*), *o* (*gallop*), *u* (*circus*). Several multisyllabic words beginning with *a* as their first unaccented syllable contain this sound. Above is a list of these words. The schwa sound appears in most multisyllabic words and is the most common sound in English.

r-controlled vowel /â/ as in *chair*

air	pair	dare	mare	spare	swear
chair	stair	fare	pare	square	wear
fair	bare	flare	rare	stare	
flair	blare	glare	scare	bear	
hair	care	hare	share	pear	

Multisyllabic /â/ Words

affair	compare	midair	repair	welfare
airfare	debonair	millionaire	silverware	wheelchair
aware	declare	nightmare	solitaire	
beware	despair	prepare	underwear	
billionaire	impair	questionnaire	warfare	

Note: The /â/ sound is an r-controlled vowel sound. The diacritical mark above the *a* is known as a circumflex.

r-controlled sound /û/ as in *bird*

blur	purr	circle	squirm	fern	person
burn	purse	circus	squirt	germ	river
burst	spur	dirt	stir	her	serve
church	surf	dirty	swirl	herd	sister
churn	Thursday	fir	third	jerk	stern
curb	turkey	firm	thirst	letter	swerve
curl	turn	first	twirl	merge	term
curse	turtle	flirt	whirl	mother	under
curve	urge	girl	after	nerve	verb
fur	bird	quirk	better	other	verge
hurt	birth	shirt	certain	over	verse
nurse	birthday	sir	clerk	perch	water
purple	chirp	skirt	ever	perk	winter

More Multisyllabic /û/ Words

adverb	converge	heartburn	observe	rebirth	sunburn
blackbird	disturb	intern	overturn	reserve	superb
concern	diverge	midterm	preserve	return	unhurt
conservative	headfirst	nightshirt	proverb	suburb	

Note: The /û/ sound is an *r*-controlled vowel sound. The diacritical mark above the *u* is known as a circumflex.

r-controlled sound /ä/ as in *car*

arch	card	farm	march	shark	tart
ark	cart	guard	mark	sharp	yard
arm	charge	hard	marsh	smart	yarn
art	charm	harm	mart	spark	Arctic
bar	chart	harp	park	star	artist
bark	dark	jar	party	start	garden
barn	dart	lard	scar	starch	party
car	far	large	scarf	tar	

More Multisyllabic /ä/ Words

aardvark	bazaar	cigar	guitar	leotard	recharge
ajar	bodyguard	depart	impart	lifeguard	seminar
alarm	bombard	discard	jaguar	outsmart	superstar
backyard	bookmark	disembark	junkyard	postcard	trademark
ballpark	caviar	enlarge	landmark	postmark	upstart

Note: The /ä/ sound is often an *r*-controlled vowel sound. The diacritical mark above the *a* is known as a dieresis.

Variant or *r*-controlled sound /ö/ as in *ball*

bore	north	sworn	small	Paul	law
born	or	thorn	stall	pause	lawn
chore	porch	torch	tall	sauce	lawyer
chord	pore	tore	wall	sausage	paw
cord	pork	torn	audience	taught	pawn
core	port	wore	August	vault	raw
cork	scorch	worn	author	awful	saw
corn	score	halt	autumn	bawl	shawl
door	scorn	malt	because	brawl	slaw
dorm	shore	salt	caught	caw	sprawl
for	short	chalk	cause	claw	squawk
force	snore	stalk	clause	crawl	straw
fork	sore	talk	daughter	dawn	strawberry
form	sort	walk	dinosaur	draw	thaw
fort	sport	all	fault	drawn	yawn
forth	store	ball	fraud	fawn	
horn	stork	call	haul	flaw	
horse	storm	fall	haunt	gnaw	
more	sword	hall	launch	hawk	
morning	swore	mall	laundry	jaw	

More Multisyllabic /ô/ Words

assault	default	exalt	jigsaw	snowball
baseball	distraught	football	pitfall	withdraw
boardwalk	enthrall	install	seesaw	

Note: The /ô/ sound is referred to as the broad o sound. The diacritical mark above the o is known as a circumflex.

Diphthong /oi/ as in *boy*

avoid	hoist	point	annoy	enjoy	soy
boil	join	poison	boy	joy	toy
broil	joint	rejoice	cowboy	joyful	voyage
choice	moist	soil	coy	loyal	
coil	moisture	spoil	decoy	ploy	
coin	noise	toil	destroy	Roy	
foil	oil	voice	employ	royal	

More Multisyllabic /oi/ Words

ahoy	checkpoint	overjoy	recoil	tenderloin	viewpoint
appoint	corduroy	pinpoint	rejoin	turmoil	
ballpoint	disappoint	purloin	sirloin	turquoise	

Diphthong /ou/ as in *house*

about	grouch	pouch	spout	crown	plow
bounce	ground	pound	sprout	down	powder
bound	hound	pout	trout	drown	power
cloud	house	proud	allow	fowl	prowl
couch	loud	round	bow	frown	sow
count	mound	scout	brow	gown	towel
crouch	mouse	shout	brown	growl	tower
doubt	mouth	snout	chow	how	town
flour	noun	sound	clown	howl	vow
foul	ouch	sour	cow	now	wow
found	out	south	crowd	owl	

More Multisyllabic /ou/ Words

abound	blowout	downtown	hometown	slowdown
account	breakdown	dropout	lighthouse	spellbound
aloud	campground	dugout	lookout	sundown
amount	campout	earthbound	loudmouth	surround
announce	compound	eyebrow	mispronounce	thundercloud
around	countdown	fallout	newfound	touchdown
astound	devour	firehouse	paramount	warehouse
background	devout	foreground	pronounce	without
ball gown	discount	hangout	runabout	workout
blackout	doghouse	holdout	runaround	

Variant /ōō/ as in *moon*

bloom	hoot	root	too	chew	June
boo	igloo	school	tool	crew	prune
boom	loom	scoop	toot	dew	reduce
boot	loop	scoot	tooth	drew	rude
broom	loose	shampoo	troop	flew	rule
coo	loot	shoo	zoo	grew	tube
cool	moo	shoot	zoom	knew	tune
coop	mood	sloop	blue	new	duty
doom	moon	smooth	clue	news	July
food	moose	snoop	due	screw	junior
fool	noon ooze	soon	glue	shrew	numeral
gloom	pool	spook	sue	stew	solution
goose	proof	spool	true	threw	truth
groom	roof	spoon	blew	crude	tuna
hoop	room	stool	brew	flute	

More Multisyllabic /o͞o/ Words

afternoon	cartoon	courtroom	mushroom	seafood
aloof	cashew	curfew	outgrew	switcheroo
anew	childproof	fireproof	overdo	taboo
baboon	classroom	harpoon	platoon	tattoo
balloon	cockatoo	interview	raccoon	troubleshoot
bathroom	cocoon	kangaroo	renew	typhoon
caboose	corkscrew	macaroon	review	withdrew

Note: The /o͞o/ sound is referred to as the long sound of *oo*.

Variant /o͝o/ as in *book*

afoot	crook	hood	notebook	stood	wool
book	foot	hoof	rook	took	
brook	football	hook	rookie	wood	
cook	good	look	shook	wooden	
cookie	good-bye	nook	soot	woof	

More Multisyllabic /o͝o/ Words

brotherhood	driftwood	mistook	redwood	understood
checkbook	fatherhood	motherhood	scrapbook	unhook
childhood	likelihood	notebook	sisterhood	underfoot
deadwood	livelihood	outlook	textbook	

Note: The /o͝o/ sound is referred to as the short sound of *oo*.

Two *oo's*

The letters *oo* can stand for two sounds about the same percentage of time (the long sound a bit more frequently). Therefore, I often advise students to try both sounds when confronted with an unfamiliar word that contains this spelling. If the word is in their speaking or listening vocabularies, then the approximation resulting from trying one of the sounds will help the students figure out the word. On the Word Wall, I write the /o͞o/ words on moon shapes and the /o͝o/ words on book shapes as visual reminders of the sound the letters *oo* stand for in each word listed.

Teaching Phonograms

A **phonogram** is a letter or series of letters that stands for a sound, syllable, or series of sounds without reference to meaning. For example, the phonogram *-ay* contains two letters and stands for the long *a* sound. It can be found in words such as *say*, *may*, and *replay*. The phonogram *-ack* contains three letters, stands for two sounds (/a/ /k/), and can be found in words such as *pack*, *black*, and *attack*. Phonograms are often referred to as **word families**. The words *face*, *space*, and *replace* belong to the same word family because they all contain the ending *-ace*. The ending *-ace* is a phonogram. During the past few decades, increased attention has been paid to phonograms and their use in reading instruction. In the classrooms I visit, I see more and more word walls containing word lists organized primarily around phonograms.

A linguistic term sometimes substituted for phonogram is **rime**. Rime is generally used in combination with the term **onset**. Onset and rime refer to the two parts of a syllable. In a syllable, a rime is the vowel and everything after it. For example, in the one syllable word *sat*, the rime is *-at*. The onset is the consonant, consonant blend, or digraph that comes before the rime in a syllable. In the words *sat*, *brat*, and *chat*, the onsets are *s*, *br*, and *ch*, respectively. A two-syllable word, such as *pancake*, has two onsets and two rimes. What are the onsets in the word *pancake*? (*p, c*) What are the rimes? (*-an, -ake*) Some words such as *at*, *out*, and *up* contain no onset.

Phonograms Provide a Reading Boost

Phonograms have been used in reading and spelling instruction dating as far back as the *New England Primer* and *Webster's Blue Back Spelling Books* of the 1600s, 1700s, and 1800s. Phonograms have been used during spelling instruction because word patterns are the most effective vehicle for teaching spelling. The most common phonograms appear in many of the words students will encounter in elementary stories. Teaching students that words contain recognizable chunks, and teaching them to search for these word parts or patterns, is an important step in developing reading fluency. As students encounter more and more multisyllabic words, they gain an understanding that words may contain recognizable parts (phonograms, suffixes, prefixes, smaller words). This insight is critical to decoding words quickly and efficiently.

Another value of phonograms is that they are reliable and generalizable. Of the 286 phonograms that appeared in the primary-level texts reviewed in one classic study, 272 (95%) were pronounced the same in every word in which they were found (Durrell, 1963). In addition, these 272 reliable phonograms can be found in 1,437 of the words common to the speaking vocabularies of primary-age children (Murphy, 1957).

Many educators have noted the utility of phonograms in early reading instruction, as is illustrated by the abundance of word walls containing word lists organized by phonograms. In fact, a relatively small number of phonograms can be used to generate a large number of words. According to Wylie and Durrell (1970), nearly 500 primary-grade words can be derived from only 37 phonograms:

ack	ap	est	ing	ot
ail	ash	ice	ink	uck
ain	at	ick	ip	ug
ake	ate	ide	it	ump
ale	aw	ight	ock	unk
ame	ay	ill	oke	
an	eat	in	op	
ank	ell	ine	ore	

Wylie and Durrell also made some important instructional findings about phonograms:

- Long-vowel phonograms (-*eat*, -*oat*) were learned as easily as short-vowel phonograms (-*ed*, -*op*).
- Long-vowel phonograms with final *e* (-*ake*, -*ide*, -*ope*) were as easily learned as other long-vowel phonograms.

- Phonograms containing variant vowels (*-ood, -ook*), r-controlled vowels (*-ear, -are*), and diphthongs (*-out, -oint*) were almost as easy to learn as long- and short-vowel phonograms.
- Phonograms ending in a single consonant (*-at, -ot*) were easier to learn than phonograms ending in consonant blends (*-ast, -imp*).

How to Teach With Phonograms

One instructional method that uses phonograms is **decoding by analogy** (Cunningham, 1975–76; Fox, 1996; Wagstaff, 1994). When decoding by analogy, students look for recognizable chunks within a word to help them figure it out. Cunningham (1995) contends that our brain works as a "pattern detector." As we develop as readers and our knowledge of English orthography increases, we detect more and more of these spelling patterns. Teaching students to decode by analogy helps make them aware of the patterns in our written language. Below is how one teacher might model the use of analogies to decode the word *sticking*.

Decoding by Analogy: A Model

When I look at this word, I see three parts that remind me of other words I know. First I see the letters *st*, as in the word *stop*. These two letters stand for the /st/ sounds. I also see the word part *-ick* as in the word *pick*. Then I see the common vowel ending *-ing*. If I blend together these three word parts, I get the word *sticking*.

Using phonograms in phonics instruction also helps some students internalize more complex phonics concepts, such as *r*-controlled vowels (Wagstaff, 1994). To explain to students how the *r* in the word *far* affects the sound that the *a* stands for is difficult. However, teaching students the phonogram *-ar* and providing them practice reading words such as *bar, car, far, jar,* and *star* is simpler and arguably more efficient.

Phonogram Cautions

Although phonograms can provide a boost to early reading instruction, I offer a **strong word of caution**. Never make phonograms the sole focus of reading instruction, especially early reading instruction; they provide the developing reader only limited independence in word analysis. Beginning readers who rely primarily on phonograms to decode by analogy are less skilled at word identification than beginning readers who analyze words fully (Bruck & Treiman, 1990a, 1990b). Fully analyzing words focuses students' attention on all of the word's sound-spelling relationships. Once students have practiced fully analyzing words, working with phonograms during spelling and word sorts helps to train students' eyes to see larger word chunks and this is quite effective in helping them transition to reading longer, multisyllabic words. But full analysis must occur first.

As you can see, analyzing words in their entirety is essential. Much of what students learn about English orthography (the spelling patterns of English) comes from constantly analyzing words and being exposed to lots and lots of print. Eventually, multiple exposures to words enable the reader to recognize words by sight and recognize common spelling patterns in unfamiliar words—an important goal in developing reading fluency. The best explanation of how this happens can be gleaned from the work of Ehri (1995). She provides us with a clear model of the **four phases** students go through in making every word a sight word:

1. **Pre-alphabetic phase (logographic):** Children recognize symbols, such as the "golden arches" of McDonald's, and attach a word or meaning to them. Or, they might recognize a special feature of a word. For example, a child might remember the word *yellow* because it contains two "sticks" in the middle.

2. **Partial alphabetic phase:** Children are beginning to learn sound-spelling relationships, yet are using only some phonic cues to figure out words. For instance, a child may guess the word *kitten* based on his use of picture clues and his knowledge of

the sounds associated with the letters *k* and *n*. However, this same child probably wouldn't be able to distinguish the word *kitten* from the word *kitchen* because he can't fully analyze the word.

3. **Full alphabetic phase:** Children are using their knowledge of sound-spelling relationships and analyzing words in their entirety. Much practice decoding and multiple exposures to print help children begin to develop an awareness of spelling patterns.

4. **Consolidated alphabetic phase (orthographic):** The awareness of spelling patterns is stronger, and children are beginning to use this knowledge to decode words they don't know quickly and accurately. Now, when a child sees the word *stack*, instead of analyzing the word sound by sound, she almost instantly recognizes the familiar *st* combination from words such as *step* and *stop*, and the word part *-ack*. The efficiency with which this child decodes words is greater than in the previous phase. This child has had many opportunities to fully analyze words, decode many words, and attend to word parts within words.

As children repeatedly encounter words, many are learned as sight words. This is the ultimate goal of fast, efficient decoding. Some children require as few as 4–5 exposures to new words to learn them by sight. For struggling readers, that number jumps to 50–100 (Honig, 1996). Learning words by sight requires analyzing many words in their entirety and wide reading. Beginning readers who are taught to look only for phonograms, or other word chunks, are being treated as skilled readers instead of the developing readers they are. In addition, no reading program can teach the vast number of phonograms children will encounter in words. Therefore, although using phonograms to decode by analogy is helpful, it is not sufficient. Students must be able to use a variety of decoding strategies, including decoding by analogy, blending, recognizing sight words, and using context clues, to figure out the complete range of words in the English language.

How to Use the Phonogram Lists

You can use the phonogram lists on pages 126–191 to develop word lists for phonics and spelling instruction. It is best to link phonics and spelling in early literacy instruction. However, as students progress through the intermediate grades, you will need to focus on problematic spelling patterns and organize spelling lists so they get progressively more complex developmentally. Resources by Louisa Moats (2010) and Bear et al. (2016) can assist you. The lists that follow contain one-syllable and multisyllabic words and are organized by vowel sound. Within each list, the words and phrases are listed in alphabetical order beginning with single consonant words, then proceeding to multisyllabic words.

Long-*a* Phonograms

–ace				
brace	place	deface	misplace	unlace
face	race	disgrace	replace	workplace
grace	space	embrace	retrace	
lace	trace	everyplace	shoelace	
mace	anyplace	fireplace	staircase	
pace	birthplace	horse race	suitcase	

–ade				
blade	trade	charade	lampshade	ready-made
fade	wade	crusade	lemonade	renegade
glade	accolade	custom-made	marmalade	serenade
grade	arcade	decade	masquerade	shoulder blade
jade	barricade	escapade	parade	tirade
made	blockade	grenade	persuade	unmade
shade	cavalcade	homemade	promenade	upgrade
spade	centigrade	invade	razor blade	

-age

age	stage	enrage	offstage	space age
cage	wage	front page	old age	teenage
page	backstage	ice age	outrage	upstage
rage	bird cage	middle age	rampage	
sage	engage	minimum wage	rib cage	

-aid

aide	paid	bridesmaid	mermaid	unafraid
braid	raid	first aid	nursemaid	underpaid
laid	afraid	foreign aid	overpaid	unpaid
maid	band-aid	hearing aid	repaid	visual aid

-ail

ail	mail	trail	derail	pigtail
bail	nail	wail	detail	prevail
Braille	pail	Abigail	dovetail	retail
fail	quail	airmail	fan mail	shirttail
frail	rail	blackmail	fingernail	thumbnail
Gail	sail	cocktail	hangnail	toenail
hail	snail	cottontail	monorail	
jail	tail	curtail	nature trail	

-ain

brain	slain	ascertain	explain	retain
chain	Spain	birdbrain	freight train	scatterbrain
drain	sprain	bloodstain	maintain	sustain
grain	stain	complain	migraine	tearstain
main	strain	contain	obtain	terrain
Maine	train	disdain	refrain	Ukraine
pain	vain	domain	regain	unchain
plain	abstain	Elaine	remain	
rain	acid rain	entertain	restrain	

-aint

faint	paint	quaint	saint	taint

-aise

raise	praise	mayonnaise

-ait

bait	gait	strait	trait	wait	await

-ake

bake	lake	stake	earthquake	namesake
brake	make	take	fruitcake	overtake
cake	quake	wake	handshake	pancake
drake	rake	awake	intake	rattlesnake
fake	sake	cheesecake	keepsake	remake
flake	shake	clambake	milkshake	shortcake
Jake	snake	cupcake	mistake	snowflake

-ale

bale	sale	whale	for sale	nightingale
Dale	scale	exhale	garage sale	tattletale
gale	stale	fairy tale	impale	telltale
mail	tale	female	inhale	upscale
pales				

-ame

blame	flame	name	aflame	inflame
came	frame	same	ball game	nickname
dame	game	shame	became	overcame
fame	lame	tame	defame	surname

-ane

cane	pane	airplane	hurricane	weather vane
crane	plane	candy cane	inhumane	windowpane
Jane	sane	cellophane	insane	
lane	vane	Great Dane	mundane	
mane	wane	humane	profane	

-ange

change	strange	exchange	long-range	rearrange
grange	arrange	interchange	prearrange	shortchange
range	downrange			

-ape

cape	nape	tape	escape	red tape
drape	scrape	agape	fire escape	reshape
gape	shape	egg-shape	landscape	shipshape
grape				

-ase

base	vase	briefcase	home base	suitcase
case	bookcase	erase	staircase	data base
chase				

-aste

baste	haste	paste	taste	waste

-ate

ate	alienate	communicate	dominate	first-rate
crate	alleviate	complicate	donate	fluctuate
date	allocate	concentrate	duplicate	formulate
fate	amputate	confiscate	educate	frustrate
gate	animate	congratulate	elaborate	fumigate
grate	annihilate	contaminate	elate	generate
hate	anticipate	contemplate	elevate	graduate
Kate	appreciate	cooperate	eliminate	gravitate
late	asphyxiate	coordinate	emancipate	gyrate
mate	assassinate	create	emigrate	hallucinate
plate	associate	cultivate	equate	helpmate
rate	birthrate	debate	escalate	hesitate
skate	blind date	decorate	estate	hibernate
slate	calculate	dedicate	estimate	humiliate
state	candidate	deflate	evacuate	hyphenate
abbreviate	captivate	delegate	evaluate	ice skate
accelerate	carbohydrate	deliberate	evaporate	illuminate
accommodate	celebrate	demonstrate	exaggerate	illustrate
accumulate	cellmate	detonate	exasperate	imitate
activate	cheapskate	devastate	excavate	immigrate
advocate	checkmate	deviate	exhilarate	impersonate
aggravate	circulate	discriminate	exterminate	indicate
agitate	classmate	dislocate	fascinate	infiltrate

inflate	liquidate	out-of-date	regulate	suffocate
ingrate	locate	overate	reiterate	tailgate
initiate	lubricate	overrate	relate	terminate
inmate	mandate	overstate	retaliate	tolerate
inoculate	manipulate	participate	reverberate	translate
insinuate	medicate	penetrate	roller skate	underrate
instigate	meditate	percolate	rotate	update
integrate	migrate	playmate	second-rate	up-to-date
interrogate	motivate	populate	sedate	vacate
intimidate	mutilate	primate	segregate	vaccinate
intoxicate	narrate	procrastinate	separate	validate
investigate	nauseate	pulsate	situate	vibrate
invigorate	navigate	punctuate	speculate	vindicate
irrigate	nominate	radiate	stagnate	violate
isolate	officiate	real estate	stalemate	
legislate	operate	rebate	stimulate	
liberate	ornate	recuperate	strangulate	

-ave				
brave	grave	shave	brainwave	misbehave
cave	knave	slave	engrave	shock wave
crave	pave	wave	forgave	tidal wave
Dave	rave	aftershave	heat wave	
gave	save	behave	microwave	

-ay				
bay	gray	nay	say	sway
clay	hay	pay	slay	tray
day	jay	play	spray	way
fray	lay	pray	stay	away
gay	may	ray	stray	birthday

blue jay	hallway	okay	someway	tooth decay
decay	headway	one-way	stairway	underway
delay	highway	railway	stingray	weekday
display	holiday	relay	stowaway	x-ray
essay	hooray	repay	subway	yesterday
everyday	ice tray	role-play	Sunday	
faraway	milky way	runaway	throwaway	
halfway	Norway	runway	today	

-aze

blaze	faze	graze	raze	stargaze
craze	gaze	haze	ablaze	trailblaze
daze	glaze	maze	amaze	

-eak

break	beefsteak	daybreak	housebreak	newsbreak
steak	coffee break	heartbreak	jailbreak	outbreak

-eigh

neigh	weigh	sleigh

-ey

hey	prey	whey	obey	survey
grey	they	disobey		

Long-*e* Phonograms

-e

be	he	me	she	we

-ea

flea	plea	tea	deep-sea	sweet pea
pea	sea			

-each

beach	breach	peach	reach	impeach
bleach	leach	preach	teach	outreach

-ead

bead	lead	read	mislead	speed-read
knead	plead	lip-read	proofread	

-eak

beak	freak	sneak	streak	misspeak
bleak	leak	speak	tweak	pip-squeak
creak	peak	squeak	weak	Chesapeake

-eal

deal	seal	zeal	fair deal	ordeal
heal	squeal	appeal	for real	piecemeal
meal	steal	big deal	ideal	reveal
peal	teal	conceal	misdeal	unreal
real	veal	congeal	oatmeal	

-eam

beam	scream	bloodstream	drill team	pipe dream
cream	seam	daydream	ice cream	sour cream
dream	steam	double-team	mainstream	sunbeam
gleam	stream	downstream	moonbeam	whipped cream
ream	team			

-ean

bean	glean	mean	dry clean	jelly bean
clean	Jean	wean	green bean	
dean	lean			

-eap

cheap	heap	leap	reap	junk heap

-ear

clear	near	tear	crystal-clear	pierced ear
dear	rear	year	disappear	reappear
fear	shear	all clear	far and near	Shakespeare
gear	smear	appear	leap year	unclear
hear	spear			

-ease

cease	lease	elbow grease	press release	time-release
crease	decease	increase	release	
grease	decrease			

-east

beast	least	Far East	Middle East	Near East
feast	yeast			

-eat

beat	heat	seat	deadbeat	overeat
bleat	meat	treat	defeat	repeat
cheat	neat	wheat	heartbeat	retreat
cleat	peat	backseat	mistreat	upbeat
feat	pleat	browbeat	off-beat	

-eath

heath	wreath	beneath	bequeath	underneath
sheath				

-eave

cleave	leave	sheave	weave	sick leave
heave				

-ee

bee	tee	degree	oversee	sugar-free
fee	three	disagree	pedigree	tax-free
flee	tree	emcee	peewee	tee-hee
free	wee	employee	queen bee	teepee
glee	absentee	fiddle-de-dee	referee	Tennessee
knee	agree	guarantee	refugee	worry-free
Lee	bumblebee	home-free	shopping spree	
see	caffeine-free	jamboree	sightsee	
spree	carefree	nominee	spelling bee	

-eech

beech	leech	speech	free speech	figure of speech
breech	screech			

-eed

bleed	greed	tweed	full speed	refereed
breed	heed	weed	guaranteed	seaweed
creed	need	agreed	indeed	succeed
deed	reed	disagreed	nosebleed	tumbleweed
feed	seed	exceed	overfeed	up to speed
freed	speed	force-feed	proceed	

-eek

cheek	leek	reek	week	cheek-to-cheek
creek	meek	seek	midweek	hide-and-seek
Greek	peek	sleek		

-eel

feel	peel	wheel	Ferris wheel	high heel
heel	reel	cartwheel	genteel	newsreel
kneel	steel			

-eem

deem	seem	teem	esteem	redeem	self-esteem

-een

green	teen	evergreen	Kathleen	sixteen
keen	between	fifteen	movie screen	smokescreen
queen	canteen	fourteen	preteen	sunscreen
screen	colleen	go-between	prom queen	thirteen
seen	eighteen	Halloween	seventeen	unseen

-eep

beep	jeep	sheep	weep	oversleep
cheep	keep	sleep	asleep	skin-deep
creep	peep	steep	beauty sleep	
deep	seep	sweep	knee-deep	

-eer

deer	sneer	root beer	engineer	pioneer
jeer	steer	auctioneer	musketeer	racketeer
peer	career	buccaneer	mutineer	volunteer
queer	reindeer			

-eet				
beet	meet	street	bittersweet	indiscreet
feet	sheet	sweet	cold feet	parakeet
fleet	skeet	tweet	discreet	Wall Street
greet	sleet			

-eeze				
breeze	sneeze	tweeze	antifreeze	freezer
freeze	squeeze	wheeze	deep freeze	sea breeze

-iece				
niece	apiece	centerpiece	hairpiece	timepiece
piece				

-ief				
brief	thief	debrief	fire chief	handkerchief
chief	belief	disbelief	good grief	relief
grief				

-ield				
field	shield	yield	mine field	windshield

Long-*i* Phonograms

-ibe				
bribe	tribe	diatribe	inscribe	subscribe
scribe	describe	imbibe	prescribe	transcribe

-ice				
dice	price	thrice	device	sacrifice
lice	rice	twice	entice	self-sacrifice
mice	slice	vice	sale price	
nice	splice	advice	suffice	

-ide

bride	snide	confide	misguide	worldwide
glide	stride	decide	outside	coincide
hide	tide	divide	provide	insecticide
pride	wide	fireside	reside	
ride	bedside	inside	riptide	
side	chloride	joyride	roadside	
slide	collide	landslide	subside	

-ie

die	tie	bow tie	mud pie	apple pie
lie	vie	hog-tie	necktie	underlie
pie	black tie	magpie	tongue-tie	

-ied

cried	clarified	glorified	notified	replied
died	deep-fried	horrified	occupied	satisfied
dried	defied	identified	pacified	supplied
fried	denied	implied	personified	terrified
lied	dignified	justified	petrified	tongue-tied
spied	disqualified	magnified	preoccupied	unsatisfied
tried	dissatisfied	modified	qualified	untied
applied	exemplified	multiplied	relied	verified

-ier

brier	crier	drier	flier

-ies

cries	lies	ties	butterflies	demystifies
dies	pies	tries	certifies	denies
dries	skies	applies	clarifies	disqualifies
flies	spies	beautifies	defies	dissatisfies

				-ies *continued*
dragonflies	implies	mystifies	preoccupies	solidifies
drip-dries	justifies	neckties	qualifies	specifies
exemplifies	lullabies	notifies	ratifies	stupefies
family ties	magnifies	occupies	relies	supplies
French fries	modifies	outcries	replies	terrifies
glorifies	mortifies	pacifies	satisfies	unifies
horrifies	mud pies	personifies	signifies	unties
identifies	multiplies	pigsties	simplifies	verifies

-ife

fife	rife	wife	jackknife	nightlife
knife	strife	housewife	larger-than-life	wildlife
life				

-igh

high	nigh	sigh	thigh

-ight

blight	slight	firelight	limelight	searchlight
bright	tight	fistfight	midnight	skintight
fight	airtight	flashlight	moonlight	stage fright
flight	all right	foresight	night-light	starlight
fright	all-night	forthright	not quite	stoplight
knight	birthright	good night	out-of-sight	sunlight
light	bullfight	green light	outright	tonight
might	civil right	headlight	overnight	twilight
night	copyright	highlight	oversight	upright
plight	daylight	hindsight	playwright	uptight
right	delight	insight	prizefight	
sight	eyesight			

-ike

bike	Mike	alike	hunger strike	motorbike
dike	pike	childlike	ladylike	unlike
hike	spike	dislike	lifelike	warlike
like	strike	hitchhike	look-alike	

-ild

child	wild	brainchild	hog wild	stepchild
mild				

-ile

file	vile	exile	reconcile	woodpile
mile	while	infantile	reptile	worthwhile
Nile	awhile	juvenile	senile	
pile	bibliophile	meanwhile	single file	
smile	crocodile	nail file	stockpile	
tile	domicile	profile	turnstile	

-ime

chime	slime	lifetime	part-time	springtime
crime	time	maritime	pastime	sublime
dime	anytime	meantime	peacetime	summertime
grime	bedtime	nighttime	prime time	wartime
lime	big time	old-time	showtime	
mime	daytime	overtime	small-time	
prime	dinnertime	pantomime	sometime	

-ind

bind	kind	change of mind	never mind	unkind
blind	mind	colorblind	one-track mind	unwind
find	rind	humankind	peace of mind	
grind	wind	lemon rind	remind	
hind	behind	mastermind	snow-blind	

-ine

dine	alpine	deadline	hot line	refine
fine	assign	decline	incline	shoeshine
line	baseline	define	intertwine	sideline
mine	beeline	divine	iodine	skyline
nine	borderline	entwine	lifeline	storyline
pine	canine	feline	neckline	streamline
shine	checkout line	goal line	outline	sunshine
shrine	clothesline	gold mine	outshine	underline
spine	cloud nine	grapevine	picket line	undermine
swine	coal mine	guideline	pipeline	valentine
vine	coastline	hairline	porcupine	
whine	combine	headline	punch line	
airline	confine	hemline	recline	

-ipe

gripe	snipe	wipe	peace pipe	tailpipe
pipe	stripe	bagpipe	pinstripe	unripe
ripe	swipe	overripe	sideswipe	windpipe

-ire

fire	aspire	crossfire	inspire	satire
hire	attire	desire	live wire	spitfire
spire	backfire	entire	on fire	surefire
tire	barbed wire	expire	overtire	transpire
wire	bonfire	flat tire	perspire	umpire
acquire	campfire	haywire	require	vampire
admire	cease-fire	hot-wire	retire	
afire	conspire	inquire	sapphire	

–ise

guise	chastise	disguise	likewise	televise
rise	clockwise	enterprise	otherwise	unwise
wise	comprise	exercise	revise	
advertise	compromise	franchise	sunrise	
advise	despise	high-rise	supervise	
arise	devise	improvise	surprise	

–ite

bite	white	frostbite	overbite	Snow White
kite	write	ignite	parasite	socialite
mite	appetite	impolite	polite	termite
quite	black-and-white	incite	recite	unite
rite	dynamite	invite	reunite	
site	excite	meteorite	satellite	
sprite	finite	not quite	snakebite	

–ive

chive	live	beehive	high dive	survive
dive	strive	connive	high five	take five
drive	thrive	contrive	nine-to-five	test drive
five	alive	crash-drive	nosedive	
hive	archive	deep-sea dive	revive	
jive	arrive	deprive	skydive	

–uy

buy	guy	wise guy

–y

by	fly	ply	sky	try
cry	fry	pry	sly	why
dry	my	shy	spy	ally

amplify	dignify	identify	occupy	signify
apply	disqualify	imply	outcry	simplify
beautify	dissatisfy	intensify	pacify	small fry
blow-dry	dragonfly	July	passerby	solidify
butterfly	drip-dry	justify	personify	specify
camera-shy	electrify	lullaby	petrify	standby
certify	exemplify	magnify	pigsty	stupefy
clarify	falsify	modify	preoccupy	supply
classify	firefly	mortify	purify	terrify
comply	fortify	multiply	qualify	testify
crucify	glorify	mummify	ratify	tsetse fly
deep-fry	gratify	mystify	rectify	unify
defy	horrify	nearby	rely	verify
demystify	horsefly	notify	reply	war cry
deny	hush-a-by	nullify	satisfy	

-ye				
bye	lye	bye-bye	good-bye	private eye
dye	rye	eye to eye	Popeye	shut-eye
eye	bull's eye			

Long-*o* Phonograms

-o				
go	dynamo	Mexico	pueblo	stop and go
no	get-up-and-go	Navajo	radio	studio
pro	golf pro	New Mexico	ratio	to and fro
so	gung ho	no-go	ready, set, go	Tokyo
ago	heave-ho	no-no	rodeo	touch and go
Alamo	hello	piccolo	Romeo	video
buffalo	Idaho	Pinocchio	so-so	yes and no
calico	info	pistachio	status quo	yo-yo
do-si-do	long ago	portfolio	stereo	

-oach

broach	poach	approach	reproach	stagecoach
coach	roach	cockroach		

-oad

load	carload	hit the road	railroad	unload
road	crossroad	overload	truckload	workload
toad	freeload			

-oak

cloak	croak	oak	soak	poison oak

-oal

coal	foal	goal	charcoal

-oam

foam	loam	roam

-oan

groan	Joan	loan	moan

-oast

boast	roast	toast	pot roast	coast-to-coast
coast				

-oat

bloat	goat	cutthroat	raincoat	steamboat
boat	moat	dreamboat	rock the boat	sugarcoat
coat	oat	lifeboat	rowboat	turncoat
float	throat	overcoat	scapegoat	
gloat	afloat	petticoat	sore throat	

-obe

globe	probe	bathrobe	earlobe	wardrobe
lobe	robe	disrobe	space probe	

-ode

code	rode	area code	episode	Morse code
lode	strode	decode	erode	penal code
mode	à la mode	dress code	explode	zip code
node	abode	electrode	implode	

-oe

doe	hoe	toe	mistletoe	tic-tac-toe
foe	Joe	woe	Sloppy Joe	tippy-toe

-oke

broke	smoke	yoke	cowpoke	provoke
choke	spoke	artichoke	dead broke	slowpoke
coke	stoke	awoke	go for broke	sunstroke
joke	stroke	cloud of smoke	heatstroke	
poke	woke			

-old

bold	old	billfold	household	stronghold
cold	scold	blindfold	ice-cold	threshold
fold	sold	choke hold	out cold	toehold
gold	told	common cold	pot of gold	unfold
hold	age-old	enfold	retold	untold
mold	behold	foothold	stranglehold	withhold

-ole

dole	whole	Creole	loophole	porthole
hole	buttonhole	cubbyhole	manhole	pothole
mole	cajole	fishing pole	north pole	tadpole
pole	camisole	flagpole	parole	totem pole
role	casserole	foxhole	peephole	
stole	console	keyhole	pigeonhole	

-oll

droll	roll	toll	egg roll	rock and roll
knoll	scroll	troll	enroll	steamroll
poll	stroll	drum roll	payroll	unroll

-olt

bolt	jolt	volt	lightning bolt	revolt
colt	molt	deadbolt		

-ome

chrome	home	Rome	metronome	palindrome
dome	Nome	foster home	mobile home	syndrome
gnome				

-one

bone	stone	car phone	headphone	pay phone
clone	tone	cobblestone	headstone	pinecone
cone	zone	condone	hormone	postpone
drone	accident-prone	cyclone	jawbone	rhinestone
hone	alone	dethrone	microphone	saxophone
lone	backbone	dial tone	milestone	sno-cone
phone	baritone	end zone	monotone	stepping-stone
prone	birthstone	funny bone	outshone	T-bone
shone	buffer zone	grindstone	ozone	telephone

time zone	twilight zone	wishbone	Yellowstone
tombstone	war zone	xylophone	

-ope

cope	nope	slope	horoscope	stethoscope
dope	pope	antelope	jump rope	telescope
hope	rope	elope	microscope	tightrope
mope	scope	envelope	periscope	towrope

-ose

chose	prose	enclose	open and close	pug nose
close	rose	expose	oppose	runny nose
hose	those	fire hose	overexpose	suppose
nose	decompose	impose	panty hose	
pose	dispose	nose-to-nose	propose	

-ost

ghost	post	goalpost	innermost	topmost
host	almost	guidepost	outpost	trading post
most	bedpost	hitching post	signpost	utmost

-ote

note	vote	antidote	keynote	promote
quote	wrote	devote	misquote	remote
rote	anecdote	footnote	outvote	

-ove

clove	drove	stove	wove	by Jove
cove	grove	trove	alcove	

-ow

blow	low	stow	game show	right-to-know
bow	mow	tow	high and low	scarecrow
crow	row	aglow	low blow	sideshow
flow	show	below	no show	skid row
glow	slow	blow by blow	outgrow	talent show
grow	snow	ebb and flow	overflow	talk show
know	sow	fashion show	rainbow	undertow

-own

blown	known	sown	full-blown	well-known
flown	mown	thrown	full-grown	windblown
grown	shown	disown	homegrown	

Short-*a* Phonograms

-ab

blab	drab	jab	slab	rehab
cab	flab	lab	stab	sand crab
crab	gab	nab	tab	taxicab
dab	grab	scab	backstab	

-ack

back	pack	tack	drawback	jumping jack
black	quack	track	feedback	knapsack
clack	rack	whack	flapjack	laugh track
crack	sack	attack	flashback	lumberjack
hack	shack	backpack	fullback	off-track
Jack	slack	backtrack	haystack	one-track
knack	smack	blackjack	heart attack	panic attack
lack	snack	camelback	hijack	paperback
Mack	stack	crackerjack	icepack	piggyback

quarterback	railroad track	setback	soundtrack	unpack
racetrack	ransack	sidetrack	thumbtack	wisecrack

-act

fact	artifact	enact	interact	riot act
pact	attract	exact	matter of fact	subtract
tact	compact	extract	overact	transact
tract	contract	impact	overreact	
abstract	distract	in fact	react	

-ad

bad	fad	pad	granddad	shoulder pad
Brad	glad	sad	ink pad	Sinbad
Chad	had	tad	ironclad	too bad
clad	lad	doodad	launching pad	Trinidad
dad	mad	egad	nomad	undergrad

-aft

craft	graft	waft	life raft	spacecraft
daft	raft	aircraft	mine shaft	witchcraft
draft	shaft			

-ag

bag	lag	tag	lollygag	sleeping bag
brag	nag	wag	mailbag	tea bag
crag	rag	bean bag	name tag	trash bag
drag	sag	dishrag	price tag	washrag
flag	shag	grab bag	ragtag	windbag
gag	snag	jet lag	saddlebag	zigzag
jag	stag	litterbag	sandbag	

-am

am	Pam	swam	flimflam	telegram
clam	ram	tam	grand slam	traffic jam
cram	Sam	yam	in a jam	Uncle Sam
dam	scam	Abraham	madam	
gram	scram	anagram	milligram	
ham	sham	diagram	outswam	
jam	slam	exam	program	

-amp

camp	cramp	ramp	tramp	summer camp
champ	damp	scamp	vamp	writer's cramp
clamp	lamp	stamp	postage stamp	

-an

ban	plan	cancan	hangman	overran
bran	ran	caravan	Japan	Pakistan
can	scan	catamaran	lawman	sandman
clan	span	caveman	life span	sedan
Dan	tan	deadpan	madman	spic-and-span
fan	than	dishpan	moving van	suntan
flan	van	dustpan	oat bran	time span
man	attention span	frying pan	orangutan	trashcan
pan	began	handyman	outran	

-ance

chance	prance	circumstance	finance	romance
dance	stance	enhance	folk dance	song and dance
France	trance	entrance	freelance	square dance
glance	advance	fat chance	last chance	tap dance
lance	break dance	fighting chance	rain dance	

–anch

blanch	branch	ranch

–and

band	armband	crash-land	handstand	quicksand
bland	baby grand	demand	headband	reprimand
brand	backhand	disband	helping hand	rubber band
gland	bandstand	dreamland	homeland	secondhand
hand	beforehand	expand	kickstand	shorthand
land	close-at-hand	fantasy land	longhand	Thailand
sand	command	firsthand	misunderstand	understand
stand	contraband	grandstand	name-brand	wasteland
strand	cowhand	hand-in-hand	offhand	

–ang

bang	gang	rang	sprang	chain gang
clang	hang	sang	twang	mustang
fang	pang	slang	boomerang	overhang

–ank

bank	frank	sank	blankety-blank	military rank
blank	Hank	shrank	blood bank	outrank
clank	lank	spank	data bank	point-blank
crank	plank	tank	draw a blank	savings bank
dank	prank	thank	fish tank	think tank
drank	rank	yank	gangplank	

–ant

ant	pant	slant	enchant	power plant
can't	plant	disenchant	gallivant	supplant
chant	rant	eggplant	implant	transplant
grant	scant			

-ap

cap	sap	backslap	gift wrap	overlap
chap	scrap	baseball cap	gingersnap	recap
clap	slap	bottle cap	handicap	road map
flap	snap	burlap	hubcap	thinking cap
gap	strap	catnap	kidnap	tourist trap
lap	tap	dunce cap	kneecap	unwrap
map	trap	firetrap	madcap	wiretap
nap	wrap	gender gap	mishap	
rap	yap	generation gap	mousetrap	

-ash

bash	gash	slash	balderdash	succotash
brash	hash	smash	corned beef hash	whiplash
cash	lash	stash	diaper rash	
clash	mash	thrash	eyelash	
dash	rash	trash	mishmash	
flash	sash	backlash	news flash	

-ask

ask	cask	flask	mask	task

-asm

chasm	plasm	spasm	enthusiasm	sarcasm

-asp

clasp	gasp	grasp	hasp	rasp

-ast

blast	last	vast	at last	contrast
cast	mast	aghast	bombast	downcast
fast	past	all-star cast	broadcast	enthusiast

flabbergast	gymnast	miscast	outlast	steadfast
forecast	half-mast	newscast	overcast	telecast
full blast	iconoclast	outcast	sandblast	typecast

-at

at	mat	vat	cowboy hat	muskrat
bat	pat	acrobat	democrat	nonfat
brat	rat	alley cat	dingbat	pack rat
cat	sat	aristocrat	diplomat	place mat
chat	scat	baby fat	doormat	thermostat
fat	slat	bureaucrat	format	tomcat
flat	spat	chitchat	habitat	welcome mat
gnat	splat	combat	hardhat	wildcat
hat	that	copy cat	laundromat	wombat

-atch

batch	match	thatch	cabbage patch	mismatch
catch	patch	arm patch	detach	mix and match
hatch	scratch	attach	dispatch	reattach
latch	snatch	boxing match	knee patch	unlatch

-ath

bath	path	aftermath	bubble-bath	steam bath
math	wrath	birdbath	psychopath	warpath

-ax

ax	lax	tax	climax	relax
fax	max	wax	earwax	
flax	sax	candle wax	income tax	

Short-*e* Phonograms

-ead				
bread	thread	drop dead	homestead	redhead
dead	tread	egghead	instead	sleepyhead
dread	ahead	figurehead	knucklehead	spearhead
head	arrowhead	forehead	letterhead	straight ahead
lead	bald head	French bread	misread	widespread
read	behead	gingerbread	overhead	
spread	blockhead	hardhead	proofread	

-ealth		
health	stealth	wealth

-eath				
death	bad breath	out of breath	scared to death	starve to death
breath	kiss of death			

-eck				
check	neck	bottleneck	pain in the neck	rubberneck
deck	peck	double-check	paycheck	shipwreck
fleck	speck	hit the deck	rain check	spot-check
heck	wreck	neck and neck	roughneck	turtleneck

-ed				
bed	red	bobsled	inbred	underfed
bled	shed	bottle-fed	infrared	unwed
bred	shred	bunk bed	moped	water bed
fed	sled	city-bred	newlywed	well-bred
fled	sped	coed	overfed	well-fed
Fred	Ted	deathbed	sickbed	
led	wed	early to bed	spoon-fed	
Ned	biped	ill-bred	thoroughbred	

-edge

dredge	hedge	pledge	wedge	on edge
edge	ledge	sledge		

-eft

cleft	left	theft

-eg

beg	leg	Meg	peg	Winnipeg
keg				

-eld

held	weld	hand-held	upheld	withheld
meld	beheld			

-elf

elf	shelf	herself	itself	yourself
self	bookshelf	himself	myself	

-ell

bell	sell	yell	gazelle	school bell
cell	shell	bombshell	inkwell	show and tell
dell	smell	dinner bell	jail cell	sleigh bell
dwell	spell	doorbell	misspell	unwell
fell	swell	dumbbell	nutshell	very well
jell	tell	eggshell	oil well	wishing well
Nell	well	farewell	retell	

-elp

help	kelp	yelp

-elt

belt	felt	melt	welt	seat belt
dwelt	knelt	pelt	heartfelt	

-em

gem	hem	stem	them

-en

Ben	Ken	then	amen	mother hen
den	men	when	bullpen	now and then
glen	pen	wren	hang ten	pigpen
hen	ten	yen	lion's den	playpen

-ence

fence	pence	commence	consequence	evidence
hence	whence			

-ench

bench	French	trench	monkey wrench	unclench
clench	quench	wrench	park bench	
drench	stench			

-end

bend	spend	attend	dividend	recommend
blend	tend	bitter end	end-to-end	suspend
end	trend	comprehend	extend	transcend
fend	vend	dead end	intend	unbend
lend	amend	defend	offend	upend
mend	apprehend	depend	overspend	wit's end
send	ascend	descend	pretend	

-ength

length	strength

-ense

dense	defense	immense	no-nonsense	self-defense
sense	dispense	incense	nonsense	sixth sense
tense	expense	intense	offense	suspense
common sense	false pretense	make sense	pretense	
condense	good sense			

-ent

bent	spent	content	frequent	misspent
cent	tent	descent	heaven sent	percent
dent	vent	discontent	implement	present
gent	went	dissent	indent	prevent
Kent	air vent	event	intent	repent
lent	cement	evident	invent	represent
rent	circus tent	experiment	lament	resent
scent	compliment	extent	malcontent	torment
sent	consent	for rent	misrepresent	underwent

-ep

pep	rep	strep	bicep	overstep
prep	step	yep	doorstep	sidestep

-ept

crept	swept	concept	intercept	rainswept
kept	wept	except	overslept	windswept
slept	accept	inept		

-esh

flesh	mesh	enmesh	in the flesh	refresh
fresh	Bangladesh	gooseflesh		

-ess

Bess	access	duress	outguess	regress
bless	address	excess	overdress	repossess
chess	air express	express	pony express	repress
dress	bench-press	full-court press	possess	second-guess
guess	caress	impress	printing press	success
less	confess	more or less	profess	suppress
mess	depress	nevertheless	progress	undress
press	digress	nonetheless	recess	unless
stress	distress	oppress		

-est

best	rest	blood test	hope chest	protest
blest	test	bulletproof vest	hornet's nest	request
chest	vest	conquest	invest	screen test
crest	west	contest	level best	second best
jest	wrest	crow's nest	life vest	suggest
lest	zest	decongest	manifest	treasure chest
nest	arrest	detest	medicine chest	under arrest
pest	beauty rest	fun-fest	next best	Wild West
quest	bird nest			

-et

bet	let	wet	alphabet	clarinet
Chet	met	yet	bassinet	dragnet
fret	net	abet	bayonet	duet
get	pet	all set	better yet	forget
jet	set	all wet	cadet	jet set

-et *continued*				
Juliet	not yet	reset	sunset	Tibet
minuet	quartet	safety net	teacher's pet	upset
mosquito net	regret	Soviet		

-etch				
etch	retch	stretch	wretch	homestretch
fetch	sketch			

-ext		
next	text	context

Short-*i* Phonograms

-ib				
bib	fib	rib	prime rib	sparerib
crib	glib	ad lib		

-ick				
brick	pick	trick	handpick	sidekick
chick	quick	wick	heartsick	slapstick
click	Rick	airsick	homesick	toothpick
Dick	sick	broomstick	lipstick	yardstick
flick	slick	card trick	lovesick	candlestick
kick	stick	chopstick	nit-pick	dirty trick
lick	thick	drumstick	seasick	
nick	tick			

-id				
bid	lid	squid	hybrid	overdid
did	mid	amid	Madrid	pyramid
grid	rid	arachnid	outbid	redid
hid	skid	eyelid	outdid	whiz kid
kid	slid	forbid		

-iff

cliff	sniff	tiff	midriff	scared stiff
miff	stiff	whiff		

-ift

drift	shift	airlift	night shift	snowdrift
gift	sift	face-lift	shoplift	spendthrift
lift	swift	makeshift	ski lift	uplift
rift	thrift			

-ig

big	gig	sprig	wig	oil rig
brig	jig	swig	bigwig	shindig
dig	pig	twig	guinea pig	thingamajig
fig	rig			

-ilk

bilk	ilk	milk	silk	buttermilk

-ill

bill	Jill	thrill	freewill	standstill
chill	kill	trill	fulfill	treadmill
dill	mill	twill	goodwill	uphill
drill	pill	will	ill will	whippoorwill
fill	quill	anthill	instill	windmill
frill	sill	Capitol Hill	Jack and Jill	windowsill
gill	skill	chlorophyll	oil spill	
grill	spill	dollar bill	overkill	
hill	still	downhill	refill	
ill	till	fire drill	run-of-the-mill	

-ilt				
built	jilt	lilt	spilt	tilt
hilt	kilt	quilt	stilt	wilt

-im				
brim	him	prim	swim	whim
dim	Jim	rim	Tim	sink or swim
grim	Kim	slim	trim	

-imp				
blimp	crimp	primp	skimp	wimp
chimp	limp	shrimp		

-in				
bin	sin	bobby-pin	next of kin	stand-in
chin	skin	bowling pin	pigskin	tailspin
din	spin	break-in	rolling pin	thick and thin
fin	thin	cave-in	Rumpelstiltskin	trash bin
grin	tin	double chin	safety pin	unpin
in	twin	drive-in	sheepskin	violin
kin	win	hairpin	shoo-in	within
pin	begin	mandolin	snakeskin	
shin	Berlin			

-ince				
mince	prince	since	wince	convince

-inch				
cinch	finch	inch	pinch	inch by inch
clinch	flinch			

–ing

bring	sing	wing	class ring	porch swing
cling	sling	wring	drawstring	shoestring
ding	spring	zing	earring	something
fling	sting	anything	everything	static cling
king	string	bee sting	first-string	wing-ding
ping	swing	Beijing	offspring	
ring	thing	boxing ring	plaything	

–inge

binge	fringe	singe	tinge	infringe
cringe	hinge			

–ink

blink	link	slink	hoodwink	rinky-dink
brink	mink	stink	hot pink	roller rink
clink	pink	think	missing link	soft drink
drink	rink	wink	pen and ink	tickled pink
ink	shrink	cuff link	rethink	
kink	sink			

–int

flint	print	tint	footprint	peppermint
glint	splint	blueprint	imprint	shin splint
hint	sprint	fine print	misprint	spearmint
lint	squint	fingerprint	newsprint	U.S. Mint
mint	stint			

-ip

blip	ship	bean dip	fellowship	penmanship
chip	sip	catnip	field trip	potato chip
clip	skip	censorship	fingertip	round trip
dip	slip	championship	friendship	salesmanship
drip	snip	chocolate chip	guardianship	scholarship
flip	strip	citizenship	hardship	spaceship
grip	tip	comic strip	internship	sportsmanship
hip	trip	companionship	kinship	stiff upper lip
lip	whip	courtship	leadership	unzip
nip	zip	dictatorship	membership	
quip	apprenticeship	double-dip	ownership	
rip	battleship	equip	paper clip	

-is

his	is			

-ish

dish	squish	wish	goldfish	jellyfish
fish	swish			

-isk

brisk	frisk	whisk	floppy disk	slipped disk
disk	risk	asterisk	high risk	

-isp

crisp	lisp	wisp

-iss

bliss	kiss	Swiss	dismiss	near miss
hiss	miss	amiss	hit or miss	

-ist

fist	twist	checklist	exist	resist
gist	wrist	coexist	insist	shopping list
list	assist	consist	persist	tongue twist
mist	blacklist	enlist	price list	

-it

bit	skit	bit by bit	moonlit	submit
fit	slit	bottomless pit	nitwit	sunlit
flit	spit	close-knit	omit	switch-hit
grit	split	cockpit	outfit	tar pit
hit	wit	commit	outwit	throw a fit
kit	acquit	counterfeit	perfect fit	tight fit
knit	admit	first aid kit	permit	tool kit
lit	armpit	legit	pinch-hit	transmit
pit	baby-sit	lickety-split	smash hit	unfit
quit	banana split	misfit	snake pit	
sit	benefit			

-itch

ditch	itch	switch	bewitch	master switch
glitch	pitch	twitch	fever pitch	unhitch
hitch	stitch	witch	light switch	

-ive

give	live	forgive	outlive	relive

-ix

fix	nix	cake mix	quick fix	transfix
mix	six			

Short-*o* Phonograms

-ob				
blob	job	slob	corn on the cob	hobnob
Bob	knob	snob	corncob	inside job
cob	lob	sob	doorknob	snow job
glob	mob	throb	heartthrob	thingamabob
gob	rob	con job		

-ock				
block	rock	cell block	laughingstock	shamrock
clock	shock	cuckoo clock	livestock	shell shock
crock	smock	culture shock	mental block	Sherlock
dock	sock	deadlock	o'clock	stumbling block
flock	stock	gridlock	out of stock	sunblock
frock	tock	hard rock	padlock	tick-tock
hock	aftershock	headlock	peacock	unlock
knock	alarm clock	Hitchcock	roadblock	woodblock
lock	auction block	knock-knock	round-the-clock	writer's block
mock				

-od				
clod	nod	rod	cattle prod	lightning rod
cod	plod	sod	fishing rod	pea pod
God	pod	trod	goldenrod	slipshod
mod	prod	Cape Cod	hot rod	tripod

-oft	
loft	soft

-og

bog	fog	smog	groundhog	top dog
clog	frog	bulldog	hound dog	underdog
cog	hog	bullfrog	leapfrog	watchdog
dog	jog	catalog	road hog	
flog	log	chili dog	ship's log	

-omp

chomp	pomp	stomp	tromp	whomp
clomp	romp			

-ond

blond	fond	beyond	fishpond	vagabond
bond	pond	correspond	respond	

-op

bop	slop	box top	karate chop	shortstop
chop	sop	bus stop	kerplop	teardrop
cop	stop	coffee shop	lemon drop	tiptop
crop	top	cough drop	lollipop	traffic-stop
drop	Aesop	cream of the crop	mountaintop	treetop
flop	barbershop	doorstop	name-drop	truck stop
hop	bebop	eavesdrop	nonstop	window shop
mop	bellhop	flattop	pawnshop	workshop
plop	belly flop	flip-flop	pit stop	
pop	big top	gumdrop	pork chop	
prop	blacktop	hilltop	rain drop	
shop	body shop	hip hop	rooftop	

-ot

blot	cot	got	jot	lot
clot	dot	hot	knot	not

plot	beauty spot	forget-me-not	long shot	snapshot
pot	big shot	forgot	mascot	teapot
rot	blind spot	gunshot	melting pot	thanks a lot
shot	bloodshot	hit the spot	on the dot	tie the knot
slot	boiling hot	hot shot	on the spot	tight spot
spot	Camelot	hot to trot	parking lot	whatnot
tot	cannot	inkblot	polka dot	
trot	coffee-pot	jackpot	red-hot	
apricot	flowerpot	Lancelot	slingshot	

-otch

blotch	crotch	notch	hopscotch	topnotch
botch				

-ough

cough	trough

-ox

box	cash box	jack-in-the-box	outfox	soap box
fox	chatterbox	lunch box	paradox	toy box
lox	chickenpox	mailbox	sandbox	unorthodox
ox	detox	music box	shadowbox	Xerox
pox	Fort Knox	orthodox		

Short-*u* Phonograms

-ome

come	some	become	outcome	overcome

-on

son	ton	won	grandson

-ough

rough	tough	fair enough	rough and tough	sure enough
slough	enough			

-ove

dove	shove	labor of love	puppy love	turtledove
glove	above	none of the above	self-love	
love	boxing glove			

-ub

club	hub	snub	bathtub	hubbub
cub	nub	stub	billy club	lion cub
dub	rub	sub	fan club	nightclub
flub	scrub	tub	hot tub	ticket stub
grub	shrub	back rub		

-uch

much	such	not much	pretty much	such and such

-uck

buck	puck	beginner's luck	lame duck	stagestruck
Chuck	struck	dumbstruck	lovestruck	starstruck
cluck	stuck	fire truck	moonstruck	thunderstruck
duck	suck	good luck	out of luck	tough luck
luck	truck	hockey puck	pass the buck	tow truck
muck	tuck	horror-struck	potluck	woodchuck
pluck	awestruck	lady luck	sitting duck	

-ud

bud	dud	spud	thud	stick in the mud
crud	mud	stud	rosebud	taste bud
cud				

-udge

budge	grudge	sludge	trudge	misjudge
drudge	judge	smudge	hot fudge	prejudge
fudge	nudge			

-uff

bluff	gruff	scuff	blindman's bluff	kid stuff
buff	huff	sluff	cream puff	overstuff
cuff	puff	snuff	handcuff	powder puff
fluff	ruff	stuff	huff and puff	rebuff

-ug

bug	lug	slug	bedbug	humbug
chug	mug	smug	chugalug	jitterbug
drug	plug	snug	doodlebug	ladybug
dug	pug	thug	earplug	litterbug
hug	rug	tug	fireplug	unplug
jug	shrug	bear hug		

-ulk

bulk	hulk	skulk	sulk

-ull

cull	gull	lull	skull	sea gull
dull	hull	mull	numskull	

-um

bum	hum	slum	bubble gum	fee-fie-fo-fum
chum	mum	strum	chewing gum	ho-hum
drum	plum	sum	chrysanthemum	humdrum
glum	rum	yum	eardrum	yum-yum
gum	scum	beach bum		

-umb

crumb	plumb	cookie crumb	green thumb	succumb
dumb	thumb	deaf and dumb	rule of thumb	Tom Thumb
numb				

-ump

bump	grump	pump	trump	speed bump
chump	hump	rump	broad jump	stomach pump
clump	jump	slump	city dump	trash dump
dump	lump	stump	goose bump	tree stump
frump	plump	thump	ski jump	triple jump

-un

bun	shun	begun	home run	rerun
fun	spun	blowgun	homespun	shotgun
gun	stun	dog run	honey bun	top gun
pun	sun	hamburger bun	jump the gun	trial run
run	Attila the Hun	hit-and-run	outrun	

-unch

brunch	hunch	punch	honeybunch	school lunch
bunch	lunch	scrunch	out to lunch	whole bunch
crunch	munch	fruit punch		

-ung

clung	rung	stung	wrung	high-strung
flung	sprung	sung	egg foo yung	iron lung
hung	strung	swung	far-flung	unsung
lung				

-unk

bunk	drunk	flunk	junk	shrunk
chunk	dunk	hunk	plunk	skunk

-unk *continued*

slunk	stunk	trunk	kerplunk	slam dunk
spunk	sunk	chipmunk	preshrunk	

-unt

blunt	grunt	punt	stunt	treasure hunt
bunt	hunt	runt	manhunt	witch hunt

-up

cup	buildup	dress up	mix-up	shut up
pup	buttercup	foul-up	paper cup	stickup
sup	checkup	giddy-up	pick-me-up	teacup
all shook up	close-up	grown-up	pickup	throw up
backup	coffee cup	hang-up	roundup	toss-up
blowup	cover-up	hiccup	runner-up	touch-up
breakup	crackup	lineup	setup	washed-up
buckle up	cutup	makeup		

-us

bus	pus	us	nonplus	school bus
plus	thus			

-ush

blush	gush	plush	bum's rush	hairbrush
brush	hush	rush	cheek blush	hush-hush
crush	lush	slush	gold rush	toothbrush
flush	mush	thrush		

-ust

bust	gust	rust	adjust	coal dust
crust	just	thrust	bite the dust	combust
dust	must	trust	brain trust	crop dust

disgust	gold dust	pie crust	sawdust	unjust
distrust	mistrust	robust	stardust	wanderlust
entrust				

–ut

but	nut	clear-cut	King Tut	uncut
cut	rut	coconut	open and shut	undercut
glut	shut	haircut	precut	uppercut
gut	strut	halibut	rebut	
hut	catgut	in a rut	shortcut	
jut	chestnut			

–utch

clutch	crutch	Dutch	hutch	rabbit hutch

–utt

butt	mutt	putt	scuttlebutt

Variant Vowel /âr/ Phonograms

–air

air	pair	dentist chair	midair	repair
chair	stair	despair	millionaire	rocking chair
fair	affair	fresh air	no fair	solitaire
flair	billionaire	high chair	on the air	unfair
hair	county fair	impair	questionnaire	wheelchair
lair	debonair			

–are

bare	care	fare	glare	mare
blare	dare	flare	hare	pare

rare	stare	child care	intensive care	unaware
scare	ware	compare	nightmare	warfare
share	airfare	declare	prepare	welfare
snare	aware	Delaware	silverware	
spare	beware	fair and square	threadbare	
square	bus fare	fanfare	Times Square	

-ear

bear	swear	outerwear	underwear	wash and wear
pear	wear	teddy bear		

Variant Vowel /ûr/ Phonograms

-earn

earn	learn	yearn	live and learn

-erb

herb	verb	adverb	proverb	superb

-erge

merge	verge	diverge	emerge	submerge
serge	converge			

-erk

jerk	clerk	perk	berserk

-erm

germ	term	long-term	midterm	pachyderm

-ern

fern	stern	concern	intern

-erve

nerve	brown-and-serve	deserve	preserve	self-serve
serve	conserve	observe	reserve	unnerve
swerve				

-ir

fir	stir	whir	astir	yes sir
sir				

-ird

bird	early bird	jailbird	lovebird	one-third
third	hummingbird	ladybird	mockingbird	songbird
blackbird				

-irk

quirk	shirk	smirk

-irl

girl	twirl	awhirl	cover girl	dream girl
swirl	whirl			

-irst

first	thirst	die of thirst	feet-first	headfirst

-irt

dirt	skirt	miniskirt	pay dirt	stuffed shirt
flirt	squirt	nightshirt	redshirt	undershirt
shirt	hula skirt			

-irth

birth	girth	mirth	childbirth	rebirth

-ur				
fur	slur	concur	demur	occur
blur	spur			

-urb				
curb	disturb	news blurb	perturb	suburb
blurb	do not disturb			

-urge		
urge	purge	splurge

-url			
curl	furl	hurl	unfurl

-urn				
burn	urn	out of turn	sojourn	toss and turn
churn	downturn	overturn	sunburn	upturn
spurn	heartburn	return	tax return	U-turn
turn	nocturne	slow burn		

-urk	
lurk	murk

-urse			
curse	nurse	purse	reimburse

-urt				
curt	blurt	spurt	Frankfurt	unhurt
hurt				

Variant Vowel /är/ Phonograms

-ar				
bar	scar	boxcar	falling star	salad bar
car	spar	cable car	guitar	seminar
char	star	candy bar	handlebar	snack bar
czar	tar	caviar	jaguar	so far
far	ajar	cigar	movie star	streetcar
jar	all-star	cookie jar	near and far	superstar
mar	bazaar	costar	registrar	Zanzibar
par	bizarre	disbar		

-ard				
card	backyard	boulevard	disregard	regard
guard	barnyard	coast guard	flash card	report card
hard	baseball card	credit card	graveyard	safeguard
lard	birthday card	crossing guard	junkyard	scorecard
yard	blowhard	cue card	leotard	shipyard
armed guard	bodyguard	diehard	lifeguard	St. Bernard
avant-garde	bombard	discard	postcard	vanguard

-arge				
barge	large	enlarge	recharge	take charge
charge	discharge	overcharge		

-ark				
bark	park	baseball park	disembark	remark
Clark	shark	birthmark	double-park	skylark
dark	spark	bookmark	earmark	theme park
hark	stark	Central Park	landmark	trademark
lark	aardvark	check mark	postmark	
mark	ballpark	Denmark	question mark	

		-arm		
arm	harm	disarm	fire alarm	lucky charm
charm	alarm	false alarm	firearm	underarm
farm	arm in arm			

		-arn
barn	darn	yarn

		-arp	
carp	harp	sharp	tarp

		-art		
cart	start	eye chart	impart	restart
chart	tart	fall apart	jump-start	running start
dart	à la carte	false start	martial art	shopping cart
mart	apart	folk art	mini-mart	street smart
part	counterpart	go cart	Mozart	upstart
smart	depart	golf cart	outsmart	work of art

Variant Vowel /ô/ Phonograms

		-all		
all	appall	curtain call	know it all	shopping mall
ball	baseball	downfall	meatball	snowball
call	basketball	enthrall	nightfall	snowfall
fall	birdcall	eyeball	oddball	spitball
hall	blackball	football	off-the-wall	stonewall
mall	butterball	free fall	overall	study hall
small	cannonball	free-for-all	phone call	toll call
squall	city hall	goofball	pinball	volleyball
stall	close call	gum ball	pitfall	wake-up call
tall	cotton ball	handball	rainfall	wall-to-wall
wall	crystal ball	install	recall	waterfall

-alk

balk	back talk	fast-talk	outtalk	small talk
chalk	beanstalk	girl talk	pep talk	space walk
stalk	boardwalk	jaywalk	sidewalk	sweet talk
talk	crosswalk	nature walk	sleepwalk	
walk	double talk			

-alt

halt	malt	salt	asphalt	exalt

-aught

caught	naught	taught	distraught	self-taught
fraught				

-aunch

haunch	launch	paunch	staunch

-aunt

daunt	gaunt	haunt	jaunt	taunt
flaunt				

-ault

fault	assault	default	pole-vault	somersault
vault				

-aw

caw	gnaw	raw	straw	outlaw
claw	jaw	saw	hem and haw	seesaw
draw	law	slaw	jigsaw	southpaw
flaw	paw	squaw	last straw	withdraw

-awl

bawl	crawl	drawl	scrawl	shawl
brawl				

-awn

brawn	fawn	pawn	yawn	overdrawn
dawn	lawn	prawn	crack of dawn	withdrawn
drawn				

-ong

bong	tong	belong	hop-a-long	sarong
dong	prong	folk song	lifelong	sing-along
gong	strong	headlong	oblong	so long
long	wrong	headstrong	Ping-Pong	tagalong
song	along	Hong Kong	prolong	

-oss

boss	loss	across	double-cross	memory loss
cross	moss	crisscross	hearing loss	Red Cross
floss	toss	dental floss	lip gloss	ring toss
gloss				

-ost

cost	lost	at any cost	defrost	low-cost
frost				

-oth

broth	froth	sloth	chicken broth	three-toed sloth
cloth	moth			

-ought

bought	fought	sought	afterthought	store-bought
brought	ought	thought	food for thought	

/ô/ With *r* Phonograms

-oar

boar	roar	soar	uproar

-oor

door	door-to-door	next-door	outdoor	trapdoor
floor	indoor			

-orch

porch	torch	scorch

-ord

chord	lord	discord	record	smorgasbord
cord	sword	harpsichord	rip cord	spinal chord
fjord	afford	landlord	slumlord	tape-record
ford				

-ore

bore	snore	apple core	explore	outscore
chore	sore	ashore	eyesore	restore
core	spore	Baltimore	folklore	seashore
fore	store	before	forevermore	Singapore
gore	swore	carnivore	galore	sophomore
more	tore	cold sore	ignore	Theodore
pore	wore	drugstore	nevermore	therefore
score	adore	encore	no more	underscore
shore	anymore	evermore		

-ork

cork	pork	York	New York	pitchfork
fork	stork			

-orm

dorm	barnstorm	deform	misinform	snowstorm
form	brainstorm	dust storm	perform	thunderstorm
norm	co-ed dorm	free-form	platform	transform
storm	conform	inform	reform	uniform

-orn

born	torn	ear of corn	Matterhorn	shoehorn
corn	worn	first-born	native-born	timeworn
horn	acorn	foghorn	newborn	unborn
morn	adorn	foreign-born	outworn	unicorn
scorn	airborne	forlorn	popcorn	weatherworn
sworn	bullhorn	greenhorn	reborn	well-worn
thorn	Capricorn	inborn		

-ort

fort	airport	distort	import	seaport
port	bad sport	escort	last resort	spoilsport
sort	cavort	export	passport	support
short	cohort	good sport	report	transport
snort	contort	heliport	resort	
sport	deport			

-our

four	pour	downpour	ten-four	troubadour

Diphthong /oi/ Phonograms

-oil				
boil	foil	spoil	hard-boil	tinfoil
broil	oil	toil	recoil	turmoil
coil	soil			

-oin				
coin	join	Des Moines	purloin	sirloin
groin	loin	flip a coin	rejoin	tenderloin

-oint				
joint	ballpoint	focal point	out of joint	viewpoint
point	checkpoint	high point	pinpoint	West Point
appoint	disappoint	needlepoint	starting point	

-oise			
noise	poise	traffic noise	turquoise

-oist		
foist	hoist	moist

-oy				
boy	Roy	annoy	enjoy	overjoy
buoy	soy	corduroy	killjoy	pride and joy
coy	toy	destroy	life buoy	real McCoy
joy	Troy	employ	oh boy	
ploy	ahoy			

Diphthong /ou/ Phonograms

		-ouch		
couch	grouch	pouch	slouch	vouch
crouch	ouch			

		-oud		
cloud	proud	out loud	thundercloud	war cloud
loud	aloud	rain cloud		

		-ounce		
bounce	ounce	trounce	mispronounce	pronounce
flounce	pounce	announce	ounce for ounce	renounce

		-ound		
bound	abound	chow hound	inbound	profound
found	aground	compound	lost and found	rebound
ground	all around	dog pound	merry-go-round	runaround
hound	around	dumbfound	muscle-bound	snowbound
mound	astound	earthbound	newfound	solid ground
pound	background	fool around	outbound	spellbound
round	battleground	foreground	outward bound	surround
sound	bloodhound	greyhound	pitcher's mound	underground
wound	campground	honor bound	playground	year-round

		-ount		
count	account	bank account	head count	tantamount
mount	amount	discount	paramount	

		-our		
flour	scour	dinner hour	noon hour	sweet and sour
hour	sour	lunch hour	rush hour	
our	devour			

-ouse

blouse	bird house	firehouse	madhouse	powerhouse
douse	cat and mouse	full house	Mickey Mouse	roughhouse
house	church mouse	haunted house	on the house	warehouse
louse	clubhouse	house-to-house	outhouse	White House
mouse	courthouse	lighthouse	penthouse	
spouse	doghouse			

-out

bout	stout	down and out	in and out	shoot-out
clout	tout	dropout	inside out	sold-out
gout	trout	dugout	knockabout	stakeout
out	about	fade-out	knockout	standout
pout	blackout	falling-out	lookout	take-out
rout	blowout	fallout	odd man out	talent scout
scout	brussels sprout	far out	over and out	throughout
shout	campout	handout	pass out	tryout
snout	cookout	hangout	roundabout	without
spout	devout	holdout	runabout	workout
sprout	do without			

-outh

mouth	big mouth	deep south	loudmouth	word of mouth
south	blabbermouth	hand-to-mouth		

-ow

bow	now	allow	here and now	powwow
brow	plow	anyhow	know-how	snowplow
chow	sow	bowwow	kowtow	solemn vow
cow	vow	cat's meow	meow	somehow
how	wow	eyebrow	Moscow	take a bow

-owl				
fowl	howl	scowl	on the prowl	wise old owl
growl	prowl			

-own				
brown	ball gown	crosstown	letdown	small-town
clown	breakdown	downtown	lowdown	splashdown
crown	broken-down	face-down	meltdown	sundown
down	cap and gown	ghost town	nightgown	touchdown
drown	Chinatown	hand-me-down	out-of-town	trickle-down
frown	circus clown	hoe-down	put-down	up and down
gown	countdown	hometown	renown	upside down
town	crackdown	knockdown	slowdown	wedding gown

Variant Vowel /o͞o/ Phonograms

-ew				
blew	grew	threw	curfew	renew
brew	knew	anew	interview	review
chew	mew	bird's-eye view	on view	skeleton crew
crew	new	book review	outgrew	unscrew
dew	pew	brand-new	panoramic view	withdrew
few	screw	cashew	point of view	world-view
flew	stew	corkscrew	quite a few	

-o				
do	ado	misdo	redo	well-to-do
to	hairdo	no can do	two by two	whoop-de-do
two	how-to	outdo	undo	
who	into	overdo	unto	

-oo

boo	zoo	bugaboo	hullabaloo	switcheroo
coo	ah-choo	choo-choo	kangaroo	taboo
goo	ballyhoo	cock-a-doodle-doo	kazoo	tattoo
moo	bamboo	cockatoo	peek-a-boo	toodle-oo
shoo	boo-boo	cuckoo	shampoo	voodoo
too	boo-hoo	goo-goo	stinkaroo	yoo-hoo
woo	buckaroo			

-ood

brood	mood	dog food	in the mood	seafood
food	baby food	fast food		

-oof

goof	roof	aloof	fireproof	soundproof
proof	spoof	childproof	foolproof	

-ool

cool	school	April fool	Liverpool	tide pool
drool	spool	car pool	nursery school	toadstool
fool	stool	cesspool	preschool	whirlpool
pool	tool	high school	swimming pool	

-oom

bloom	groom	bathroom	elbow room	mushroom
boom	loom	bride and groom	gloom and doom	powder room
broom	room	bridegroom	heirloom	rest room
doom	zoom	classroom	leg room	sonic boom
gloom	baby boom	courtroom	locker room	

-oon

boon	swoon	cocoon	lampoon	raccoon
coon	afternoon	full moon	macaroon	saloon
croon	baboon	harpoon	maroon	spittoon
loon	balloon	high noon	monsoon	too soon
moon	bassoon	honeymoon	platoon	twelve noon
noon	buffoon	hot-air balloon	pontoon	tycoon
soon	Cameroon	lagoon	pretty soon	typhoon
spoon	cartoon			

-oop

coop	hoop	sloop	swoop	hula hoop
droop	loop	snoop	troop	inside scoop
goop	scoop	stoop	alley-oop	nincompoop

-oose

goose	noose	hang loose	on the loose	silly goose
loose	caboose	mongoose	papoose	vamoose
moose	footloose	Mother Goose		

-oot

boot	moot	shoot	outshoot	troubleshoot
hoot	root	snoot	overshoot	uproot
loot	scoot	toot	square root	

-ooth

booth	kissing booth	snaggletooth	sweet tooth	voting booth
tooth	phone booth			

-ooze

ooze	snooze

-oup				
croup	soup	in-group	pressure group	regroup
group	chicken soup	peer group		

-ube				
cube	tube	Danube	ice cube	test tube
lube				

-uce				
Bruce	spruce	deduce	introduce	reduce
deuce	truce	induce	produce	reproduce

-ude				
crude	allude	elude	include	multitude
dude	altitude	exclude	interlude	protrude
nude	aptitude	exude	latitude	seclude
prude	conclude	gratitude	longitude	solitude
rude	delude			

-ue				
blue	true	misconstrue	past due	revue
clue	avenue	miscue	postage due	subdue
cue	barbecue	navy blue	pursue	tried and true
due	black-and-blue	on cue	red, white, and blue	true blue
glue	construe	out of the blue	residue	untrue
hue	counter-sue	overdue	revenue	
Sue	curlicue			

-uke				
duke	Luke	nuke	puke	rebuke
fluke				

-ule				
mule	gag rule	majority rule	module	overrule
rule	golden rule	minuscule	molecule	ridicule
yule	home rule			

-ume				
fume	assume	costume	perfume	resume
plume	consume	exhume	presume	

-une				
dune	tune	immune	Neptune	out of tune
June	commune	loony tune	opportune	
prune	fine tune			

-ure				
cure	assure	ensure	manicure	premature
lure	brochure	immature	mature	reassure
pure	curvature	impure	obscure	secure
sure	demure	insecure	overture	unsure
aperture	endure	insure	pedicure	

-use				
fuse	abuse	confuse	excuse	refuse
muse	accuse	defuse	infuse	short fuse
ruse	amuse	effuse	misuse	
use	blow a fuse	enthuse	peruse	

-ute				
brute	absolute	deaf mute	ill repute	refute
chute	acute	destitute	institute	repute
cute	astute	dilute	minute	resolute
flute	attribute	dispute	parachute	salute
jute	commute	electrocute	persecute	substitute
lute	compute	execute	pollute	tribute
mute	constitute			

-uth				
Ruth	truth	Baby Ruth	moment of truth	untruth
sleuth	youth	half-truth	naked truth	

Variant Vowel /o͝o/ Phonograms

-ood				
good	childhood	Hollywood	neighborhood	Robin Hood
hood	deadwood	likelihood	no-good	sainthood
stood	driftwood	livelihood	pretty good	sisterhood
wood	falsehood	misunderstood	Red Riding Hood	so far so good
brotherhood	fatherhood	motherhood	redwood	understood

-ook				
book	look	checkbook	handbook	overlook
brook	nook	comic book	mistook	scrapbook
cook	rook	dirty look	notebook	textbook
crook	shook	fishhook	outlook	unhook
hook	took	gobbledygook		

-oot				
foot	afoot	Big Foot	tenderfoot	underfoot
soot	barefoot	hotfoot		

-ould		
could	should	would

-ull				
bull	pull	pit bull	push-pull	Sitting Bull
full	chock-full			

-ush			
bush	push	ambush	rosebush

What About Rules?

Use *i* before *e* except after *c*. When two vowels go walking, the first does the talking. Don't hit your sister. Sit up straight, Wiley! These and other rules swim around in my head when I think about my childhood. When it comes to reading, I often wonder how many rules I actually recall and use as a skilled reader and writer. This list is probably quite small.

"Effective decoders see words not in terms of phonics rules, but in terms of patterns of letters that are used to aid in identification" (Stahl, 1992). Through phonics instruction that focuses students' attention on each letter in a word, teaches blending, and highlights common spelling patterns, students will begin to internalize rules, or generalizations, about words. For example, when students encounter words in which the letter *c* stands for either the /s/ sound or the /k/ sound, we want them to be able to generalize the conditions under which each is likely to occur. Rules can be used to help students attend to a specific spelling pattern or organize their thinking about it. As time goes by, and we give students more and more opportunities to review and apply a rule, they'll internalize it.

In addition, teachers of reading need to be aware of rules so that they can verbalize them for students who would benefit from them (Durkin, 1993). However, since few rules are 100% reliable, they should never be taught as absolutes. That's why I prefer the term *generalization*, rather than rule.

Guidelines for Using Rules/Generalizations

- **Don't make rules/generalizations the emphasis of phonics instruction.** Instead, use them as one tool to help students focus on important spelling patterns and recognize unfamiliar words.
- **Teach only those rules/generalizations that are most useful.** For example, teaching students that the spelling pattern *-ough* can stand for up to six sounds is wasteful. In addition, avoid generalizations that are wordy or full of technical language.
- **Emphasize applying the rules/generalizations rather than verbalizing them.** Remember that once students can apply the generalizations, there's no need to spend instructional time on them.
- **Don't teach the rules/generalizations too soon or too late.** Teach them at a point when students can best understand and apply them.
- **Never teach rules as absolutes.** Since students tend to think of rules as absolutes, it's better to use the term *generalization*. And be sure to make the students aware of exceptions to the generalizations.

The classic study on generalizations and their utility was conducted in 1963 (Clymer). Clymer examined 45 generalizations (rules) taught by basal reading programs. He found that many of the generalizations commonly taught were of limited value. In fact, less than half of the rules worked as much as 75% of the time. The chart that follows shows the generalizations he examined. I've updated the wording of some of them so that they're consistent with the language used in today's basals.

Utility of Phonics Generalizations

Generalizations		Example	Exception	% Utility
1.	When two of the same consonants appear side by side in a word, only one is heard.	berry	suggest	99
2.	When the letter *c* is followed by the letter *o* or *a*, the *c* stands for the /k/ sound.	cat		100
3.	When the letters *c* and *h* appear next to each other in a word, they stand for only one sound.	rich		100
4.	The digraph *ch* is usually pronounced /ch/ as in *watch* and *chair*, not /sh/.	batch	machine	95
5.	The letter *g* often has a sound similar to that of the letter *j* in *jump* when it comes before the letter *i* or *e*.	ginger	give	64
6.	When the letter *c* is followed by the letter *e* or *i*, the /s/ sound is likely to be heard.	cent	ocean	96
7.	When a word ends in the letters *ck*, it has the /k/ sound as in *book*.	sick		100
8.	When the letters *ght* appear together in a word, the letters *gh* are *silent*.	fight		100
9.	When a word begins with the letters *kn*, the letter *k* is silent.	know		100
10.	When a word begins with the letters *wr*, the letter *w* is silent.	write		100
11.	If there is one vowel letter in an accented syllable, it has a short sound.	city	lady	61
12.	When a word has only one vowel letter, the vowel sound is likely to be short.	lid	mind	57
13.	When two vowels appear together in a word, the long sound of the first one is heard and the second is usually silent.	seat	chief	45
14.	When a vowel is in the middle of a one-syllable word, the vowel is short.	best	gold	62
15.	The letter *r* gives the preceding vowel a sound that is neither long nor short.	torn	fire	78
16.	When there are two vowels, one of which is final *e*, the first vowel is long and the *e* is silent.	hope	come	63

	Generalizations	Example	Exception	% Utility
17.	The first vowel is usually long and the second silent in the digraphs *ai, ea, oa,* and *ui.*	nail/said 64% bead/head 66% boat/cupboard 97% suit/build 6%		66
18.	When words end with silent *e,* the preceding *a* or *i* is long.	bake	have	60
19.	When the letter *y* is the final letter in a word, it usually has a vowel sound.	dry	tray	84
20.	When the letter *y* is used as a vowel in words, it sometimes has the sound of long *i.*	fly	funny	15
21.	When *y* or *ey* appears in the last syllable that is not accented, the long *e* sound is heard.		baby	0
22.	The letter *a* has the same sound as /ô/ when followed by *l, w,* and *u.*	fall	canal	48
23.	The letter *w* is sometimes a vowel and follows the vowel digraph rule.	snow	few	40
24.	When there is one *e* in a word that ends in a consonant, the *e* usually has a short sound.	pet	flew	76
25.	In many two- and three-syllable words, the final *e* lengthens the vowel in the last syllable.	invite	gasoline	46
26.	Words having double *e* usually have the long *e* sound.	feet	been	98
27.	The letters *ow* stand for the long *o* sound.	own	town	59
28.	When the letter *a* follows the letter *w* in a word, it usually has the sound that *a* stands for as in *was.*	watch	swam	32
29.	In the vowel spelling *ie,* the letter *i* is silent and the letter *e* has the long vowel sound.	field	friend	17
30.	In *ay* the *y* is silent and gives *a* its long sound.	play	always	78
31.	If the only vowel letter is at the end of a word, the letter usually stands for a long sound.	me	do	74
32.	When the letter *e* is followed by the letter *w,* the vowel sound is the same as represented by *oo* (/$\overline{oo}$/).	blew	sew	35

	Generalizations	Example	Exception	% Utility
33.	When the letter *a* is followed by the letter *r* and final *e*, we expect to hear the sound heard in *care*.	dare	are	90
34.	When the letter *i* is followed by the letters *gh*, the letter *i* usually stands for its long sound and the *gh* is silent.	high	neighbor	71
35.	If the first vowel sound in a word is followed by two consonants, the first syllable usually ends with the first of the two consonants.	bullet	singer	72
36.	If the first vowel sound in a word is followed by a single consonant, that consonant usually begins the second syllable.	over	oven	44
37.	In a word of more than one syllable, the letter *v* usually goes with the preceding vowel to form a syllable.	cover	clover	73
38.	If the last syllable of a word ends in *le*, the consonant preceding the *le* usually begins the last syllable.	tumble	buckle	97
39.	When the first vowel in a word is followed by *th, ch*, or *sh*, these symbols are not broken when the word is divided into syllables, and they may go with either the first or second syllable.	dishes		100
40.	In most two-syllable words, the first syllable is accented.	famous	polite	85
41.	When the last syllable is the sound /r/, it is unaccented.	butter	appear	95
42.	In most two-syllable words that end in a consonant followed by *y*, the first syllable is accented and the last is unaccented.	baby	supply	96
43.	If *a, in, re, ex, de*, or *be* is the first syllable in a word, it is usually unaccented.	above	insect	87
44.	When *tion* is the final syllable in a word, it is unaccented.	nation		100
45.	When *ture* is the final syllable in a word, it is unaccented.	picture		100

Syllabication: The Challenge at the Intermediate Grades

Reading multisyllabic words can be challenging for many of our students. Some students, even those who seem to effortlessly decode one-syllable words, struggle when faced with longer, harder words because they haven't fully mastered those basic spelling patterns. That is, these readers lack the speed and automaticity required with those patterns to apply them to longer, more complex words. Other students struggle when analyzing and breaking down a longer word into recognizable chunks that would aid in decoding. For example, rather than decoding a word such as *uncomfortable* sound by sound, we need students to instantly recognize the larger chunks *un*, *comfort* (or *com* and *fort*) and *able* to more easily tackle the word. Dealing with three or four pieces of information (*un*, *com*, *fort*, *able*) is much easier than dealing with 11 or more (*u, n, c, o, m, f, or, t, a, b, le*). The good news is that we can systematically and efficiently transition students from reading one-syllable to multisyllabic words if we take advantage of what they already know and make explicit those connections. Also, by focusing on high-utility decoding skills, syllables, and syllable patterns, we can tailor our instruction so that it is fast, efficient, and effective.

Key Information for Teaching Syllabication

- A syllable is a unit of pronunciation. Each syllable contains only one vowel sound. Finding the vowels in a word is an important starting point for breaking it apart by syllables. However, each syllable may have more than one vowel. For example, the word *boat* contains one vowel sound, therefore one syllable. However, the vowel sound is represented by the vowel digraph *oa*.

- Whether a group of letters forms a syllable depends on the letters that surround it (Adams, 1990). For example, the letters *par* form a syllable in the word *partial*, but not in the word *parade*.

- One syllable in a multisyllabic word receives more emphasis or stress. The vowel sound in this syllable is heard most clearly. Stress is indicated in dictionary pronunciation keys by accent marks. In addition to one primary accent, some words also have one or more secondary accents. Vowels in unstressed syllables become schwas (/ə/). Generally, in words with prefixes and suffixes, the prefix or suffix forms a separate syllable and the accent falls on the root (base) word. In compound words, the accent generally falls on or within the first word. The accent in most two-syllable words falls on the first syllable.

- To decode multisyllabic words, students must be able to divide words into recognizable chunks. Some readers develop a sense of syllabication breaks independently through their exposures to print; others have great difficulty and need instruction (Just & Carpenter, 1987). Some students' phonics skills break down when confronted by multisyllabic words because they can't readily identify syllable boundaries (Eldredge, 1995).

- Students need training in dividing words according to syllables. They must (1) understand how to figure out the vowel sound in one-syllable words [teach them common one-syllable spelling patterns such as CVC and CVCe], and (2) understand that a syllable has only one vowel sound, but that the vowel sound may be spelled using more than one vowel.

- Students can use syllabication strategies to approximate a word's pronunciation. This approximation is generally close enough for the reader to recognize the word if it's in his speaking or listening vocabularies. This demonstrates how important it is to help students develop their speaking and listening vocabularies and to combine building their background knowledge with vocabulary instruction.

- Some words can be divided in more than one way. For example: *treat-y*, *trea-ty*, *tr-ea-ty*. The fewer chunks into which a word is divided, the easier it is to decode the word.

- Traditional syllabication strategies can be ineffective. Clapping syllables in words, for example, doesn't work because the student must already know the word before she can clap the syllables (Johnson & Bauman, 1984). Similarly, memorizing countless syllabication rules has little effect on a reader's ability to decode multisyllabic words. (Note: *Syllabication* and *syllabification* are synonymous.)

- Few syllabication generalizations are very useful to students, but some are worth pointing out (Chall & Popp, 1996). State them in simple, clear terms. Focus on applying them, not reciting them:

  - If the word is a compound word, divide the word between the two words that comprise it. If either or both of these words has more than one syllable, follow the syllabication generalizations below.

  - Inflectional endings such as *ing*, *er*, *est*, and *ed* often form separate syllables. The remaining portion of the word is the root (base) word. Looking for these and other meaning units in words is known as morphemic analysis. A morpheme is a meaning unit. There are free morphemes—whole words that can stand alone and cannot be divided into other meaning units (i.e., root words). There are also bound morphemes—word parts that can't stand alone and must be combined with a free morpheme (i.e., suffixes and prefixes). Bound morphemes alter the meaning of the free morphemes to which they are attached (example: *un + happy = unhappy*).

- When two or more consonants appear in the middle of a word, divide the word between them (CVC + CVC words). Then try the short sound for the vowel in the first syllable. This generalization doesn't apply if the two (or three) consonants form a digraph such as *ch, tch, ck, ph, sh,* or *th*. These digraphs cannot be separated across syllable boundaries.

- When only one consonant appears between two vowels, divide the word before the consonant. Then try the long sound of the first vowel (examples: *tiger, pilot*). This works about 55% of the time. If a recognizable word is not formed using the long sound, divide the word after the consonant and try the short sound for the first syllable (examples: *exit, second*). This works about 45% of the time.

- When a two-syllable word ends in a consonant plus *le*, the consonant and *le* form the last syllable. If the preceding syllable ends in a consonant, try the short sound of the vowel (examples: *wiggle, sample*). If the preceding syllable ends with a vowel, try the long sound of the vowel (examples: *table, bridle*).

- When a two-syllable word ends in a consonant plus *re*, the consonant and *re* form the last syllable. If the preceding syllable ends with a vowel, try the long sound of that vowel (example: *acre*).

- Never break apart vowel digraphs or diphthongs across syllable boundaries.

Tips for Teaching Syllabication

- **Syllabication instruction should begin in grade 1** by pointing out compound words, words with double consonants, and words with common prefixes and suffixes such as *un, re, s, es, ing,* and *ed.* In the intermediate grades, additional prefixes and suffixes, as well as common root words become the focus of instruction. In addition, practice in recognizing common syllabic units is beneficial.

- **Teach syllabication strategies using known words,** then provide ample opportunities for students to apply the strategy in context.

- **Use dictionaries with caution.** Most dictionaries divide words according to how the word should be broken across lines. This sometimes has little to do with the division of the word into its syllables for the purpose of pronunciation.

Sample pronounciations:

/rēd/

/rīt/

/fon´iks/

Syllabication Lessons

Begin teaching syllabication by providing explicit, multisensory lessons on the concept of a syllable.

What Is a Syllable?

Phonic Principle: A syllable is a unit of pronunciation. A word can be divided into syllables.

1. Distribute small mirrors to your students or have them find a partner to watch as he or she pronounces words.

2. Together, say aloud a series of words of varying lengths as students look in the mirrors. Have students count the number of times their mouths open when saying the word. Explain that this is the number of syllables in the word. Another way to count the syllables is to have them count the number of times their jaw drops when they say a word.

3. Ask students to identify which part of the word causes their mouth to open (the vowel sound). Point out to students that a syllable has one vowel sound.

4. Conclude by choosing one or all of the following activities:

   - Ask students to generate a list of short words, then a list of long words. Write the words on the board and compare them. Most long words contain more letters and more syllables.

- Ask students to repeat a series of words you say. As they pronounce each word, have students clap or tap the number of syllables. Start with compound words, progress to two-syllable words, then to three- and four-syllable words.

- Ask students to repeat a series of words you say. As they pronounce each word, have them move a counter for each syllable they hear. Have them count the number of counters moved. Provide modeling as necessary.

- Ask students to repeat a series of words you say. For each word, have them delete the first syllable. For example, "Say *sunflower* without the *sun*," or "Say *robot* without the *ro*." Go on to have them delete the ending syllables.

Lessons for the Most Common Syllable Spelling Patterns

Once students have mastered the concept of the syllable, you can begin teaching the six most common syllable spelling patterns. Learning these common patterns will give students insight into how words are put together. In a series of intervention studies, Shefelbine (1990) found that when students were taught how to pronounce common syllables and then practiced reading multisyllabic words with these syllables, their ability to read multisyllabic words in general improved. Since closed syllables are the most frequent, begin instruction there (Stanbach, 1992). I suggest the following sequence:

- closed syllables
- open syllables
- VCe (final *e*, VCe)
- vowel team
- *r*-controlled
- consonant + *le*

I've included a sample lesson and a reteach lesson for each syllable type.

Six Basic Syllable Spelling Patterns (Moats, 1995a)

1. **closed:** These syllables end in a consonant. The vowel sound is generally short (examples: *rabbit, napkin*).

2. **open:** These syllables end in a vowel. The vowel sound is generally long (examples: *tiger, pilot*).

3. **vowel–silent e (VCe):** These syllables generally represent long-vowel sounds (examples: *compete, decide*).

4. **vowel team:** Many vowel sounds are spelled with vowel digraphs such as *ai, ay, ea, ee, oa, ow, oo, oi, oy, ou, ie,* and *ei*. The vowel digraphs appear in the same syllable (examples: *boat, explain*).

5. ***r*-controlled:** When a vowel is followed by *r*, the letter *r* affects the sound of the vowel. The vowel and the *r* appear in the same syllable (examples: *bird, turtle*).

6. **consonant + le:** Usually when *le* appears at the end of a word and is preceded by a consonant, the consonant + *le* form the final syllable (examples: *table, little*).

Closed Syllables
Syllabication Spelling Pattern

Key Concept: Explain to your students that every syllable in a word has only one vowel sound. Write *napkin* and *subject* on the board. Divide the words syllable by syllable. Point out that the first syllable in each word ends in a consonant and explain that this is called a **closed syllable**. Most closed syllables have a short vowel sound.

Teacher Model: Write the word *fabric* on the board. Do not say the word, but give your students time to examine its parts. Then model how to use syllabication strategies to read the word.

Think-Aloud: *I know that each syllable has one vowel sound. I see two vowels in this* word separated by two consonants. If I divide the word between the consonants I get f-a-b and r-i-c. Both of these syllables are closed syllables since they end in a consonant. Therefore, I will try the short vowel sound when pronouncing each syllable: /fab/ /rik/. When I put these two syllables together, I get fabric.

Blending Practice: Write the following words on the board. Have students chorally read each word. Provide modeling as necessary.

absent	atlas	comet
husband	kitten	fossil
velvet	zigzag	plaster
habit	sunset	tidbit

Reteach Lesson: Closed Syllables

1. Write the following words on the board: *sat, run, lid, nest*. Say: *Look at these words. How many vowels do you see in each?*
2. Then ask: What does each word end with? (One consonant.)
3. Have students read the words aloud, noting their pronunciation. Ask: *How did you pronounce the words at the end?* (Tongue, teeth, or lips closed.)
4. Ask: *What would be a good name for this syllable?* (Closed, since the mouth is closed at the end.)
5. Define closed syllable for students. (A closed syllable ends in at least one consonant; the vowel sound is short.)
6. Write the following sentences on the board for students to complete: A closed syllable ends in at least one _____. The vowel sound is _____.
7. Extend the lesson by writing two-syllable words with a closed first syllable (e.g., *napkin, candid, subject*). Help students blend each syllable to read the words.

Teacher note: Short vowel sounds in unaccented syllables, particularly before *m, n,* or *l,* may be distorted and sound like a schwa. Also, short vowel sounds before the nasal sounds /m/, /n/, and /ng/ may seem distorted (e.g., *ram, ant, sank, sing*).

Closed Syllable Word List

absent	cannot	denim	gossip	madcap
active	canvas	dental	habit	magnet
admit	canyon	dentist	hangar	manner
album	catnap	dismal	hatbox	mantel
anklet	catnip	distant	hectic	mascot
antic	channel	dollar	helmet	mental
atlas	chicken	eggnog	hiccup	metric
attic	cluster	engine	hidden	midget
axis	comet	exit	hostel	mishap
basket	comic	fabric	husband	mitten
beggar	common	falcon	index	muffin
beverage	contact	fasten	inlet	napkin
blanket	content	fatten	insect	nectar
blister	contest	fender	instinct	nostril
bobbin	context	fidget	insult	padlock
bonnet	cosmic	figment	jacket	panic
budget	cottage	filter	jogger	pasture
button	cotton	fossil	kingdom	pencil
cabin	crimson	frantic	kitchen	picnic
cactus	culprit	gallon	kitten	picture
campus	custom	goblet	lesson	pigment
cancer	cutlet	goblin	limit	plaster
candid	dapple	gospel	litmus	plastic

plumber	random	splendor	tandem	upset
pocket	ransom	splinter	tantrum	valid
pollen	rapid	subject	tendon	velvet
practice	ribbon	submit	tennis	victim
pregnant	robin	sudden	ticket	vivid
pretzel	rotten	suffix	tidbit	vulture
princess	rustic	summit	timid	welcome
problem	sadden	sunset	tonsil	witness
public	sandwich	suntan	tractor	zigzag
publish	satin	sunup	transit	
pumpkin	septic	suspect	tremor	
puppet	signal	tablet	tunnel	
rabbit	socket	tactic	until	

Open Syllables
Syllabication Spelling Pattern

Key Concept: Explain to your students that every syllable in a word has only one vowel sound. Write *favor* and *tiger* on the board. Divide the words syllable by syllable. Point out that the first syllable in each word ends in one vowel. Explain that this is called an **open syllable**. Most open syllables have a long vowel sound.

Teacher Model: Write the word *secret* on the board. Don't say the word, but give students time to examine its parts. Then model how to use syllabication strategies to read the word.

Think-Aloud: *I know that each syllable has one vowel sound. I see two vowels in this word separated by two consonants. If I divide the word between the consonants, I get* s-e-c *and* r-e-t. *Both of these syllables are closed syllables since they end in a consonant.*

Therefore, I will try the short vowel sound when pronouncing each syllable: /sek/ /ret/. When I put these two syllables together, I don't get a word I know. So, I'll separate the word between the letters e *and* c. *The first syllable becomes an open syllable since it ends in a vowel. The vowel sound will be long. When I pronounce the syllables, I get* /sē/ /kret/—secret. *This is a real word.*

Blending Practice: Write the following words on the board. Have students chorally read each word. Provide modeling as necessary.

baby	cedar	cider
diver	frozen	female
hijack	human	lady
motor	prefix	social

Reteach Lesson: Open Syllables

1. Write the following words on the board: *me, hi, no, she.* Ask students: *How many vowels do you see in each word?*
2. Then ask: *What does each word end with?* (One vowel.) *Can these be closed syllables?* (No, a closed syllable ends in a consonant.)
3. Have students read the words, paying attention to the way each is pronounced. Ask: *How are the words pronounced at the end?* (The mouth is open.)
4. Ask: *What would be a good name for the syllable?* (Open, since the mouth is open at the end.)
5. Define open syllable for students. (An open syllable ends in a vowel; the vowel sound is long.)

6. Write the following sentences on the board for students to complete: An open syllable ends in a _____. The vowel sound is _____.

7. Extend the lesson by writing two-syllable words with an open first syllable (e.g., *tiger*, *lady*, *secret*). Help students blend each syllable to read the words.

Open–Syllable Word List

agent	cupid	future	locust	polo
baby	data	global	major	pony
bacon	decent	gracious	migraine	prefix
bagel	demon	gravy	minus	primate
basal	depot	grocery	mogul	probate
basic	diver	halo	moment	profile
basin	donate	helix	motor	program
basis	donor	hijack	mucus	propane
biceps	donut	holy	museum	pupil
bison	edict	human	music	raven
blatant	ego	humid	mutate	rebate
bogus	equal	idol	nasal	recent
bonus	even	irate	nature	regal
butane	evil	iris	naval	rhino
cedar	fatal	item	navy	rival
cider	favor	label	obese	rodent
cobalt	feline	lady	odor	saber
cobra	female	latent	open	sacred
cogent	final	latex	oval	secret
colon	finite	lazy	ozone	senile
cozy	focal	legal	penal	sequence
cradle	focus	lethal	phony	sequin
crazy	fragrant	lilac	photo	silent
crisis	frequent	local	pilot	silo
cubic	frozen	locate	pliers	sinus

siren	stamen	titan	vacant	yo-yo
slogan	table	token	vagrant	zebra
social	tidal	total	vinyl	
solo	tidy	totem	virus	
spinal	tiger	tribal	vital	
spiral	tirade	unit	vocal	

SAMPLE LESSON

Final *e* (VCe)
Syllabication Spelling Pattern

Key Concept: Explain to students that every syllable in a word has only one vowel sound. Write *compete* and *inflate* on the board. Divide the words syllable by syllable. Point out that the last syllable in each word ends in vowel, consonant, final *e*. Explain that this is called a final *e*, or VCe, syllable. The final *e* is silent and the vowel sound before it is long.

Teacher Model: Write the word *female* on the board. Don't say the word, but give students time to examine the word's parts. Then model how to use syllabication strategies to read the word.

Think-Aloud: *I know that each syllable has one vowel sound. I see three vowels in this word.*

However, the word ends in an e. Therefore, I will keep the e and the vowel before it in the same syllable. This syllable will have a long vowel sound. If I divide the word between the e and m, I get an open syllable (f-e) and a VCe syllable (m-a-l-e). When I pronounce these two syllables, I get /fē/ /māl/— female.

Blending Practice: Write the following words on the board. Have students chorally read each word. Provide modeling as necessary.

alone	amuse	complete
delete	expose	hopeless
invade	refine	shameful
stampede	suppose	unmade

Reteach Lesson: Final *e* (VCe)

1. Write the following words on the board: *make, bike, cute, hope.* Ask students: *How many vowels do you see in each word?*

2. Then ask: *What does each word end with?* (The letter e.) *What comes between the vowel and the final e?* (A consonant.)

3. Have students read the words, paying particular attention to the vowel sound. Ask: *What happens to the final* e? (It's silent.) *How are the vowels pronounced?* (Each has a long sound.)

4. Say: *Each of these words ends in a vowel, a consonant, and a final* e. *What would be a good name for this syllable?* (VCe or final *e.*)

5. Define VCe syllable for students. (It ends in a vowel, a consonant, and *e*; the vowel sound is long.)

6. Write the following sentences on the board for students to complete: A VCe syllable ends in a _____, a _____, and an _____. The vowel sound is _____.

7. Extend the lesson by writing two-syllable words with VCe final syllable (e.g., *alone, debate, invite*). Help students blend each syllable to read the words.

VCe Word List

abuse	compete	device	excuse	imbibe
accuse	compile	devote	explode	immune
advice	complete	dictate	explore	impede
advise	concise	diffuse	expose	impose
alone	concrete	disclose	extreme	incite
amaze	confuse	disgrace	fanfare	incline
amuse	connote	dispose	feline	inflate
athlete	console	dispute	female	innate
blockade	convene	divine	finely	insane
boneless	cyclone	donate	finite	inside
calcite	debate	efface	franchise	insulate
captivate	deflate	empire	fructose	invade
cascade	degrade	entice	frustrate	invite
collide	delete	erase	galore	iodine
combine	describe	erode	graphite	locate
commode	desire	escape	hopeless	lonesome
commune	despite	estate	humane	membrane
compare	dethrone	excite	ignite	mistake

negate	prepare	refine	secrete	suppose
ninety	profane	refuse	severe	supreme
notebook	profile	regulate	shameful	tadpole
obscene	propose	relate	sidewalk	textile
octane	provide	remote	sincere	translate
oppose	rebate	replete	stampede	trombone
ozone	rebuke	reptile	sublime	unmade
phoneme	recede	retire	subscribe	widespread
pomade	recite	sapphire	subside	xylophone

SAMPLE LESSON

Vowel Digraphs
(Vowel Teams) Syllabication Spelling Pattern

Key Concept: Explain to your students that sometimes two letters together stand for one vowel sound. Write the words *met*, *meat*, and *metal* on the board. Say each word and ask the students how many syllables they hear. Explain that every syllable in a word has only one vowel sound. Point out that the **vowel digraph** (or **vowel team**) *ea* stands for the long *e* sound in *meat*. Explain that when two vowels appear in a long word, such as *meaningful*, they often stay in the same syllable. This is called a vowel digraph, or vowel team, syllable.

Teacher Model: Write the word *beanbag* on the board. Don't say the word, but give students time to examine its parts. Then model how to use syllabication strategies to read the word.

Think-Aloud: *I know that every syllable has one vowel sound. In this word I see two vowels side-by-side,* ea. *I know that when two vowels team up in a word, I need to keep them in the same syllable. Therefore, I can divide this word into two parts:* bean *and* bag. *The letters* ea *stand for the long* e *sound. When I put these two parts together, I get the word* beanbag.

Blending Practice: Write the following words on the board. Have students chorally read each word. Provide modeling as necessary. Remind students that the letters *y* and *w* can stand for a vowel sound in vowel teams such as *ay* and *ow*.

mailbox	maintain	snowing
paycheck	freedom	seaweed
sleepless	highway	soaking
railroad	oatmeal	leaving

Reteach Lesson: Vowel Digraphs (Vowel Teams)

1. Write the following words on the board: *pea, zoo, rain, boat, leaf*. Ask students: *How many vowels do you see in each?* (Two.)

2. Ask: *What does each word end with?* (Some with a consonant, some with two vowels.) Then ask: *Can these be closed syllables?* (No, a closed syllable has only one vowel and must end in a consonant.) *Can these be open syllables?* (No, an open syllable must end in only one vowel.)

3. Have students read the words. Ask: *What is the same about the vowel sound in each word?* (It's long.) *What is the same about the way the vowel sound is written?* (It is always written with a vowel pair or team.)

4. Next ask: *What would be a good name for this syllable?* (Vowel team or vowel pair.)

5. Define a vowel-team syllable for students. (A vowel-team syllable contains two vowels next to each other; the vowel sound is sometimes long, unless the vowel team is a variant vowel or diphthong.) Explain to students that when they're looking at a long word, they should put the vowel team in the same syllable.

6. Write the following sentences on the board for students to complete: A vowel-team syllable contains _____. The vowel sound is _____.

7. Extend the lesson by writing two-syllable words with a vowel-team syllable (e.g., *trainer, mushroom, repeat*). Help students blend each syllable to read the words.

Vowel-Team (Vowel-Digraph) Word List

abound	aloud	away	chimney	convey
about	amount	baboon	classroom	cuckoo
account	annoy	ball gown	cocoon	decay
affair	appeal	balloon	coffee	devour
agree	appear	beneath	complain	discount
agreed	appoint	blackmail	complaint	display
airfare	approach	canteen	compound	donkey
allow	assault	cartoon	contain	dugout

Vowel–Team (Vowel–Digraph) Word List *continued*

elbow	freeload	monkey	release	turmoil
emcee	galley	moonbeam	remain	unafraid
employ	halfway	mushroom	repeat	unclear
enjoy	handbook	oatmeal	retreat	unfair
essay	hockey	obtain	reveal	unreal
esteem	holiday	overpaid	seesaw	valley
exclaim	impeach	pedigree	shallow	viewpoint
exhaust	indeed	pillow	spoilage	volunteer
explain	mermaid	poison	subway	window
exploit	midair	prevail	Sunday	withdraw
fellow	midweek	proceed	tattoo	yellow
fingernail	mislead	raccoon	textbook	
follow	mistreat	railroad	thirteen	
fourteen	Monday	raincoat	trainer	

SAMPLE LESSON

r-Controlled Vowels
Syllabication Spelling Pattern

Key Concept: Explain to your students that when the letter *r* follows a vowel, it affects the sound the vowel usually stands for. When dividing a word into syllables, the vowel plus the *r* usually stay in the same syllable.

Teacher Model: Write the word *snorkel* on the board, but don't say the word aloud. Ask students to identify the vowel that precedes the letter *r*. Then model how to use that information to figure out how to pronounce the word.

Think-Aloud: *I see two vowels in the word, so it probably has two syllables. I see an r*

following an o as in the word or. I can put these sounds together with s-n to get snor-. If I combine that with the second syllable, -kel, I say the word snorkel.

Blending Practice: Write the following words on the board. Have students chorally read each word. Provide modeling as necessary.

circus	barber	charter
dirty	floral	forty
garlic	hermit	marshal
perfect	target	thirsty

Reteach Lesson: *r*-Controlled Vowels

1. Write the following words on the board: *red, men, hen, her*. Ask: *How many vowels do you see in each?* (One.)

2. Then ask: *What does each word end with?* (One consonant.) *What kind of syllable ends in one consonant?* (A closed syllable.)

3. Have students read the words, paying particular attention to the vowel sound in each. Ask: *How are they pronounced?* (All with a short vowel sound, except the last word.) Ask: *Why can't the last word be read with a short vowel sound?* (The *r* controls the vowel sound.)

4. Ask: *What would be a good name for this syllable?* (An *r*-controlled syllable.)

5. Define *r*-controlled syllable for students. (An *r*-controlled syllable contains a vowel plus *r*; these two letters are kept in the same syllable.)

6. Write the following sentences on the board for students to complete. An *r*-controlled syllable contains _____. The vowel sound is affected by the letter _____.

7. Extend the lesson by writing two syllable words with an *r*-controlled vowel (e.g., *harvest, circus, normal*). Help students blend each syllable to read the words.

r-Controlled Vowel Words

aboard	anger	birthday	cashmere	chorus
absorb	ardent	blister	cellar	circus
adhere	arson	blizzard	center	clover
admire	artist	border	certain	clutter
adore	assert	burden	certify	color
adorn	barber	burlap	chairperson	comfort
afford	batter	butter	chapter	concert
after	before	cancer	charcoal	confer
airplane	berry	carbon	charter	consort
alarm	better	carton	cherish	copper

courtship	fortress	kernel	offer	shelter
cursor	forty	labor	otter	sheriff
curtain	fourteen	ladder	parcel	silver
dairy	further	lantern	pardon	sister
desert	galore	laser	pattern	skipper
differ	garden	lemur	pearly	skirmish
dinner	garlic	letter	pepper	slender
dirty	garnish	litter	perfect	slipper
discard	gerbil	liver	peril	snorkel
distort	girded	lumber	person	soared
disturb	glimmer	lunar	plaster	soccer
doctor	glory	manner	platter	solar
dollar	guitar	margin	portal	sordid
dormant	hairbrush	market	porthole	spider
dreary	hammer	marshal	pouring	splinter
duration	harness	master	prairie	spurious
earliest	harvest	matter	purchase	stairway
effort	herald	member	razor	stardom
endurance	herbal	merchant	rebirth	sterling
enter	hereby	merit	rehearse	suburb
entire	hermit	merriment	resource	summer
error	hoarding	mister	restore	supper
expert	hopper	modern	return	target
explore	hornet	monster	revere	temper
fairway	hunger	morning	rubber	tender
favor	ignore	mortal	rumor	terrace
filter	immerse	murmur	scarlet	terrible
finger	import	never	scatter	thermos
fireman	infer	normal	scoreless	thirsty
flirtatious	inspire	northwest	searchlight	thunder
floral	invert	number	servant	timber
formal	jargon	nurture	severe	torture

tractor	under	vapor	virtue	winter
tumor	unstirred	varnish	whether	
turkey	urban	vendor	whirlwind	
turnip	urgent	vertical	whisker	

Words with Consonant + *-le, -al, -el*
Syllabication Spelling Pattern

Key Concept: Explain to your students that every syllable in a word has only one vowel sound. Write *dimple, colossal,* and *counsel* on the board. Review that *-le, -al,* and *-el* all stand for the same sounds: /əl/. Explain that these letter pairs and the consonant that precedes them usually form the last syllable in a word.

Teacher Model: Write the word *rumble* on the board. Don't say the word, but give students time to examine the word's parts. Then model how to use syllabication strategies to read the word.

Think-Aloud: *I know that -le and the consonant before it form the last syllable in a word. Therefore, the last syllable in* r-u-m-b-l-e *is* ble. *That stands for* /bəl/. *This leaves* r-u-m, *which is pronounced* /rum/. *When I put the two word parts together, I get* rumble.

Blending Practice: Write the following words on the board. Have students chorally read each word. Provide modeling as necessary.

table	bundle	sparkle
sizzle	pickle	little
mantle	middle	global
hospital	model	chapel

Reteach Lesson: Words Ending With *-le, -al, -el*

1. Write the following words on the board: *table, bridle, puzzle, middle.*
2. Ask students: *What is the same in each of these words?* (They end in a consonant + *-le.*)
3. Have students read the words. Ask: *How many syllables do you hear?* (Two.)
4. Say: *The second syllable is spelled with the consonant + le. What sound does the e stand for?* (It's silent.)
5. Ask: *What would be a good name for this syllable?* (Consonant + *le.*)

6. Define consonant + *le* syllable for students. (A consonant + *le* syllable ends in a consonant + *le*. Whenever you see a consonant + *le* in a long word, keep them together in the same syllable.)

7. Write the following sentence on the board for students to complete: A consonant + *le* syllable ends in _____.

8. Extend the lesson by writing two-syllable words with a consonant + *le* final syllable (e.g., *table, bridle, puzzle*). Help students blend each syllable to read the words.

Teacher note: The consonant + *le* syllables (along with the syllables *-ture*, *-age*, *-sion*, and *-tion*) are **stable final syllables**. These are good syllables to include in instruction from grade 3 on up. Directly teach the sounds that each consonant + *le* syllable represents. For example, list on the board these spelling patterns: *tle, ple, zle, ble, gle, dle*. Read aloud each syllable [e.g., /dəl/]. Then have students chorally repeat.

Consonant + *–le* Words

boggle	circle	dribble	grapple	jingle
bottle	coddle	drizzle	griddle	joggle
bridle	crackle	durable	gristle	jumble
bristle	crinkle	dwindle	grumble	jungle
brittle	cripple	eagle	guzzle	kettle
bubble	crumble	enable	handle	kibble
buckle	cuddle	fable	heckle	kindle
bugle	curable	fickle	hobble	knuckle
bundle	curdle	fiddle	honeysuckle	little
bungle	dawdle	fizzle	huddle	mantle
bustle	dazzle	freckle	humble	maple
cable	debacle	fumble	hurdle	marble
cackle	diddle	gentle	hurtle	meddle
castle	dimple	giggle	hustle	middle
cattle	disable	girdle	icicle	mingle
chronicle	doodle	gobble	incurable	muddle
chuckle	double	goggle	jiggle	muffle

mumble	puzzle	securable	stubble	triple
muscle	quadruple	settle	stumble	trouble
muzzle	quibble	shackle	swashbuckle	truffle
needle	ramshackle	shingle	swindle	tumble
nibble	rattle	shuffle	tabernacle	turtle
noble	resemble	shuttle	table	tussle
noodle	riddle	sickle	tackle	twiddle
nuzzle	ripple	simple	tattle	twinkle
ogle	rubble	single	temple	unable
paddle	ruffle	sizzle	thimble	uncle
pebble	rumble	skedaddle	thistle	unstable
peddle	rustle	snuffle	throttle	vehicle
periwinkle	sable	spackle	tickle	waddle
pickle	saddle	sparkle	timetable	whistle
piddle	sample	spindle	tingle	whittle
pimple	scramble	sprinkle	title	wiggle
pinochle	scribble	squabble	toddle	wobble
poodle	scruple	squiggle	treble	wrinkle
prattle	scuffle	steeple	tremble	
puddle	scuttle	straddle	trickle	
purple	Seattle	struggle	tricycle	

Consonant + –al or –el Words

accidental	focal	mental	chisel
acquittal	fraternal	metal	drivel
bifocal	fundamental	monumental	duffel
brutal	global	nocturnal	kernel
coincidental	hospital	ornamental	label
committal	illegal	parental	mislabel
conical	incidental	paternal	model
continental	instrumental	pedal	mussel
cymbal	internal	petal	nickel
dental	ironical	regal	strudel
detrimental	jackal	rental	pumpernickel
dismissal	journal	sentimental	rebel
environmental	judgmental	temperamental	shrivel
eternal	legal	transcendental	snivel
experimental	local	transmittal	swivel
external	maternal	vocal	yokel
feudal	medal	chapel	

Helping Students Recognize Common Syllables

As students develop in their reading ability, they begin to notice larger word parts, or **orthographic chunks** (Moats, 1998). "Once a reader perceives a syllable, he begins searching the memory for a word that matches those letters, simultaneously beginning to sound out the letter combinations" (Hall & Moats, 1999). Instead of sounding out each letter, students can more easily sound out and blend larger portions of the word, making decoding more efficient. "As whole words, morphemes, and print patterns become increasingly familiar, knowledge of these larger units of print allows students to read efficiently and spend less and less attention on sounding out words letter by letter" (Share, 1995). For some students this is quite easy and natural; for others it is a daunting task.

There's a great deal teachers can do to help students learn to focus on larger parts of longer words and thus struggle less with decoding. Unfortunately, little is done in most classrooms to build this orthographic awareness that is so critical to reading multisyllabic words. In several studies, Shefelbine (1990; Shefelbine, Lipscomb & Hern, 1989) examined students' (a) ability to read common syllables by sight, (b) flexible identification of multisyllabic word patterns (open and closed syllables), and (c) oral vocabularies. His studies revealed that through systematic, focused instruction on, and flexible use of, common syllable patterns, students' ability to read longer words can be improved. However, he notes that students' oral vocabularies must be well developed so that many words they encounter while reading are already in their speaking and listening vocabularies. As teachers, we can help students sound out words, but if they don't know the words' meanings or have no way of figuring them out, we've only partially done our job of developing skilled readers.

Shefelbine's research provides a powerful argument for developing a strong nonfiction, read-aloud component in every reading curriculum, beginning in the earliest grades and continuing in the intermediate grades. The more words we can expose our students to, the better off they'll be when they begin to read more complex, vocabulary-laden texts in the upper elementary grades and beyond. Thus phonics and vocabulary instruction go hand in hand. Not only can we increase students' oral vocabularies through reading aloud to them and discussing novel words, we can also highlight orthographic regularities among these words to make students aware of how words are similar. For example, when you're reading a text about ocean life, you might point out that all the words beginning with *aqua* have something to do with water, or that all the words beginning with *sub* have something to do with the concept of "under." Write a few of these words on the board and have students comment on the spelling patterns common to the words. Moats (1998) contends that "attention to the internal structure of words, in both speech and spelling, supports whole-word identification; it is linguistic awareness, not rote visual memory, that underlies memory for sight words . . . ." Research has shown that learning the structure of words at the syllable and morpheme levels supports word recognition, spelling, and vocabulary development (Nagy and Anderson, 1984).

Read aloud at least two nonfiction books (or a portion of a book, such as an interesting spread or chapter) a week to expand student's vocabulary and world knowledge.

Cunningham & Stanovich (1991) suggest that teachers can help students become "word detectives" and notice common spelling and pronunciation patterns among related words. The activities that follow are designed to achieve that goal. Since word parts, such as prefixes and suffixes, are much easier to recognize, point these out first. Leave other spelling patterns, such as long-vowel spellings, which are harder to recognize visually, until later. Remember, in order to read multisyllabic words easily, students must be able to (CORE, 2000):

- quickly recognize as "chunks" the phonics patterns they learned in single-syllable words
- understand the concept of a syllable and how to identify vowels and consonants
- recognize various syllable types and their pronunciations
- know where syllables divide (syllable patterns)
- recognize common prefixes, suffixes, and base words
- break apart a word and arrive at an approximate pronunciation, then use context to resolve ambiguity and confirm the word

To help students learn to read multisyllabic words, display a chart like the one in Resource 4.1 (see right) on a classroom wall and model the process, as described below. Encourage students to refer to the chart as they read independently.

Introducing Decoding Big Words Strategy

1. Distribute a copy of the Decoding Big Words Strategy Reference Sheet (Resource 4.1; see image at right) to each student. Post a copy on a classroom wall or bulletin board.
2. Tell students that this strategy is a simple five-step process for decoding an unfamiliar word. They will practice this strategy throughout their word study lessons this year and while they read.

Decoding Big Words

1. Look for the word parts (prefixes) at the beginning of the word.
2. Look for the word parts (suffixes) at the end of the word.
3. In the base word, look for familiar spelling patterns. Think about the six syllable-spelling patterns you have learned.
4. Sound out and blend together the word parts.
5. Say the word parts fast. Adjust your pronunciation as needed. Ask yourself: "Is it a real word?" "Does it make sense in the sentence?"

The Decoding Big Words Strategy Reference Sheet (Resource 4.1) can be downloaded from www.scholastic.com/phonicsintermediate. See page 367 for details on how to access.

3. Walk students through the Decoding Big Words Strategy, using the word *unlisted*. Write the word *unlisted* on the board, but do not pronounce it. Rather say, "Let's look at the word *u-n-l-i-s-t-e-d* [spell it aloud] to see how we can break it apart into recognizable or manageable chunks. This will help us read the whole word." See the sample lesson below.

Decoding Big Words Strategy

STEP 1
Look for the word parts (prefixes) at the beginning of the word. Explain that many common word parts can be found at the beginning of a word, such as *un-*, *dis-*, *re-*, and *pre-*. These word parts are called prefixes. They are added to a base word and change the word's meaning. Circle the prefix *un-* in the word *unlisted* and pronounce it.

STEP 2
Look for words parts (suffixes) at the end of the word. Explain that many common word parts can be found at the ending of a word, such as *-ed*, *-ing*, *-ful*, and *-ment*. These word parts are called suffixes. They are added to a base word and often change the word's part of speech. Circle the suffix *-ed* in the word *unlisted* and pronounce it.

STEP 3
In the base word, look for familiar spelling patterns. Think about the six syllable spelling patterns you have learned. Tell students that what is left (what isn't circled) is the base word. They should use their decoding skills to sound out this part of the word. Underline the base word *list* and pronounce it. Explain to students that this year they will also learn six common syllable types that will help them sound out the base word if they don't already recognize it.

STEP 4
Sound out and blend together the word parts. Slowly decode the word: *un-list-ed*.

STEP 5
Say the word parts fast. Adjust your pronunciation as needed. Ask yourself, "Is it a real word? Does it make sense in the sentence?" Read the word *unlisted* at a natural pace. Adjust the pronunciation as needed. (Note: This will be necessary in many multisyllabic words as one or more of the syllables will be unaccented.) Tell students that if they were reading a passage, they would check to see if this word made sense in the sentence they were reading. You will model this as they read throughout the year.

Throughout the year, use the Decoding Big Words Strategy Practice Sheet (see image at right) to guide students to apply the strategy and discuss with partners how the strategy helped them read new words. This is a great partner activity for students to complete using some of the words from an upcoming story or book they are reading in class. This activity can be completed as a warm-up to the introduction of these words, or as a self-directed activity when you are working with other students in small groups to provide differentiated instruction.

Helping Students Who Struggle With Syllabication

Use the following routine with students who struggle to identify syllables. Model it frequently with important multisyllabic words from selections your students will be reading.

The Decoding Big Words Strategy Practice Sheet (Resource 4.2) can be downloaded from www.scholastic.com/ phonicsintermediate. See page 367 for details on how to access.

Model Routine for Dividing Words

Routine	Teacher–Student Dialogue
1. Select a word with recognizable word parts according to the six common syllable-spelling patterns.	Write the word *fantastic* on the board.
2. Underline, loop your finger under, or reveal the first syllable of the word. Help students pronounce the syllable.	**Teacher:** Let's look at the first part of this word: *f-a-n*. How would you pronounce this syllable? **Students:** fan **Teacher:** That's right. This is a closed syllable, since it ends in a consonant. Closed syllables usually have a short vowel sound.
3. Continue syllable by syllable for the rest of word.	**Teacher:** Let's look at the next syllable: *t-a-s*. How would you pronounce this syllable? **Students:** tas **Teacher:** Great! How is this syllable like the first syllable in the word? **Students:** They are both closed syllables; they both have short vowel sounds. **Teacher:** Super! Now let's read the last syllable in the word: *t-i-c*. It's a closed syllable, too. **Students:** tic
4. When you have finished working through every syllable, have students blend the syllables together to pronounce the word. During reading, finish the model by asking: "Is that a real word? Does it make sense in the sentence?"	**Teacher:** You read *fan-tas-tic*. Let's put these syllables together to read the whole word. **Students:** fantastic **Teacher:** That's right. The word is *fantastic*.

Syllabication Activities

The following quick, fun activities can heighten students' awareness of syllable divisions (Carreker, 1999). Use the Common Syllable Frequency Charts on pages 229–236 to select syllables for the activities.

1 Separated-Syllables Read Write words on the board syllable by syllable, leaving enough space between the word parts for students to see syllable divisions. Ask students to use their knowledge of common syllable spelling patterns (e.g., closed syllables, open syllables, consonant + -le) to read each word. Model blending as necessary by discussing syllable generalizations. When there's a question about a syllable's pronunciation, be sure to have students explain why they pronounced it as they did. It is critical that students be able to verbalize all six syllable-spelling patterns. When they've read each syllable in a word, have students read the word at a natural pace (Gillingham & Stillman, 1997).

fan tas tic	fa ble	ab sent
pump kin	ad ven ture	croc o dile

2 Related-Syllables Read Write on the board a series of related open and closed syllables, such as *re, rem, em.* Have students use their knowledge of open and closed syllables to read each. **Alternative:** Create syllable lists using all prefixes, all suffixes, all consonant + -le syllables, or some other grouping.

re rem em	lo lom om
fi fim im	bo bot ot

3 Multisyllabic Words Manipulation Divide words you've selected from upcoming reading selections into syllables. Write each syllable on a note card. Display the syllables that make up one of the words in jumbled order (e.g., *tas fan tic*). Have students arrange the syllables to form the word. When necessary, discuss the pronunciation and spelling generalizations of any confusing syllables.

4 Syllable Scoop On a reproducible master, write 20 multisyllabic words from an upcoming story. Have students work with a partner to draw an arc, or to scoop with their finger, under each syllable as they read each word aloud. Then have them code each syllable by type (e.g., draw a macron over all open syllables with long vowel sounds, circle all the prefixes). **Alternative:** Have students code a specific type of syllable—circle all consonant + -*le* syllables or underline all closed syllables—and then read the words. Visually identifying the common syllable-spelling pattern makes reading the entire word easier.

table

Resources 4.3 and 4.4 provide sample speed drills*.

5 Speed Drills These quick-paced, timed drills are fun; Resources 4.3 and 4.4 provide sample speed drills (see images at left). One drill contains 20 common syllables in random order. The other contains words with a specific syllable-spelling pattern (consonant + -*le*). Before timing students, give them a chance to practice reading the syllables or words on the drill. Then, give them one minute to read as many syllables or words as they can. This must be done one-on-one with each student. I suggest selecting five students each day to test. On a copy of the drill, mark the syllables or words the students mispronounce. Have students count the number of syllables or words read correctly and mark this on a progress chart. Students find it highly motivating to track their own progress.

Resources 4.5 and 4.6 provide sample What's My Word? activities*.

6 What's My Word? These word completion activities combine a focus on key syllable patterns with word meanings. These activities can be completed for any syllable pattern and make ideal partner activities. Begin by writing a clue for each target word, then providing the spelling of the word, with key letters left out (replaced by blank lines for students to fill in). Resources 4.5 and 4.6 provide sample What's My Word activities for closed syllables and consonant + *le* syllables. See images at right and access online.

7 **Unscramble It!** Like the Multisyllabic Words Manipulation activity, students are required to look at a series of common syllables and combine them to form words. This makes a great independent or partner activity. Use words from upcoming (or current) stories or words containing syllables that are the current focus of instruction. Activity sheets can also be created for review skills and vocabulary words to build mastery over time. See the sample at right.

Resource 4.7:
Closed Syllables:
Unscramble It!*

How Can Teaching Syllables Help Students Decode Multisyllabic Words?

To decode multisyllabic words, students must be able to divide words into recognizable chunks. Some readers develop a sense of syllabication breaks independently through their exposures to print; others have great difficulty and need instruction. When confronted with multisyllabic words, some students' phonics skills break down because they can't readily identify syllable boundaries. Students can use syllabication strategies to approximate a word's pronunciation. This approximation is generally close enough for the reader to recognize the word if it's in the student's speaking or listening vocabularies. This demonstrates how important it is to help students develop their speaking and listening vocabularies and to combine building their background knowledge with vocabulary instruction. Decoding instruction and vocabulary instruction are not mutually exclusive. In fact, at this level they overlap in very significant ways. Therefore, it is important to intertwine phonics and vocabulary instruction in order to maximize learning.

*Resources can be downloaded from www.scholastic.com/phonicsintermediate.
See page 367 for details on how to access.

What About High-Utility Syllables?

When I travel to elementary classrooms across the country, I notice the countless hours spent helping students master the alphabet (the ABCs and their associated sounds) as well as the various spellings for the 44 sounds in English (e.g., the letters *oa* stand for the long *o* sound). These high-utility sound-spellings aid students in becoming efficient decoders of one-syllable words. However, I rarely see any time spent on teaching and reviewing high-utility syllables—those building blocks for multisyllabic words. For some reason, we stop. Let's not! On the following pages, you will find a list of the 322 most frequent syllables in the 5,000 most frequent English words (Fry, Sakiey, Goss & Loigman, 1980). By focusing on these syllables, we can give our students a leg up in their decoding of longer, more complex words. Over time, students will begin to automatically recognize these common syllables in words and use that knowledge to aid in their decoding. Numerous weekly activities can be created around these syllables (Blevins, 2011).

Research Behind the Common Syllable Frequency Charts

One chart contains the **100 Most Common Non-word Syllables**. The other contains the **322 Most Frequent Syllables in the 5,000 Most Common Words in English**. Of these syllables, 222 or 69% are non-word syllables and 100 or 31% are word syllables. These syllables account for over 70% of the syllables used in these 5,000 words. Fry et al. (1980) have shown that 92% of the syllables found in primary-grade basal readers have no more than two pronunciations; 66% of the syllables have only one pronunciation. Therefore, because these syllables are so regular and are used so often, knowing them will give students great flexibility and agility in reading multisyllabic words.

102 Most Common Non-Word Syllables

ing	num	ca	gan	en	tions
der	ent	ap	ry	ture	cal
la	por	tion	ar	ern	cov
coun	al	mer	ning	nev	u
er	peo	fol	bod	di	ther
tle	ven	stud	de	fer	mu
el	fi	re	ma	ny	ger
mon	ed	wa	col	ure	con
i	ble	ful	tence	bout	fore
ber	ev	ad	ver	dif	moth
n't	bers	o	ri	cit	nit
pe	es	ment	par	mem	per
y	af	na	ward	com	est
ty	ac	tween	ex	pa	pic
si	sec	oth	sen	po	un
lar	e	pro	dis	ters	fa
ter	ers	tain	hap	ple	im

322 Most Common Syllables in the 5,000 Most Frequent English Words (With Sample Words for Instruction)

1. **ing** (picking, writing, forthcoming)
2. **er** (never, recover, practitioner)
3. **a** (alive, abandon, adapt)
4. **ly** (silly, gladly, happily)
5. **ed** (acted, decided, stranded)
6. **i** (idea, iron, radio*)
7. **es** (boxes, beaches, touches)
8. **re** (recycle, reinforce, receptionist)
9. **tion** (nation, motionless, relationship)
10. **in** (inside, individual, reinstate)
11. **e** (election, enormous, eliminate)
12. **con** (contact, construct*, concentration)
13. **y** (stormy, pushy, rubbery)
14. **ter** (terrific, external, bitterly)
15. **ex** (exit, export, external)
16. **al** (colonial, memorial, territorial)
17. **de** (define, design, decompose)
18. **com** (comment, complex, accommodate)
19. **o** (radio, rodeo, studio)
20. **di** (diner, dilate, diversity)
21. **en** (energy, enforce, environment)
22. **an** (answer, anticipate, analyze)
23. **ty** (property, priority, authority)
24. **ry** (carry, furry, summary)
25. **u** (uniform, unique, unify)
26. **ti** (title, tiger, tidy)
27. **ri** (rifle, rival, riot)
28. **be** (become, believe, on behalf)

29. **per** (percent, persist, perspective)
30. **to** (total, tofu, totem pole)
31. **pro** (protect, professional, prohibit)
32. **ac** (accuse, acquire, accidental*)
33. **ad** (adjust, advocate, adequate)
34. **ar** (argue, architect, arbitrary)
35. **ers** (cleaners, bankers, gardeners)
36. **ment** (treatment, document, complement)
37. **or** (order, organ, orientation)
38. **tions** (definitions, traditions, abbreviations)
39. **ble** (table, flexible, visible)
40. **der** (wonderful, derby, derive)
41. **ma** (maple, major, maniac)
42. **na** (navy, nation, native)
43. **si** (silent, silo, siren)
44. **un** (under, uneven, unforgettable)
45. **at** (atlas, attitude, attach)
46. **dis** (display, distribute, distort)
47. **ca** (cable, catering, Cajun)
48. **cal** (calendar, calorie, calculate)
49. **man** (mansion, manual, manuscript)
50. **ap** (apple, application, apparatus)
51. **po** (polite, potential, repossess)
52. **sion** (television, tension, dimension)
53. **vi** (vibrate, vital, violate)
54. **el** (elevator, element, eloquent)
55. **est** (tallest, straightest, healthiest)
56. **la** (lazy, labeled, labor)

57. **lar** (larger, larva, dollar*)

58. **pa** (paper, pastry, patience)

59. **ture** (picture, mature, structure)

60. **for** (forest, fortune, forbid)

61. **is** (isn't, Islam, issue*)

62. **mer** (mercy, mercury, merchant)

63. **per** (perfect, performance, perceive)

64. **ra** (razor, radar, ratio)

65. **so** (social, solar, isolation)

66. **ta** (table, tablespoon, taper)

67. **as** (aspirin*, assume, assessment)

68. **col** (collect, collapse, collide)

69. **fi** (final, finance, finite)

70. **ful** (graceful, wonderful, doubtful)

71. **ger** (danger, gerbil, germinate)

72. **low** (below, lower, lowercase)

73. **ni** (nitrogen, denial, alumni)

74. **par** (participate, parcel, particle)

75. **son** (person, reason, arson)

76. **tle** (settle, gentle, belittle)

77. **day** (daylight, Tuesday, Wednesday)

78. **ny** (sunny, balcony, nylon*)

79. **pen** (pencil, penalty, penetrate)

80. **pre** (predict, previous, precise)

81. **tive** (captive, objective, representative)

82. **car** (cartoon, cargo, carbohydrate)

83. **ci** (cider, citation, accidental*)

84. **mo** (motion, mobile, motive)

85. **on** (online, ongoing, onomatopoeia)

86. **ous** (joyous, obvious, ambiguous)

87. **pi** (pilot, pioneer, pious)

88. **se** (secret, sequence, sequel)

89. **ten** (tennis, tender, tenant)

90. **tor** (torture, monitor, tortoise)

91. **ver** (vertical, version, verdict)

92. **ber** (November, barber, limber)

93. **can** (candle, cancer, cantaloupe)

94. **dy** (candy, bodybuilder, subsidy)

95. **et** (quiet, etcetera, etiquette)

96. **it** (edit, credit, exhibit)

97. **mu** (music, museum, mutual)

98. **no** (noble, notion, innovate)

99. **ple** (simple, couple, people)

100. **cu** (cucumber, cupid, cuticle)

101. **fac** (factory, factor, faculty)

102. **fer** (transfer, ferocious, differentiate)

103. **gen** (gentle, gender, generation)

104. **ic** (topic, classic, dynamic)

105. **land** (landmark, Iceland, landscape)

106. **light** (lightning, highlight, lightweight)

107. **ob** (object, obvious, observation)

108. **of** (often, office, offering)

109. **pos** (possible, positive, posture)

110. **tain** (maintain, obtain, retain)

111. **den** (dentist, Denmark, identical)

112. **ings** (spellings, carvings, belongings)

113. **mag** (magnet, magazine, magnify)

114. **ments** (moments, governments, supplements)

115. **set** (settle, offset, setbacks)

116. **some** (something, somewhat, somewhere)

117. **sub** (subway, substitute, subterranean)

118. **sur** (survive, survey, surgery)

* = syllable with an alternate pronunciation

119. **ters** (chapters, alters, encounters)

120. **tu** (virtual, eventual, fluctuate)

121. **af** (afternoon, African, affluent)

122. **au** (author, autumn, automate)

123. **cy** (fancy, policy, currency)

124. **fa** (fable, favorite, fatal)

125. **im** (important, image, immigrate)

126. **li** (lion, license, intelligence*)

127. **lo** (lotion, locate, psychology)

128. **men** (mention, mental, fundamental)

129. **min** (minute, minimum, administrate)

130. **mon** (monster, monsoon, monument)

131. **op** (option, cooperate, optical)

132. **out** (outside, outcome, output)

133. **rec** (record, recognize, recreation)

134. **ro** (robot, rotate, robust)

135. **sen** (sentence, Senate, sensible)

136. **side** (sidewalk, sideline, reside*)

137. **tal** (talent, tally, talon)

138. **tic** (arctic, scholastic, domestic)

139. **ties** (abilities, properties, treaties)

140. **ward** (upward, westward, straightforward)

141. **age** (ageless, agelessness, voyage*)

142. **ba** (bacon, baby-sitter, basic)

143. **but** (butter, button, rebuttal)

144. **cit** (citizen, citrus, explicit)

145. **cle** (cycle, uncle, vehicle)

146. **co** (coconut, coordination, coincide)

147. **cov** (cover, recovered, covet)

148. **da** (David, data, foundation)

149. **dif** (different, difficult, differentiate)

150. **ence** (excellence, difference, obedience)

151. **ern** (modern, government, tavern)

152. **eve** (eve, evening, uneven)

153. **hap** (happy, happen, hapless)

154. **ies** (cookies, armies, accessories)

155. **ket** (market, kettle, basketball)

156. **lec** (election, lecture, collector)

157. **main** (remain, domain, maintenance)

158. **mar** (marble, marvelous, margin)

159. **mis** (mistake, misery*, misrepresent)

160. **my** (myself*, academy, economy)

161. **nal** (journal, final, internal)

162. **ness** (illness, dizziness, bitterness)

163. **ning** (running, planning, inning)

164. **n't** (couldn't, wouldn't, shouldn't)

165. **nu** (numerous, nutritious, nuclear)

166. **oc** (October, occupy, octagon)

167. **pres** (present, presentation, presidential)

168. **sup** (supper, supplement, supple)

169. **te** (strategic, integrate, tedious)

170. **ted** (knotted, adapted, educated)

171. **tem** (item, temper, temporary)

172. **tin** (tinfoil, tinsel, continue)

173. **tri** (triangle, triumph, contribute*)

174. **tro** (astronaut, Trojan War, controversy)

175. **up** (uphill, update, upheaval)

176. **va** (vacation, vapor, vacant)

177. **ven** (venom, vendor, ventilate)

178. **vis** (visitor, revisit, vision*)

179. **am** (ambulance, amateur, amphibian)

180. **bor** (boring, border, neighbor)

181. **by** (bypass, bystanders, whereby)	212. **cor** (corner, correspond, incorporate)
182. **cat** (cattle, catalog, category)	213. **coun** (council, counselor, counterfeit)
183. **cent** (percent, accent, adjacent)	214. **cus** (custom, focus, custodian)
184. **ev** (every, evolution, evident)	215. **dan** (dandruff, bandanna, dandelion)
185. **gan** (began, gigantic, gander)	216. **dle** (cradle, saddle, bundle)
186. **gle** (eagle, angle, gurgle)	217. **ef** (effort, effect, efficient)
187. **head** (headache, headphones, arrowhead)	218. **end** (endless, bookend, unending)
188. **high** (highway, higher education, highbrow)	219. **ent** (different, excellent, apparent)
189. **il** (illegal, illustrate, illiterate)	220. **ered** (flowered, airpowered, empowered)
190. **lu** (lunar, revolution, lucrative)	221. **fin** (finish, Finland, finicky)
191. **me** (meteor, media, intermediate)	222. **form** (perform, conform, transform)
192. **nor** (normal, ignoring, governor)	223. **go** (going, gopher, undergo)
193. **part** (apart, partner, department)	224. **har** (harvest, harness, harmony)
194. **por** (portion, important, portal)	225. **ish** (childish, bluish, outlandish)
195. **read** (misread*, ready, readily)	226. **lands** (islands, wetlands, highlands)
196. **rep** (represent, repetition, replica)	227. **let** (letter, lettuce, inlet)
197. **su** (super, superbly, supersonic)	228. **long** (belong, longest, longings)
198. **tend** (attend, intend, pretended)	229. **mat** (matter, mattress, format)
199. **ther** (other, brotherly, furthermore)	230. **meas** (measure, measurement, measurable)
200. **ton** (carton, cotton, skeleton)	231. **mem** (member, membrane, remembrance)
201. **try** (entry, country, poultry)	222. **mul** (multiple, multitude, multinational)
202. **um** (umpire, umbrella, medium)	233. **ner** (nervous, beginner, partnership)
203. **uer** (rescuer*, leaguer, cataloguer)	234. **play** (playful, playground, displaying)
204. **way** (highway, driveway, wayward)	235. **ples** (apples, couples, principles)
205. **ate** (appropriate, accurate, corporate)	236. **ply** (reply, multiply, imply)
206. **bet** (better, alphabet, diabetic)	237. **port** (report, transport, import)
207. **bles** (marbles, crumbles, foibles)	238. **press** (pressing, depress, expression*)
208. **bod** (body, busybody, antibodies)	239. **sat** (Saturday, Saturn, satellite)
209. **cap** (capital, capsule, capture)	240. **sec** (second, section, sector)
210. **cial** (special, artificial, crucial)	241. **ser** (servant, service, eraser)
211. **cir** (circle, circus, circumstance)	242. **south** (Southwest, Southeast, southern*)

* = syllable with an alternate pronunciation

243. **sun** (sunshine, sunset, sundae)

244. **the** (nonetheless, nevertheless, theory*)

245. **ting** (fitting, babysitting, earsplitting)

246. **tra** (tradition, contradict, trapeze*)

247. **tures** (cultures, features, infrastructures)

248. **val** (valley, valid, evaluate)

249. **var** (vary, various, variation)

250. **vid** (video, David, individually)

251. **wil** (willow, Wilbur, wildebeest)

252. **win** (window, winner, wintergreen)

253. **won** (wonder, wonderful, wondrous)

254. **work** (workplace, framework, network)

255. **act** (overact, react, interact)

256. **ag** (agriculture, agony, aggregate)

257. **air** (airplane, airport, airtight)

258. **als** (visuals, betrayals, liberals)

259. **bat** (battle, battery, battleground)

260. **bi** (bicycle, bias, bicentennial)

261. **cate** (dedicate, replicate, communicate)

262. **cen** (center, century, incentive)

263. **char** (charcoal, charter, charity*)

264. **come** (become, income, unwelcome)

265. **cul** (culture, cultivate, culprit)

266. **ders** (ladders, wonders, elders)

267. **east** (Easter, eastern, easterly)

268. **fect** (affect, infect, disinfect)

269. **fish** (fishbowl, fisherman, goldfishes)

270. **fix** (fixing, fixture, fixation)

271. **gi** (giant, gigantic, fungi*)

272. **grand** (grandfather, grandstand, grand jury)

273. **great** (greatest, greatness, great-grandchild)

274. **heav** (heavy, heaven, heavenly)

275. **ho** (hotel, holy, hogan)

276. **hunt** (hunter, overhunted, headhunter)

277. **ion** (onion, million, union)

278. **its** (edits, credits, exhibits)

279. **jo** (banjo, Joseph, jovial)

280. **lat** (latter, Latin, latitude)

281. **lead** (leader, leadership, misleading)

282. **lect** (elect, select, collectible)

283. **lent** (excellent, relentless, equivalent)

284. **less** (restless, hopeless, carelessness)

285. **lin** (linen, gremlin, linear)

286. **mal** (normal, minimal, malnutrition)

287. **mi** (minus, minor, migrate)

288. **mil** (million, military, mildew)

289. **moth** (mother*, mammoth, behemoth)

290. **near** (nearest, nearby, nearsighted)

291. **nel** (funnel, channel, kernel)

292. **net** (networks, magnet, cabinet)

293. **new** (newly, newbie, newborn)

294. **one** (someone, one-way, anyone)

295. **point** (pointed, appoint, pointless)

296. **prac** (practice, practical, impractical)

297. **ral** (rally*, spiral, referral)

298. **rect** (direct, erect, indirect)

299. **ried** (carried, married, salaried)

300. **round** (around, roundabout, roundup)

301. **row** (rowboat, arrow, rowdy*)

302. **sa** (sensation, sabertooth tiger, saliva*)

303. **sand** (sandy, sandstorm, sandwiches)

304. **self** (myself, selfish, self-defense)

305. **sent** (absent, resentful*, consent)	314. **tom** (bottom, atomic, tomboyish)
306. **ship** (shipment, friendship, scholarship)	315. **tors** (actors, tractors, curators)
307. **sim** (simple, similar, simulate)	316. **tract** (distract, contract, extract)
308. **sions** (visions, decisions, commissions)	317. **tray** (ashtray, portray, betraying)
309. **sis** (sister, thesis, hypothesis)	318. **us** (status, sinus, ruckus)
310. **sons** (persons, poisons, bisons)	319. **vel** (velvet, Velcro, development)
311. **stand** (standard, withstand, notwithstanding)	320. **west** (westward, Midwestern, westernize)
312. **sug** (suggest, suggestion, suggestive)	321. **where** (nowhere, whereas, whereabouts)
313. **tel** (telephone, television, intelligent)	322. **writ** (written, unwritten, rewritten)

* = syllable with an alternate pronunciation

50 Sample Two-Syllable Words for Instruction

absent	dessert	inspect	paper	sandbox
action	exclaim	jolly	pencil	special
applaud	excuse	joyous	planet	stubborn
balloon	fastest	kicking	plastic	subtract
because	flavor	laughing	pocket	surprise
before	grassy	louder	pretzel	table
center	hammer	magic	pumpkin	turtle
contest	helpful	mitten	puzzle	unlock
cricket	insect	monster	question	valley
dinner	insist	notebook	railroad	water

50 Sample Three-Syllable Words for Instruction

activate	cantaloupe	crocodile	discotheque	gigantic
adventure	capable	cucumber	elephant	habitat
advisor	caravan	cumulus	fabulous	honestly
banana	carousel	curious	factory	however
bicycle	Chihuahua	different	fantastic	icicle
butterfly	committee	difficult	forever	invention

50 Sample Three–Syllable Words for Instruction *continued*

kangaroo	marshmallow	mosquito	popular	vacation
labyrinth	marvelous	multiply	terrible	watery
listening	magical	normally	tornado	whichever
magnify	millionaire	poisonous	underneath	wonderful

50 Sample Four–Syllable Words for Instruction

absolutely	conceptual	escalator	kindergarten	populated
acceptable	considerate	especially	librarian	refrigerate
activity	conversation	exaggerate	magnificent	regularly
adorable	dedicated	fortunately	material	reversible
adversary	dependable	graduation	misunderstood	spectacular
affectionate	demonstration	hysterical	motorcycle	stationery
alligator	differences	independent	mysterious	tarantula
calculator	energetic	information	necessary	transformation
caterpillar	enjoyable	interested	operation	unusual
competitive	entertainment	interrupted	pepperoni	watermelon

Sample Five–Syllable Words for Instruction

abracadabra	choreography	inexcusable	representative	unacceptable
academia	claustrophobia	intellectual	schizophrenia	uncontrollable
administration	hippopotamus	irreplaceable	tonsillectomy	underachiever
auditorium	indestructible	paraphernalia	transcontinental	underdeveloped
bibliography	indisputable	reprehensible	transfiguration	Yugoslavia

Sample Six–Syllable Words

authoritarian	encyclopedia	onomatopoeia	undereducated
autobiography	incomprehensible	paleontology	unimaginable
disciplinarian	octogenarian	Tyrannosaurus Rex	unsatisfactory

Just for Fun! 14 Syllables

supercalifragilisticexpialidocious

Using the High–Frequency Syllable List

Use the 322 Most Frequent Syllables list to create weekly activities to help students readily recognize these high-utility syllables in isolation and in words. These activities, including a weekly High-Frequency Syllable Routine and Activity Sheet, also help to build wider word awareness and vocabulary. Below you will find a high-frequency syllable routine, sample activity pages, and templates for creating your own activities.

High–Frequency Syllable Routine

Distribute copies of the High-Frequency Syllable Fluency Sheet (Syllables 1-10), Resource 4.8. This sample page includes the ten most frequent syllables in English. Use the High-Frequency Syllable Fluency blank template, Resource 4.9, and the syllable list (see pages 230-235; list contains words for instruction) to create other sheets for your students. As an alternative, you can use those pre-made in *Week-by-Week Phonics & Word Study Activities in the Intermediate Grades* (Blevins, 2011). Also distribute copies of the High-Frequency Syllable Fluency Activity Sheet, Resource 4.10.

Resources 4.8 and 4.9 can be downloaded from www.scholastic.com/ phonicsintermediate. See page 367 for details on how to access.

STEP 1 For the High-Frequency Syllable Fluency Sheet (Syllables 1-10), students will underline the target syllable in each word, then use the words in a sorting activity.

STEP 2 For the High-Frequency Syllable Fluency Activity Sheet, students will look for other words with the target syllables in their weekly readings. Then they will record the meanings of five (or more) unknown words that appear on the High-Frequency Syllable Fluency Sheet (Syllables 1-10) to build vocabulary.

Some useful information about making and using High-Frequency Syllable Fluency Sheets:

Resource 4.10 can be downloaded from www.scholastic.com/ phonicsintermediate. See page 367 for details on how to access.

1. Throughout the year, students will be exposed to the 322 most common syllables in the 5,000 most frequent words in English. Learning these syllables will help students recognize them in new words while reading.

2. Some of the syllables will have a different pronunciation based on their position in a word. For example, a syllable in an unaccented syllable will be pronounced with a schwa sound.

3. The words in each column should get progressively more complex. Therefore, the words in column 3 are the most sophisticated. This is one way to differentiate the practice. If you are working with younger or struggling students, you may choose to only focus on the first or second columns, saving the third column as a challenge for more advanced students.

4. Three great sources of high-utility words to use when constructing your own sheets are Avril Coxhead's list of High-Incidence Academic Words (Coxhead, 1998), Andrew Biemiller's Words Worth Teaching lists (Biemiller, 2009), and the Harris-Jacobson Basic Reading Vocabularies lists (Harris & Jacobson, 1972).

5. Once you introduce a set of syllables for the week, create a set of Syllable Fluency Flash Cards. Each day, flip through the cards quickly as students chorally read them. (You can also create or add sample words with the syllables.) Each week, add the new set of cards to the growing flash card set. This fast, 2-minute warm-up drill will help students gain automaticity in reading these common syllables and further help them recognize these syllables while reading.

6. Record these syllables on a chart in the classroom or a word wall. As students find words with these syllables in their weekly readings, have them add the words to the chart or word wall. You might wish to provide a prize each week for the students who find the most words (e.g., special book to take home). This will help create an interest in and excitement about words and make students active observers of words and their important parts.

Word Study (Structural Analysis)

When they begin reading increasingly complex texts, students will encounter growing numbers of multisyllabic words. Teaching students word analysis gives them additional strategies they need to tackle those longer, more difficult words.

Word Study Teaching Guidelines

- **Introduce, or reinforce, the concept that words can be made up of several elements.** Define these elements, such as prefixes, suffixes, and roots, for students, but focus primarily on how students can use word parts to sound out a word and figure out its meaning. The word part *un*, for example, is very common; students should be able to recognize it immediately in unfamiliar words. Teach students to recognize the word part and explain that its meaning affects the meaning of the whole word. Some examples include *unhappy, unsuccessful*, and *unable*. Contrast these words with non-examples such as *uncle* and *until*.

- **Be sure your instruction is explicit.** Tell students why they are learning a specific skill, show when they can use it, and provide many opportunities for them to practice using it.

- **During instruction, rely more on concrete, known examples, rather than abstract rules, principles, or definitions.** Illustrate all generalizations with countless examples. During reading, focus students' attention on the relationship between a word's internal structure and its role in a sentence. For example, although it's not particularly useful to teach the meanings of suffixes, knowing that a particular suffix changes a word from an adjective to a noun can be important in understanding a word's role in a sentence.

- **Alert students to the diversity of English words.** Provide instruction in Anglo-Saxon, Greek, and Roman roots and clarify the differences among them. Also, teach prefixes and suffixes differently. For example, although learning the meanings of prefixes is important, learning the meanings of suffixes has less value.

- **Be sure students are aware of the limitations of structural analysis.** For example, not all words that begin with *un* begin with a prefix (e.g., *unhappy* vs. *under*). Remind students that after they analyze a word to determine its pronunciation and meaning they should check to see if it makes sense in the sentence.

- **Apply! Apply! Apply!** Use all reading experiences as an opportunity for students to use their knowledge of word parts to pronounce and determine the meanings of unfamiliar words.

The following pages provide teaching guidelines, lessons and activities, and word lists for the following word-study skills:

1. Compound Words
2. Prefixes
3. Suffixes (including plurals and inflectional endings)
4. Homophones
5. Greek and Latin Roots

Compound Words

A compound word is a word made up of two smaller words. Often its meaning can be derived from the meaning of the two smaller words that comprise it: a *doghouse* is a "house for a dog." However, there are notable exceptions such as *butterfly*. There are three types of compound words: open (*fire drill*), closed (*doghouse*), and hyphenated (*by-pass*).

Teaching Guidelines
- Encourage students to look for smaller words in larger words to help them pronounce and, sometimes, figure out the meanings of the larger words. Compound-word instruction serves as an introduction to this concept.

Word–Study Research

"The term word study refers to the process of learning everything about words, including their spelling, meaning, pronunciation, historical origin, and relationship with other words" (Moats, 2000). Skilled readers use phonics to determine a word's pronunciation, context clues to infer a word's meaning, and structural analysis, or knowledge of word parts, to determine both a word's meaning and pronunciation. Nagy & Anderson (1984) estimated that as many as 60% of English words have meanings that can be predicted from the meanings of their parts. For another 10% of English words, word parts may give useful, though incomplete, information. This is critical when you consider that the average fifth-grader reads 1 million words of text a year (Anderson, Wilson, & Fielding, 1998). Of these 1 million words, they'll see 10,000 only once—1,000 are truly novel words not related to words they've previously encountered. Therefore, the majority of the words are related to known words, and structural analysis can play a key role in figuring out their pronunciations and meanings. For example, 4,000 of the words are derived from more frequent words (e.g., *romantic/unromantic, debt/indebtedness*) and 1,300 are inflections (*merit/merited, merge/merges*).

In a study by Henry (1988), on-level students knew far too little about the major structures of words, including syllable and morpheme patterns. Below-level students knew virtually nothing about word structure. As Henry states: "Unfortunately, decoding instruction largely neglects syllable and morpheme patterns, perhaps because these techniques are primarily useful for the longer words found in literature and subject matter text beyond grade 2 or 3, at which point decoding instruction becomes virtually nonexistent in most schools. Without recognizing the value of syllabic and morphological patterns, the student is constrained from using clues available to identify long, unfamiliar words." Although some on-level students can use knowledge of structural analysis to determine the meanings of new words (Tyler & Nagy, 1989), many fail to apply their knowledge of word parts where it would be helpful (White, Power, & White, 1989; Wysocki & Jenkins, 1987). Therefore, instruction in structural analysis, or key word parts, can improve students' ability to interpret, remember the meanings of, and spell new multisyllabic words.

However, it's important to encourage children to look for words with more than two or three letters in a larger word. Identifying a two-letter word in a larger word isn't always useful. For example, finding the word *to* in *town* or *tornado* is useless for both determining pronunciation and meaning.

- Point out that when a compound word is divided, each remaining smaller word must be able to stand on its own.

Use these books to add fun to your lessons on compound words:

- *Once There Was a Bullfrog* by Rick Walton
- *Thumbtacks, Earwax, Lipstick, Dipstick: What Is a Compound Word?* by Brian Cleary & Brian Gable
- *Flying Butter: A Rookie Reader* by Patricia Trattles
- *If You Were a Compound Word* by Trisha Shasken
- *Cloudy with a Chance of Meatballs* by Judi and Ron Barrett

Compound Words

after all	anthill	backbone	barnyard	bedroll
afternoon	anybody	backdoor	baseball	bedroom
aftershave	anyhow	backfield	basketball	bedside
air bag	anyone	background	bath mat	bedspread
air boat	anything	backpack	bathrobe	bedspring
air hole	anywhere	backseat	bathroom	bedtime
air mattress	applesauce	backstage	bathtub	beehive
airmail	armchair	backstop	bathwater	beeline
airplane	armrest	backstroke	beanbag	bird dog
airsick	back away	backyard	beanpod	birdbath
airtight	back room	bagpipe	beanpole	birdcage
anteater	backboard	bandleader	bed rest	birdcall

birdhouse	collarbone	everyone	footpath	high jump
birdseed	cookbook	everything	footprint	high noon
birthday	cornbread	everywhere	footrest	high school
blackbird	corncob	eyeball	footstep	high-rise
blackboard	cornfield	eyeglasses	footstool	hilltop
blindfold	countdown	eyelid	give-and-take	home plate
blueberry	cowboy	eyesight	goldfish	home run
bluebird	crossword	faraway	grapevine	homegrown
blueprint	cupcake	farmhouse	grasshopper	homemade
boathouse	daydream	father-in-law	greenhouse	homeroom
book bag	daylight	finger bowl	grownup	homesick
bookcase	diving board	finger hole	hairbrush	hometown
bookmark	doghouse	fingernail	haircut	homework
buttonhole	dollhouse	fingerpaint	hairnet	horseback
broomstick	doorbell	fingerprint	hairpiece	horsefly
bulldog	doorknob	fingertip	hairpin	horseshoe
bullfrog	doormat	fire drill	hairstyle	hotdog
butterfly	doorstep	fire engine	hand-feed	houseboat
buttermilk	doorway	fire escape	handbag	ice skate
by-pass	double-header	fire station	handball	ice skater
campfire	downhill	fire truck	handbook	iceberg
campground	downstairs	fire-eater	handmade	inside
candlelight	downtown	fireboat	handpick	jellyfish
candlemaker	dragonfly	firefighter	handsaw	keyhole
candlestick	dressmaker	firefly	handshake	lawnmower
cardboard	driveway	firehouse	handstand	lifetime
cheerleader	drumstick	firelight	handwrite	lighthouse
classroom	dugout	fireplace	headache	living room
clothespin	eardrum	firewood	headband	lookout
clubhouse	earthquake	fireworks	headphone	loudspeaker
coal mine	electric guitar	flowerpot	headstand	lunchroom

merry-go-round	poison ivy	seafood	someway	toeshoe
milkshake	polar bear	seaport	spaceship	toolbox
moonbeam	popcorn	seashell	spacesuit	toothache
moonlight	postcard	seashore	springtime	toothbrush
mother-in-law	railroad	seaside	starfish	toothpaste
motorboat	rainbow	seat belt	starlight	townspeople
motorcycle	raincoat	seaweed	starship	treetop
mousetrap	raindrop	send-off	steamboat	tugboat
music box	rainfall	shopkeeper	stepladder	underground
newspaper	ringmaster	shoreline	storehouse	underwater
nightgown	roadside	sidewalk	storeroom	upstairs
notebook	roof garden	sideways	storyteller	wallpaper
outdoors	rooftop	skyline	sunburn	washcloth
outfield	rosebud	skyscraper	sunflower	watchdog
outside	rosebush	smokestack	sunlight	waterfall
overlook	rowboat	snapshot	sunrise	whatever
overnight	sailboat	snowball	sunset	wheelchair
overtake	sandbox	snowfall	sunshine	windmill
pancake	sandpaper	snowflake	supermarket	windpipe
passer-by	saucepan	snowman	swimming pool	windshield
peanut	sawdust	snowplow	tablespoon	wintertime
pillowcase	scarecrow	snowshoe	teacup	wishbone
pinecone	scrapbook	snowstorm	teaspoon	without
pinwheel	sea breeze	snowsuit	tennis court	workbench
playground	sea captain	somebody	thunderstorm	workday
playhouse	sea gull	someday	tightrope	worktable
playpen	sea horse	someone	toadstool	wristwatch
pocketbook	seacoast	something	toenail	

Prefixes

A prefix is a group of letters that appears at the front of a word. A prefix affects the meaning of the root (base) word to which it is attached. To determine whether or not a group of letters is a prefix, remove them from the word. The letters are a prefix if a known word remains. For example, remove the letters *un* from the following words: *unhappy, untie, uncle, uninterested.* In which word are the letters *un* not a prefix? Yes, these letters are <u>not</u> a prefix in the word *uncle*.

Teaching Guidelines

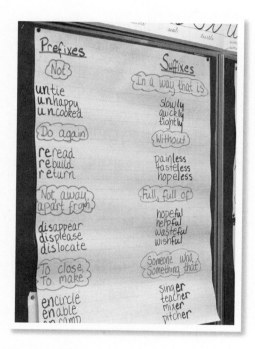

- Make students aware of the following warnings about prefixes.

  1. Most prefixes have more than one meaning. For example, the prefix *un* can mean "not" as in *unhappy*, or "do the opposite of" as in *untie*. Teach the multiple meanings of the most common prefixes, and use careful language during lessons such as, "the prefix *un* <u>sometimes</u> means *not*."

  2. Be careful of letter clusters that look like prefixes, but aren't. For example, when the letters *un* are removed from *uncle*, no recognizable root word is left. In addition, when the letters *in* are removed from *invented*, the word that remains has no relation to the whole word. The prefixes that cause the most difficulty are *re, in*, and *dis*.

  3. Don't rely solely on word-part clues to determine meaning. Use context clues as well to verify a word's meaning. For example, you might think the word *unassuming* means "not assuming/not supposing" instead of its actual meaning "modest." It is estimated that about 15 to 20% of the prefixed words students will encounter share this complexity (White et al., 1989).

- Teach only the most common prefixes. The chart below shows the most common based on a count of prefixed words appearing in the *Word Frequency Book* (Carroll et al., 1971). The prefix *un* alone accounts for almost one-third of the total. The top three on the list account for over half.

Rank	Prefix	%	Rank	Prefix	%
1.	un (not, opposite of)	26	**11.**	pre (before)	3
2.	re (again)	14	**12.**	inter (between, among)	3
3.	in, im, ir, il (not)	11	**13.**	fore (before)	3
4.	dis (not, opposite of)	7	**14.**	de (opposite of)	2
5.	en, em (cause to)	4	**15.**	trans (across)	2
6.	non (not)	4	**16.**	super (above)	1
7.	in, im (in or into)	4	**17.**	semi (half)	1
8.	over (too much)	3	**18.**	anti (against)	1
9.	mis (wrongly)	3	**19.**	mid (middle)	1
10.	sub (under)	3	**20.**	under (too little)	1

All other prefixes (about 100) accounted for only 3% of the words.

- Incorporate activities to give students practice. See the sample activities online: Prefix or Pretender (Resource 4.11).
- and Prefixes: Connect a Word (Resource 4.12).

Resources 4.11 and 4.12 can be downloaded from www.scholastic.com/ phonicsintermediate. See page 367 for details on how to access.

Prefixes

STEP 1: Define

Tell students that a prefix is a group of letters added to the beginning of a base word to make a new word. The prefix changes the word's meaning. Recognizing common prefixes can help students decode a word and figure out its meaning. For example, the word *unhappy* begins with the prefix *un-*. The prefix *un-* means "not" or "the opposite of." So, someone who is *unhappy* is not happy. Point out the following prefixes:

un- means "not" or "the opposite of"
- The little girl was *unhappy* when her balloon popped.
- We need the key to *unlock* the safe.

re- means "again" or "back/backwards"
- That villain will likely *reappear* on screen later in the movie.
- We had to *return* the movie the following week.

in-, im-, -ir-, il- mean "not" or "the opposite of" or "lack of"
- It is *inappropriate* to talk in class during an exam.
- Was it *impossible* to climb that mountain?
- Her decision to run for class president was *irreversible*.
- It is *illegal* to drive without a license.

STEP 2: Transition to Longer Words

Help students transition from reading one-syllable words to multisyllabic words. Have them read the prefix in the first column, then underline the prefix in the word in the second column. Guide students in reading the longer word and determining its meaning using the prefix.

un	unable
un	untie
un	unnecessary
re	reappear
re	remake
in	inappropriate
in	inaccessible
im	immature
ir	irresponsible
il	illogical

STEP 3: Build Words

Write the following word parts on the board: *un, re, in, im, ir, il, do, make, side, legal, mature, replace, able*. Have student pairs combine the word parts to build as many words as possible. These and other words can be formed: *undo, redo, remake, inside, illegal, immature, irreplaceable*.

STEP 4: Apply Decoding Strategy

Have students use the Decoding Big Words Strategy (see page 221) to decode the following words: *inexpensive, immortal, illiterate, reconstructed, unbelievable*. Remind them to look for prefixes in Step 1 of the strategy.

Prefix Word Lists

un (not, opposite of)				
unable	unclip	unfamiliar	unlawful	unrest
unaccustomed	uncombed	unfasten	unlike	unrestrained
unafraid	uncomfortable	unfelt	unlikely	unroll
unanswered	uncommon	unfinished	unlit	unruly
unathletic	unconscious	unfit	unload	unsafe
unattractive	uncontrollably	unfold	unlock	unsatisfactory
unaware	uncooked	unfortunate	unloved	unscrew
unbearable	uncover	unfriendly	unlucky	unseen
unbelievable	uncrate	unglue	unmade	unsnap
unbend	uncrowded	unhappy	unmake	unsold
unbind	uncut	unharmed	unmarked	unspoiled
unblock	undamaged	unhealthy	unmarried	unsteady
unborn	undecided	unheard	unmistakable	unstick
unbound	undo	unhook	unmoved	unstring
unbroken	undone	unhurt	unnamed	unsuccessful
unbuilt	undress	unidentified	unnatural	unsure
uncanny	unearth	unimaginable	unpack	untangle
uncap	uneasy	unimportant	unpaid	unthinkable
uncertain	unequal	unimpressed	unpleasant	untie
unchain	uneven	uninhabited	unprotected	untouched
unchanged	uneventful	uninteresting	unplug	unwanted
unchecked	unexpected	unkind	unravel	unwind
unclean	unexplored	unknown	unreal	unwise
unclear	unfair	unlatch	unreasonable	unwrap

re (again)

reappear	redraw	remix	reread	retrace
reapply	refigure	remove	rescore	return
rearrange	refill	rename	respond	retype
reassure	reform	renew	reseal	reunite
reattach	refreeze	reoil	resell	reuse
rebuild	refuse	reopen	resew	reveal
recall	regain	repack	reshoot	reverse
recheck	regrade	repaid	restack	revise
recook	regroup	repave	restate	rewash
recopy	rehang	repay	restuff	rewind
recount	rehearse	replace	resume	rewrite
recover	reheat	replan	retag	rewrap
recut	relearn	replenish	retie	
recycle	release	reproduce	retire	
rediscover	reload	request	retold	

in, im, ir, il (not)

illegal	impatient	inappropriate	indirect	insane
illegible	imperfect	inboard	indistinct	insatiable
illiterate	impersonal	inbounds	indoors	inseparable
imbalance	impetuous	incapable	inefficient	insight
immaterial	impolite	incase	inevitable	invaluable
immature	impossible	incompetent	inexpensive	invisible
immodest	impractical	incomplete	inexperienced	irrational
immortal	improper	inconvenient	infinite	irregular
immovable	impure	incorrect	infrequent	irresistible
impartial	inaccurate	indefinite	ingrown	irresponsible
impassable	inadequate	indignant	injustice	irrevocably

dis (not, opposite of)

disable	disarray	disengage	dislodge	displeasure
disadvantage	disbelief	disgrace	dismantle	dispute
disagree	discard	disgust	dismiss	disqualify
disagreeable	discolor	dishearten	disobey	distort
disallow	discomfort	dishonest	disorder	distract
disappear	disconnect	disintegrate	disown	distrust
disappoint	discourage	disjoin	displace	disturb
disapprove	disdain	dislike	displease	

en, em (cause to)

embark	encage	encounter	enjoy	entangle
embarrass	encamp	encourage	enlarge	entitle
embattle	encase	endear	enlighten	entrust
embedded	enchant	endure	enlist	envelop
emblazon	encircle	enfold	enrage	envision
embrace	enclose	enforce	enrich	enwind
employ	encode	engage	enroll	
enable	encompass	engulf	ensure	

non (not)

nonabrasive	nonbreakable	noncritical	nonfiction
nonabsorbent	noncentral	noncurrent	nongraded
nonacademic	noncertified	nondeductible	nonhistoric
nonacceptance	nonchalant	nondigestible	nonindustrial
nonactive	nonchallenged	nondissolved	noninfected
nonadjustable	noncombustible	nondrinkable	nonliving
nonaquatic	noncommittal	nondrip	nonpaying
nonathletic	nonconditional	noneffective	nonperfect
nonattached	nonconsecutive	nonequivalent	nonqualified
nonbeing	noncontagious	nonexplainable	nonrealistic
nonbinding	noncreative	nonfactual	nonreflecting

nonremovable	nonslip	nonsticky	nonsupporter
nonresponsive	nonsmoker	nonstop	nonwashable
nonsimilar	nonspecific		

in, im (in or into)

interior	imbue	imminent	imprison
influx	imbibe	important	imperil
inhale	immigrate	impress	impulsive

over (too much)

overact	overcast	overflow	overplan	overstep
overbake	overclean	overjoyed	overpowering	oversweet
overbeat	overcoach	overlap	overrate	overtake
overbill	overcome	overlarge	override	overthink
overboard	overcook	overlength	oversalt	overtight
overbook	overcrowded	overload	overshadow	overtip
overbusy	overdo	overnice	oversized	overuse
overcame	overdry	overpay	overslept	overwhelm

mis (wrongly)

misact	miscalculate	misdo	mislocate	misread
misaddress	mischoose	misfile	misname	mistreat
misadjust	misconnect	misguide	misnumber	mistype
misadvise	misdefine	misjudge	misorder	misunderstood
misarrange	misdiagnose	mislead	mispronounce	

sub (under)

subaquatic	subdivide	sublease	submerge	subterranean
subclass	subgroup	submarine	substandard	subway
subconscious				

pre (before)

preadult	predinner	prelunch	preplan	prestamp
prearrange	pregame	premeasure	prequalify	pretrial
precool	preharvest	premix	prerinse	pretrim
precut	preheat	prenoon	presale	prewash
predawn	prejudge	preorder	preseason	prework

inter (between, among)

interact	intercommunity	interlock	intersect
interchange	interconnect	intermix	interspace
intercollegiate	intergroup	international	interstate

fore (before)

forearm	foreground	forereach	foreshadow	forethought
forecast	forehead	forerun	foreshock	forewarn
forecheck	forejudge	foresaid	forespeak	
forego	foreknow	foresail	foretaste	
foregone	forename	foresee	foretell	

de (opposite of)

debug	deface	deform	deplane	dethrone
declaw	defang	defrost	derail	detrain
decompose	deflate			

trans (across)

transatlantic	transfer	transmit
transborder	translocate	transplant

super (above)

superable	superdifficult	superman	supersize
superabsorbent	superfast	supernatural	supersoft
superabundant	superheat	superpower	superspeed
supercharge	superhighway	supersafe	superthin
superclean	superhuman	supersensitive	superwide

semi (half)

semiactive	semidome	semiopen	semistiff
semiautomatic	semidry	semipeaceful	semiweekly
semiclosed	semifinal	semipro	
semidangerous	semifinished	semiskilled	

anti (against)

antibacterial	anticrime	antigravity	antisocial

mid (middle)

midafternoon	midland	midsize	midweek
midcourse	midnight	midterm	midwinter
midday	midrange	midway	midyear

under (too little)

underachieve	undercover	underfeed	undershirt
underage	underdeveloped	underground	undersize
underbake	underdo	undergrown	understudy
underbrush	underdog	underpay	undertake
undercharge	underdress	underperform	underwater
underclothes	underemploy	underrate	underway
undercoat	underestimate	undersea	underwear
undercook	underexpose	undersell	

Suffixes

A suffix is a letter, or group of letters, that is added to the end of a root (base) word. Common suffixes include *s, ed, ing, ly,* and *tion*. A suffix changes the meaning of the root or base word. Therefore, students need to understand the meanings of suffixes and how they affect the words they're attached to. By helping students quickly identify a suffix and visually remove it to identify the base word, you'll help them figure out the meaning of the whole word.

Teaching Guidelines

- Adding a suffix sometimes changes the spelling of a base word, and students need to be directly taught the suffixes that cause changes. The three most common spelling changes resulting from the addition of suffixes are:

  1. *Consonant doubling* (*runner, running*): The consonant is doubled so that the first syllable will form a CVC pattern. Most CVC words contain a short vowel sound. Therefore, the second consonant acts as a diacritical mark, ensuring that the short vowel sound of the root word is maintained.

  2. *Changing* y *to* i (*flies, happiest, loneliness*): Words that end in *y* change the *y* to *i* before adding a suffix. The letter *y* at the beginning of a word or syllable acts as a consonant and stands for the /y/ sound. However, the letter *y* at the end of a word either stands for a vowel sound (*fly*) or is part of a vowel digraph (*play*). The change from *y* to *i* ensures that the vowel sound the *y* stands for in the word is maintained.

  3. *Deleting the silent* e (*making*): When a word ends in silent *e*, the letter is removed before adding the suffix (except *s*). Most of the common suffixes begin with vowels and vowel doubling in this case would cause confusion; it would create a vowel digraph.

- Teach only the most commonly used suffixes. The chart on page 255 shows the 20 most frequent suffixes appearing in words in the *Word Frequency*

Book (Carroll et al., 1971). The suffixes *s, es, ed,* and *ing* account for almost two-thirds of the words. The suffixes *s* and *es* are used to form the plurals of most nouns. The suffixes *ed* and *ing* are inflectional endings added to verbs to change their tense. These suffixes are generally introduced to children in grade one and students continue to work on them throughout grade 2 and beyond (e.g., addressing spelling changes when adding these suffixes). The word lists included here are for those suffixes that need to be formally taught in the primary grades.

Rank	Suffix	%	Rank	Suffix	%
1.	s, es (plurals)	31	11.	ity, ty (state of)	1
2.	ed (/d/), ed (/ed/), ed (/t/) (past-tense verbs)	20	12.	ment (action or process)	1
3.	ing (verb form/present participle)	14	13.	ic (having characteristics of)	1
4.	ly (characteristic of)	7	14.	ous, eous, ious (possessing the qualities of)	1
5.	er, or (person connected with)	4	15.	en (made of)	1
6.	ion, tion, (act, process)	4	16.	er (comparative)	1
7.	able, ible (can be done)	2	17.	ive, ative, itive (adjective form of a noun)	1
8.	al, ial (having characteristics of)	1	18.	ful (full of)	1
9.	y (characterized by)	1	19.	less (without)	1
10.	ness (state of, condition of)	1	20.	est (comparative)	1

All other suffixes (about 160) accounted for only 7% of the words.

- Point out that different suffixes are used for different parts of speech. Increasing students' awareness of this can assist them in figuring out new words and how they are used in sentences. A common activity is to provide students with a word and have them put it in a chart divided into four sections: noun, verb, adjective, adverb. Then have students work together to create the other forms of the word to fill in the chart. For example: *agree* (verb), *agreeable* (adjective), *agreement* (noun). Note that for some words there isn't a noun, verb, adjective. and adverb form, but there will be more than one part of speech form for most words.

Noun suffixes: *age, al, ance, ant, ate, ee, ence, ent, er, or, ar, ese, ess, hood, ice, ism, ist, ment, ness, sion, tain, tion, ure*

Suffixes that form adjectives: *able, al, er, est, ette, let, ful, fully, ible, ic, ical, ish, ive, less, ous, some, worthy*

Suffixes that form adverbs: *ly, wards, ways, wide, wise*

Suffixes that create a verb form: *ate, ed, en, ing, ise, ize, yze*

- Incorporate activities to give students practice with suffixes. See the sample activity online: Suffixes: Build a Word (Resource 4.13).

Resource 4.13 can be downloaded from www.scholastic.com/ phonicsintermediate. See page 367 for details on how to access.

Suffixes

STEP 1: Define

Tell students that a suffix is a group of letters added to the end of a base word. A suffix changes the word's meaning and often its part of speech. For example, the suffix -ed is added to the word *depart* (*departed*) to indicate that the action happened in the past. Point out the following suffixes:

-s/-es used to make a word plural
(The letters -es are often used when a word ends in *ch, tch, sh, ss, zz, x.*)
- The *bugs* were all over the tree.
- We went to several *beaches* in Thailand.

-ed used to make verbs past tense
(The -ed can have one of three sounds: /d/, /t/, or /ed/.)
- I carefully *closed* my book.
- I *placed* two plates on the table.
- I have never *acted* in a play.

-ing verb form, present participle
(When adding -ing to a CVC word, you must double the final consonant. When adding -ing to a word ending in e, you must drop the e.)
- We are *painting* pictures for the show.
- I like *running* in the mornings.
- We went *racing* across the gymnasium.

STEP 2: Transition to Longer Words

Help students transition from reading one-syllable words to multisyllabic words. Have them read the word in the first column, then underline the suffix in the word in the second column. Guide students in reading the longer word.

boy	boys
globe	globes
glass	glasses
watch	watches
squint	squinted
phone	phoned
trace	tracing
cover	covering

STEP 3: Build Words

Write the following base words on the board: *catch, miss, bag, line, drift, inch*. Have student pairs add the suffixes -s, -es, -ed, and -ing to build words. Ask them to check the dictionary to confirm spellings.

STEP 4: Apply Decoding Strategy

Have students use the Decoding Big Words Strategy (see page 221) to decode the following words: *reacting, guessing, conditioning, remembering, hibernating*. Remind them to look for suffixes in Step 2 of the strategy.

Suffix Word Lists

-es (plural)					
arches	brushes	dashes	inches	peaches	sizes
ashes	buses	dishes	kisses	presses	sketches
axes	bushes	dresses	latches	prizes	smashes
batches	buzzes	fishes	mashes	pushes	splashes
beaches	cashes	fixes	matches	quizzes	teaches
benches	catches	flashes	misses	ranches	touches
bosses	circuses	gases	mixes	reaches	washes
boxes	classes	glasses	passes	riches	watches
breezes	coaches	grasses	patches	rushes	wishes

-s (plural)					
bags	cakes	dates	kites	plays	tests
beads	capes	days	lakes	plums	toads
beans	caps	dimes	masks	pots	toes
beds	cats	dots	mats	queens	toys
bees	caves	dreams	mitts	rakes	trains
bells	cents	eggs	moms	rats	trays
belts	chains	flakes	mugs	roads	trees
bibs	clocks	gifts	notes	ropes	trucks
bikes	coats	globes	oats	sacks	vans
blocks	cones	hams	paints	sinks	weeks
boats	cots	hats	pans	skates	
bones	cubes	hens	pies	skunks	
boys	cubs	jeans	pigs	socks	
braids	cups	jeeps	pits	sticks	
cabs	dads	jobs	plants	streets	

-ed /d/ (past tense)

bagged	closed	fined	nabbed	robed	snagged
banged	crammed	framed	named	ruled	staged
blabbed	craved	fumed	phoned	sagged	tamed
blamed	cubed	gazed	phrased	scanned	throbbed
bombed	dazed	glazed	planned	schemed	timed
boned	dined	grabbed	poled	scrammed	toned
bragged	doled	holed	prized	shamed	tugged
buzzed	domed	hummed	probed	shaved	tuned
caged	dozed	jammed	raged	sized	used
canned	dragged	jogged	rammed	slammed	
chimed	fanned	lined	rhymed	slugged	
cloned	filed	longed	robbed	smiled	

-ed /ed/ (past tense)

acted	drafted	handed	matted	quoted	squinted
added	drifted	hated	melted	rated	stated
banded	ended	hinted	mended	rested	stranded
batted	faded	hunted	muted	rusted	tempted
blasted	fitted	jaded	nodded	sanded	tended
budded	frosted	jotted	noted	sculpted	tilted
busted	funded	jutted	petted	shaded	toted
ceded	gifted	kidded	planted	shifted	traded
chanted	gilded	knotted	plodded	shredded	trotted
chatted	glided	landed	plotted	sided	trusted
coded	graded	lasted	printed	skated	voted
crated	granted	lifted	prodded	skidded	waded
dated	grunted	listed	prompted	slanted	
dotted	guided	mated	quilted	spotted	

-ed /t/ (past tense)

asked	chomped	guessed	paced	sloped	taped
axed	clapped	helped	passed	smacked	taxed
backed	clashed	hiked	pecked	smoked	thanked
baked	clipped	hoped	picked	snaked	traced
based	coped	hopped	pinched	sniffed	trapped
biked	cracked	iced	placed	spiked	tricked
blinked	crunched	inched	poked	spliced	tripped
boxed	dipped	itched	priced	spruced	tucked
braced	draped	joked	puffed	staked	typed
brushed	dressed	kicked	quaked	stamped	wiped
bumped	dropped	knocked	raked	stepped	wished
bussed	faced	liked	ripped	stitched	zipped
capped	fished	locked	roped	stopped	
cased	fixed	milked	rushed	strapped	
chased	flapped	missed	scraped	striped	
checked	flipped	mixed	shaped	stroked	
choked	griped	napped	sliced	swiped	

-ing (verb form/present tense)

acting	drawing	helping	planning	smashing	waiting
beating	eating	keeping	planting	soaking	walking
blocking	ending	landing	playing	speaking	washing
boating	fainting	leaking	reaching	speeding	watching
boxing	feeding	mashing	resting	sticking	winking
brushing	fishing	matching	ringing	swaying	wishing
catching	fixing	meeting	running	sweeping	
cleaning	flashing	painting	saying	teaching	
covering	floating	painting	sinking	training	
draining	heating	parking	sleeping	treating	

-ly (characteristic of)

abruptly	calmly	crumbly	firmly	mostly	weakly
absolutely	casually	deadly	fluently	nicely	widely
accidentally	certainly	deeply	freshly	possibly	yearly
anxiously	cleanly	eagerly	friendly	rarely	
bitterly	cleverly	easily	generally	sparingly	
boldly	costly	evidently	likely	uniquely	

-er (person connected with)

banker	closer	heater	player	sweeper
blocker	cooker	jogger	reader	simmer
boxer	dreamer	jumper	robber	teacher
builder	eater	leader	runner	user
caller	farmer	logger	singer	washer
catcher	flier	maker	sleeper	worker
cleaner	fryer	packer	speaker	wrapper
climber	gardener	painter	splasher	writer

-or (person connected with)

actor	collector	director	inventor	senator
advisor	conductor	governor	sailor	survivor
auditor	creator	investigator	sculptor	visitor

-ion, -tion (act, process)

abbreviation	application	calculation	commission
addition	appreciation	carnation	communication
admiration	association	celebration	companion
admission	assumption	champion	compassion
adoption	attention	circulation	compensation
ambition	attraction	civilization	competition
animation	audition	collection	completion
anticipation	aviation	collision	complication

comprehension	destruction	identification	quotation
computation	determination	illumination	radiation
concentration	devotion	illustration	reaction
concoction	digestion	implication	reception
concussion	dimension	institution	recollection
condition	direction	investigation	recreation
confirmation	distraction	mansion	reflection
congratulation	diversion	meditation	registration
congregation	education	motivation	rejection
consolation	elevation	multiplication	relation
consultation	eruption	notation	reproduction
contemplation	evaporation	obligation	reservation
conversation	exaggeration	occasion	restriction
coordination	exception	operation	salutation
corporation	excursion	passion	speculation
creation	exhibition	perspiration	subscription
declaration	expectation	plantation	suggestion
decoration	explanation	pollution	superstition
definition	explosion	population	termination
delusion	expression	precaution	tradition
demonstration	fascination	production	vegetation
depression	graduation	profusion	
description	hesitation	pronunciation	
destination	humiliation	qualification	

-able, -ible (can be done)

abominable	delectable	implausible	invincible
acceptable	despicable	impossible	irreplaceable
accessible	digestible	inaccessible	irresistible
affordable	discernible	inadmissible	irresponsible
agreeable	disposable	inadvisable	irreversible
allowable	divisible	inaudible	irritable
answerable	drinkable	incalculable	knowledgeable
applicable	durable	incomparable	liable
appreciable	edible	incomprehensible	lovable
audible	enforceable	inconceivable	malleable
beatable	enjoyable	inconsolable	manageable
bendable	enviable	incorrigible	memorable
breakable	equitable	incredible	movable
capable	erasable	indefensible	navigable
charitable	exchangeable	indelible	negligible
cleanable	fallible	indescribable	nonflammable
coercible	feasible	indestructible	nonnegotiable
collapsible	fixable	indispensable	noticeable
collectible	flammable	indisputable	peaceable
combustible	flexible	inedible	permeable
comfortable	forcible	inescapable	plausible
compatible	formidable	inexcusable	pliable
controllable	gullible	inexplicable	possible
convertible	horrible	inflexible	probable
corruptible	hospitable	innumerable	programmable
coverable	illegible	inoperable	questionable
credible	immeasurable	insatiable	readable
crushable	immovable	inseparable	redeemable
deducible	impassable	insurmountable	regrettable
deductible	impeccable	intolerable	replaceable
deferrable	impenetrable	invaluable	reproducible

-able, -ible (can be done) *continued*

reversible	tangible	uncontrollable	visible
salvageable	thinkable	undeniable	washable
sensible	traceable	unforgettable	workable
sinkable	transferable	usable	
sociable	unbelievable	valuable	

-al, -ial (having characteristics of)

accidental	continental	illegal	psychological
ancestral	conventional	impractical	quizzical
architectural	criminal	industrial	recital
artificial	crucial	ineffectual	removal
astronomical	cylindrical	internal	rhythmical
biblical	disapproval	judicial	sacrificial
bifocal	disposal	magical	seasonal
biographical	economical	mathematical	spiritual
biological	editorial	memorial	supernatural
centrifugal	educational	musical	survival
ceremonial	environmental	mythical	technological
chemical	essential	national	territorial
classical	exceptional	nautical	theatrical
clinical	federal	neutral	traditional
coastal	financial	normal	tribal
colonial	general	original	universal
comical	gradual	pastoral	withdrawal
commercial	guttural	physical	
confidential	historical	political	
conspiratorial	hysterical	potential	

-y (characterized by)

bloody	catchy	clingy	crazy	easy	foxy
bouncy	chubby	kooky	dingy	fluffy	frosty

glassy	itchy	misty	picky	squeaky	toasty
glittery	jerky	moldy	pointy	squirmy	toothy
gloomy	jumpy	mossy	pushy	steamy	tricky
goofy	leafy	musty	rainy	stocky	twisty
grainy	leaky	needy	rubbery	stormy	twitchy
grassy	leery	nosy	rusty	stringy	weighty
gusty	liquidy	oily	savory	stuffy	woody
hairy	lofty	patchy	scanty	sugary	wormy
hefty	lucky	peachy	shifty	summery	
huffy	meaty	peppery	slimy	sweaty	
humpy	messy	perky	snoopy	teary	
inky	minty	pesky	spidery	thirsty	

-ness (state of, condition of)

badness	fairness	quickness	smoothness
baldness	fondness	roughness	sourness
blackness	goodness	roundness	sweetness
brightness	greatness	sadness	thinness
closeness	happiness	shyness	tightness
dampness	illness	sickness	ugliness
darkness	kindness	silliness	unhappiness
dimness	lightness	slowness	weakness
dryness	nearness	smallness	wildness

-ity, -ty (state of)

agility	felicity	loyalty	parity	spontaneity
amnesty	honesty	mediocrity	regularity	unity
civility	humidity	necessity	safety	
falsity	inferiority	obesity	specialty	

−ment (action or process)

advertisement	contentment	entertainment	placement
agreement	detachment	equipment	puzzlement
amazement	development	government	settlement
announcement	employment	improvement	statement
appointment	engagement	movement	treatment
argument	enjoyment	pavement	
arrangement	entanglement	payment	

−ic (having characteristics of)

academic	atmospheric	fanatic	hysteric	sarcastic
acrobatic	autistic	frantic	magnetic	scientific
aeronautic	ballistic	galactic	manic	specific
alcoholic	caloric	generic	mathematics	strategic
allergic	civic	geographic	mythic	sympathetic
angelic	cosmetic	graphic	optimistic	theatrics
antiseptic	economic	gymnastic	pacific	volcanic
artistic	electric	heroic	rhythmic	
astronomic	enthusiastic	hieroglyphic	romantic	
athletic	exotic	historic	rustic	

−ous, −eous, −ious (possessing the qualities of)

adventurous	disastrous	incredulous	officious	subconscious
ambitious	enormous	infectious	precarious	superstitious
anonymous	expeditious	marvelous	presumptuous	tenacious
boisterous	fabulous	miraculous	pretentious	tremendous
cautious	flirtatious	momentous	raucous	vacuous
cavernous	furious	monotonous	repetitious	vigorous
conscientious	glorious	monstrous	scrumptious	zealous
continuous	gorgeous	nauseous	semiconscious	
curious	grievous	numerous	serious	
delicious	impetuous	nutritious	spontaneous	

-en (made of)

barren	darken	frozen	hidden	quicken	stiffen
bitten	deepen	glisten	loosen	sharpen	straighten
blacken	enlighten	harden	madden	shorten	thicken
brazen	fasten	hasten	oaken	soften	woven
broken					

-er (comparative)

bigger	faster	lesser	nicer	slower
brighter	fewer	lighter	older	smaller
busier	fresher	littler	poorer	smoother
cleaner	fuller	longer	prettier	softer
clearer	funnier	louder	quicker	sooner
colder	happier	lower	rounder	straighter
darker	higher	madder	sadder	taller
deeper	hotter	meaner	safer	thicker
earlier	kinder	narrower	shorter	warmer
fairer	larger	nearer	sicker	wider

-ive, -ative, -itive (adjective form of noun)

adaptive	digestive	ineffective	negative	representative
additive	disruptive	informative	objective	respective
captive	effective	insensitive	positive	secretive
cognitive	executive	instructive	prescriptive	sensitive
comparative	exhaustive	inventive	preventive	subjective
competitive	festive	locomotive	primitive	suggestive
consecutive	fugitive	lucrative	productive	talkative
conservative	hyperactive	massive	radioactive	tentative
deceptive	inactive	motive	reactive	
definitive	inattentive	narrative	receptive	
descriptive	incentive	native	repetitive	

-ful (full of)

armful	doubtful	healthful	playful	tasteful
beautiful	fearful	helpful	restful	thankful
bowlful	forceful	hopeful	roomful	thoughtful
careful	forgetful	joyful	skillful	truthful
cheerful	frightful	mouthful	spoonful	useful
colorful	graceful	painful	successful	willful
cupful	handful	peaceful	tankful	wonderful

-less (without)

ageless	hairless	nameless	spotless
blameless	harmless	painless	sunless
careless	headless	penniless	thoughtless
childless	helpless	pointless	timeless
cloudless	homeless	rainless	useless
colorless	hopeless	seamless	waterless
doubtless	lifeless	shapeless	weightless
endless	loveless	shirtless	windless
faceless	meatless	shoeless	worthless
fearless	mindless	sleepless	

-est (comparative)

biggest	fastest	largest	oldest	smallest
brightest	fewest	lightest	poorest	smoothest
busiest	freshest	longest	prettiest	softest
cleanest	fullest	loudest	quickest	soonest
clearest	funniest	lowest	roundest	stillest
coldest	happiest	maddest	saddest	straightest
darkest	healthiest	meanest	softest	tallest
deepest	highest	narrowest	shortest	thickest
earliest	hottest	nearest	sickest	warmest
fairest	kindest	nicest	slowest	widest

Homophones

Homophones are words that sound the same, but have different meanings and spellings. Each homophone pair (or triplet) contains the same number of phonemes, but different graphemes. The spellings of homophones are critical because they provide clues to the word's meaning. You can teach homophones at all grades. Some of the homophones students will encounter are provided in the list below. Students will improve their skills when they read and write homophones in a variety of contexts.

Use these books to add fun to your lessons on homophones:

- *A Chocolate Moose for Dinner* by Fred Gwynne
- *The King Who Rained* by Fred Gwynne
- *Eight Ate: A Feast of Homonym Riddles* by Marvin Terban
- *If You Were a Homonym or a Homophone* by Nancy Loewen
- *Did You Say Pears?* by Arlene Aida
- *Dear Deer: A Book of Homophones* by Gene Barretta
- *Aunt Ant Leaves through the Leaves* by Nancy Coffelt
- *Yaks Yak: Animal Word Pairs* by Linda Sue Park
- *How Much Can a Bare Bear Bear?: What are Homonyms and Homophones?* by Brian P. Cleary
- *A Bat Cannot Bat, a Stair Cannot Stare: More Homonyms and Homophones* by Brian P. Cleary

Homophones		
accept/except	arc/ark	beat/beet
ad/add	ate/eight	been/bin
adds/ads/adz	bail/bale	berry/bury
affect/effect	ball/bawl	billed/build
aisle/I'll/isle	based/baste	blew/blue
aloud/allowed	be/bee	board/bored
altar/alter	beach/beech	brake/break
ant/aunt	bear/bare	brews/bruise

by/buy	fairy/ferry	hole/whole
capital/capitol	fare/fair	hour/our
carat/caret/carrot	feat/feet	in/inn
caught/cot	find/fined	its/it's
ceiling/sealing	fir/fur	Jim/gym
cell/sell	flair/flare	knead/need
cellar/seller	flea/flee	knew/new/gnu
cent/sent/scent	flew/flu/flue	knight/night
cents/scents/sense	flour/flower	knot/not
cereal/serial	for/fore/four	know/no
chalk/chock	forth/fourth	knows/nose
cheap/cheep	foul/fowl	lead/led
chews/choose	gate/gait	leak/leek
choral/coral	grease/Greece	lessen/lesson
clause/claws	great/grate	lie/lye
close/clothes	groan/grown	loan/lone
core/corp	guessed/guest	made/maid
creak/creek	hail/hale	mail/male
cymbal/symbol	hair/hare	man/Maine/mane
days/daze	hall/haul	Mary/marry/merry
deer/dear	hay/hey	meat/meet
dense/dents	heal/heel/he'll	might/mite
desert/dessert	hear/here	mind/mined
dew/do/due	heard/herd	missed/mist
die/dye	here/hear	moose/mousse
doe/dough	hi/high	muscle/mussel
dual/duel	higher/hire	none/nun
earn/urn	him/hymn	oar/or/ore
ewe/yew/you	hoarse/horse	oh/owe
eye/I	hoes/hose	one/won

overdo/overdue	root/route	their/there/they're
paced/paste	rose/rows	theirs/there's
pail/pale	rote/wrote	threw/through
pain/pane	rough/ruff	throne/thrown
past/passed	rung/wrung	thyme/time
patience/patients	sail/sale	tide/tied
pause/paws	scene/seen	to/too/two
peace/piece	sea/see	toad/towed
peak/peek	seam/seem	tow/toe
peal/peel	seas/sees/seize	undo/undue
pear/pair/pare	sew/so/sow	vain/vane/vein
pedal/peddle	shear/sheer	vary/very
plain/plane	shoe/shoo	wade/weighed
pole/poll	shone/shown	waist/waste
poor/pour/pore	side/sighed	wait/weight
praise/prays/preys	sight/cite	ware/wear/where
presence/presents	some/sum	wave/waive
prince/prints	son/sun	way/weigh
principal/principle	stake/steak	we'd/weed
quarts/quartz	stare/stair	we/wee
rain/reign/rein	stationary/stationery	week/weak
raise/rays/raze	steal/steel	weather/whether
rap/wrap	straight/strait	weave/we've
read/reed	suite/sweet	weight/wait
real/reel	sundae/Sunday	which/witch
red/read	tacks/tax	who's/whose
right/rite/write	tail/tale	wood/would
ring/wring	tea/tee	you'll/Yule
road/rode/rowed	team/teem	your/you're
roll/role	teas/tease/tees	

Greek and Latin Roots

English words are derived from three primary origins—Anglo-Saxon, Romance (Latin), and Greek (see chart on page 273; Moats, 1998). About 60% of the words in English text are of Latin and Greek origin (Henry, 1997). Words with Greek roots are common in science and social studies textbooks (Bear, Templeton, Invernizzi & Johnston, 1996; Henry, 1988). Words with Latin roots are common in technical, sophisticated words found in literature and upper-elementary textbooks. Words with Anglo-Saxon roots are common in everyday speech; these words are found in primary-level texts. The following lists contain some of the most common Greek and Latin roots.

Common Latin Roots	
audi:	auditory, audience, audit, auditorium, audible, inaudible, audition
dict:	dictate, predict, dictator, edict, contradict, dictation, indict, prediction
ject:	reject, inject, projection, interjection, eject, objection, dejection
port:	transport, transportation, import, export, porter, portable, report, support
rupt:	rupture, erupt, eruption, interrupt, interruption, disruption
scrib/script:	scribe, describe, manuscript, inscription, transcript, description, prescription
spect:	spectator, inspect, inspector, respect, spectacle, spectacular
struct:	structure, construct, construction, instruct, destruction, reconstruction
tract:	tractor, traction, attract, subtraction, extract, retract, attractive
vis:	vision, visual, visit, supervisor, invisible, vista, visualize, visionary

Common Greek Roots

auto:	automatic, autograph, autobiography, automobile, autocracy
bio:	biology, biosphere, biography, biochemistry, biometrics, biophysics
graph:	graphite, geography, graphic, photograph, phonograph
hydro:	anhydrous, dehydration, hydrogen, hydrant, hydrostatic, hydrophobia, hydrotherapy, hydroplane
meter:	speedometer, odometer, metronome, thermometer, chronometer, perimeter, hydrometer
ology:	geology, theology, zoology, meteorology, phonology
photo:	photography, photocopy, photosynthesis, phototropism, photostat, photogenic
scope:	periscope, stethoscope, telescope, microscope, microscopic
tele:	telephone, telepathy, telegraph, television
therm:	thermos, thermodynamics, thermostat, thermophysics

English Word Origins (Moats, 1998)

Layer of Language	Sound	Syllable	Morpheme
Anglo-Saxon	consonants: single, blends, digraphs vowels: short, long (VCe), teams, diphthongs, r-control	closed open VCe r-control C + -le vowel team (schwa)	compounds (*highlight*) inflections (*ed, s, ing, er, est*)
Romance (Latin)			prefixes (*mis, in*) suffixes (*ment, ary*) roots (*fer, tract*) plurals (*a, ae,* as in *curricula, alumnae*)
Greek	/i/ = y (gym) /k/ = ch (chorus) /f/ = ph (photo)		combining forms (*biography, micrometer*) plurals (*es,* as in *crises, metamorphoses*)

Teaching Guidelines

- Teach common Greek and Latin roots in Grades 4–8 to give students access to a larger number of words. These roots provide clues to word meanings and help students cognitively group related words.

- Teach Greek and Latin roots in categories, such as those related to number, size, or the body (the word lists on pages 277–281 are organized this way). Such grouping will help students efficiently sort and cluster words in their memory.

- Use the following lists of related roots and sample words for instruction on pages 277–281; see Sample Lessons on pages 275–276. However, keep in mind that it isn't necessary or reasonable to teach the meanings of all the roots and their corresponding words. What's important is to teach students key words that they can use to analyze unfamiliar words. Focus on the most common, high-utility roots shown in the lists provided.

- Incorporate activities to give students practice. See the sample activities online in Resources 4.14-4.19: Greek Roots: Word Web, Greek Roots and Combining Forms: B-I-N-G-O, Greek Root and Combining Forms: Speed Drill, Latin Roots: Latin Dictionary, and Latin Roots: Speed Drill.

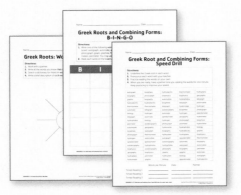

Resources 4.14-4.19 can be downloaded from www.scholastic.com/phonicsintermediate. See page 367 for details on how to access.

Greek Roots (number roots)

STEP 1: Define

Tell students that a root is a basic word part that gives a word the most important part of its meaning. Many English words have roots from Greek, the language of the peoples from ancient Greece. Sometimes Greek roots are combined to form larger words. For example, the Greek roots *auto* and *graph* are used to form the word *autograph*. Teach the meanings of the following Greek roots and combining forms:

> **hemi means "half"** (*hemisphere*)
> **mono means "one"** (*monorail*)
> **tri means "three"** (*tricycle, triplets, triangle*)
> **pent means "five"** (*Pentagon*, the five-sided government building)
> **hex means "six"** (*hexagon*, like a STOP sign)
> **oct means "eight"** (*octagon*)
> **deca means "ten"** (*decade* = ten years)

STEP 2: Transition to Longer Words

Help students transition from reading one-syllable words to multisyllabic words. Have them read the Greek root in the first column, then use that root to read the multisyllabic word in the second column. Help students use the root to determine the meaning of the word.

hemi	hemisphere
mono	monorail
tri	tricycle
pent	pentagon
hex	hexagon
oct	octopus
deca	decade

STEP 3: Build Words

Write the following word parts on the board: *mon, mono, tri, arch, poly, k, graph, rail, tone, logy, sect, cycle, llion, o, ple.* Have student pairs combine the word parts to build as many words as possible. These and other words can be formed: *monarch, monopoly, monk, monograph, monorail, monotone, trilogy, trisect, tricycle, trillion, trio, triple.*

STEP 4: Apply Decoding Strategy

Have students use the Decoding Big Words Strategy (see page 221) to decode the following words: *trisection, monopolize, monastery, octagonal, tricentennial.* Remind them to look for Greek roots in Step 3 of the strategy.

Latin Roots (audi, dict, ject, port, rupt)

STEP 1: Define

Tell students that a root is a basic word part that gives a word the most important part of its meaning. Many English words have roots from Latin, the language of the ancient Romans. For example, the Latin root *port* is used to form the word *portable*. The root *port* means "carried" or "moved." Something that is portable is easily moved from place to place. Teach the meanings of the following Latin roots:

audi means "hearing"
The audience listened to the concert in the auditorium.

dict means "speech/say/speak"
The weather forecaster predicted the terrible winter storm.

ject means "to throw"
Why did he reject our offer to help clean up?

port means "to carry"
The company imports fruit from South America to the United States.

rupt means "to break"
The pipe ruptured, filling the kitchen with water.

STEP 2: Transition to Longer Words

Help students transition from reading one-syllable words to multisyllabic

words. Have them read the Latin root in the first column, then use that root to read the multisyllabic word in the second column. Help students use the root to determine the meaning of the word. Model as needed.

audi	audience
dict	predict
ject	reject
port	export
rupt	rupture
audi	audible
dict	dictator
ject	projection
port	transportation
rupt	interruption

STEP 3: Build Words

Write the following word parts on the board: *audi, dict, ject, port, rupt, ence, pre, re, e, able, ex, im, in, ure, dis*. Have student pairs combine the word parts to build as many words as possible. These and other words can be formed: *audience, predict, reject, eject, portable, export, import, inject, rupture, disrupt.*

STEP 4: Apply Decoding Strategy

Have students use the Decoding Big Words Strategy (see page 221) to decode the following words: *inaudible, auditorium, contradict, objection, eruption.* Remind them to look for Latin roots in Step 3 of the strategy.

Number Roots

Root	Meaning	Words for Instruction
monos **(Greek)**	one	monologue, monarch, monarchy, monogram, monopoly, monopolize, monolith, monolithic, monastery, monk, monorail, monotonous, monochromatic, monocle, monogamy, monograph, monolingual, monomania, mononucleosis, monophonic, monoplane, monosyllable, monotone
unus **(Latin)**	one	unanimous, unanimity, unanimously, unilateral, unilaterally, inch, onion, ounce, unicorn, unicycle, uniform, unify, unique, unit, universal, union, unite, universe, university, unicameral, unicellular, unisex, unison, unitary, univalent
duo (Latin) **duplex** **(Latin)**	two, twofold	duplicate, double, doublet, doubloon, duplicity, duplex
bi **(Latin)**	two	bilateral, bilaterally, bipartisan, bisect, bisection, biceps, bicultural, bicycle, bifocals, bilingual, billion, bimonthly, binoculars, biracial, biweekly, biannual, bicameral, bicarbonate, bicentennial, bicuspid, biennial, bifurcate, bigamy, binomial, biped, biplane, bipolar, bivalve
tri **(Greek)** **tres** **(Latin)**	three	trilogy, trisect, trisection, trisector, triumvirate, tricycle, trillion, trimester, trio, triple, triplet, triplicate, tricentennial, trident, triennial, trinity, tripartite, triplex, triptych
quartus **(Latin)** **quatuor** **(Latin)**	fourth four	quadrant, quartet, quatrain, quadrangle, quadruple, quadruplet, quart, quarter, squad, square, quadraphonic, quadrennial, quadrille, quadripartite, quarry, quarto, quatrefoil
decem **(Latin)**	ten	decimate, decathlon, decade, December, decimal, decagram, Decalogue, deciliter, decimeter, duodecimal
centum **(Latin)**	hundred	bicentennial, centenary, cent, centennial, centimeter, centipede, century, percent, centavo, centenarian, centiliter, centime, centigrade

Body–Parts Roots

Root	Meaning	Words for Instruction
caput, capitis (Latin)	head	cap, capital, capital letter, capitalize, capitol, captain, chapter, chief, kerchief, mischief, recap, cap-a-pie, capitation, per capita, capitalist, capitalism, capitalize, capitulation, capitulate, decapitate, precipice, precipitate, precipitation, precipitous, recapitulation, recapitulate
cerebrum (Latin)	brain	cerebral, cerebrum, cerebration, cerebrate, cerebellum, cerebral cortex, cerebral palsy
facies (Latin)	face, form, shape	deface, defacement, face, face-off, face-saving, facial, surface, typeface, facing, prima facie, efface, façade, facet
frons, frontis (Latin)	front, forehead, face	front, frontage, frontal, frontier, affront, confront, frontispiece, confrontation, effrontery
gurges, gurgitis (Latin)	throat, whirlpool	gorge, gargle, gurgle, disgorge, gargantuan, gargoyle, regurgitate
supercilium (Latin)	eyebrow	supercilious
os, oris (Latin) oro, orare, orai, oratum (Latin)	mouth to speak	adore, oral, inexorable, oracle, oratorio, orotund, peroration, oracular, oration, orate, orator, oratorical, oratory, orifice, osculate, osculation
dens, dentis (Latin)	tooth	indentation, indenture, dandelion, dental, dentifrice, dentist, dentistry, denture, indent, dentate, dentin, dentition, indention, trident
odon, odontos (Greek)	tooth	periodontal, orthodontist, orthodontia, orthodontics
caro, carnis (Latin)	flesh	carnage, carnal, carnation, carnival, carnivorous, charnel, crone, incarnadine, carnality, carnally, carrion, incarnate, incarnation

Body–Parts Roots *continued*

Root	Meaning	Words for Instruction
collum (Latin)	neck	collar, accolade, décolletage, décolleté
corpus, corporis (Latin)	body	corporal, corporate, corpse, incorporate, leprechaun, corpus delicti, corpuscle, esprit de corps, corporality, corporally, corporeal, corporeity, corps, corpulent, corpulence, corpus
cor, cordis (Latin)	heart	accord, according, accordingly, corsage, courage, discord, encourage, record, cordial, concordance, concord, concordant
os, ossis (Latin)	bone	ossify, ossification
derma (Greek)	skin	derma, dermal, dermatitis, pachyderm, dermatology, dermatologist, epidermis, epidermal, epidermic
dorsum (Latin)	the back	dorsal, dossier, endorse, endorsee, endorsement, do-si-do, reredos
gaster, gastreros (Greek)	stomach, belly	gastric, gastronome
nervus (Latin)	sinew, nerve	nerve, nerve-racking, nervous, nervy, unnerve, enervate
sanguis, sanguinis (Latin)	blood	sanguine, sanguinary, sanguinity, sangfroid, consanguinity, consanguineous
sedeo, sedere, sedi, sessum (Latin)	to sit, to settle	assess, hostage, preside, president, resident, residue, sediment, session, sewer, siege, subsidize, subsidy, assiduous, assiduity, dissident, dissidence, séance, obsession, presidium, sessile, sedentary, supersede
manus (Latin)	hand	emancipate, emancipation, manacle, mandate, manifest, manifestation, manifestly, manifesto, manipulate, manipulation, manipulative, command, commend, demand, maintain, manage, maneuver, manicure, manner, manual, manufacture, manure, manuscript, amanuensis, countermand, legerdemain, manumission

Body–Parts Roots *continued*

Root	Meaning	Words for Instruction
dextra (Latin)	right hand	dexterity, dexterous, ambidextrous, ambidexterity, digitalis, digitigrade, prestidigitation
digitus (Latin)	finger	digital, digit
flecto, flectere, flexi, flexum (Latin)	to bend	flex, flexible, inflexible, reflector, reflex, flexure, reflexive, deflect, deflection, genuflect, genuflection, inflection, inflect, inflected, reflection, reflect, reflective
rapio, rapere, rapui, raptum (Latin)	to snatch	enraptured, rape, rapid, rapids, rapture, ravenous, rapacious, rapacity, rapt, raptly, raptness, surreptitious, surreptitiously, rapine, ravine, ravish, surreptitiousness
plico, plicare, plicavi, plicatum (Latin)	to fold	complicity, duplicity, accomplice, apply, complex, comply, display, duplex, duplicate, employ, multiply, pliant, plight, supply, triplicate, explicate, explicable, explication, explicative, deploy, implicate, multiplex, multiplicity, plissé, replicate, explicit, implicit, exploit, exploitable, exploitation, exploiter, imply, implication, ploy, ply, supplicate, suppliant, supplicant, supplication
prehendo, prehendere, prehendi, prehensum (Latin)	to catch, to seize, to grasp	apprehend, apprentice, comprehend, enterprise, prison, prize, surprise, misprision, prehensile, reprise, apprehensible, apprehension, apprehensive, comprise, entrepreneur, impregnable, reprehend, reprehensible, reprehension, reprisal
pes, pedis (Latin)	foot	biped, expedition, moped, pedal, pedestrian, pedicure, pioneer, quadruped, expedient, expediency, expediently, expedite, expeditious, expeditiously, impede, impediment, pedigree, pedometer, peon, peonage, cap-a-pie, expeditionary, millipede, pedicab, pied-á-terre, sesquipedalian
pous, podos (Greek)	foot	octopus, tripod, antipodes, antipodal, antipode, podiatry, podium, chiropody, platypus
gradior, gradi, gressum (Latin)	to step, to walk	aggression, aggressive, aggressiveness, degradation, congress, degree, grade, gradual, graduate, ingredient, progress, transgress, egress, ingress, degrade, degraded, digress, digression, digressive, gradation, gradient, regress, regression, regressive

Body–Parts Roots *continued*

Root	Meaning	Words for Instruction
ambulo, ambulare, ambulavi, ambulatum (Latin)	to walk around	ambulance, somnambulist, ambulatory, circumambulate, perambulate, perambulator, ambulant, ambulate, preamble
calcitro, calcitrare, calcitravi, calcitratum (Latin)	to kick	recalcitrant, recalcitrance, recalcitrantly
sto, stare, steti, statum (Latin) **statio, stationis (Latin)** **sisto, sistere, steti, statum (Latin)**	to stand a standing, a standing position to cause to stand, to put, to place	constituent, desist, destitute, destitution, interstice, obstinate, obstinacy, oust, ouster, prostitute, prostitution, restitution, restive, restiveness, stance, static, subsist, subsistence, arrest, assist, circumstance, consistency, constant, constitute, constitution, contrast, cost, distant, exist, insist, instant, obstacle, persist, resist, rest, stable, stage, stand, state, station, stationary, statistic, statue, status, substance, substitute, superstition, extant, instate, obstetrics, reinstate, stanch, stanchion, statute

Other Useful Word Lists

Additional word lists related to intermediate grade word study skills follow. Use these as needed to supplement your lessons, create spelling lists, or include in word study games and activities (see pages 295–302).

Contractions

I'm	could've	here's	aren't	let's
they're	I've	he's	can't	I'll
we're	might've	it's	couldn't	it'll
you're	should've	she's	didn't	he'll
	they've	that's	doesn't	she'll
	we've	there's	don't	that'll
	would've	what's	hadn't	they'll
I'd	you've	where's	hasn't	we'll
it'd		who's	haven't	you'll
she'd			isn't	
there'd			mustn't	
they'd			needn't	
we'd			shouldn't	
you'd			wouldn't	

Synonyms

add/total	during/while	illegal/wrong
after/following	earth/world	income/earnings
all/every	eat/consume	injure/hurt
anger/rage	end/finish	insult/offend
appear/look	enough/sufficient	job/occupation
appreciative/thankful	error/mistake	jump/leap
arrive/reach	fat/chubby	just/fair
ask/question	fetch/get	keep/save
baby/infant	find/locate	kind/considerate
back/rear	fix/mend	large/big
before/prior	forgive/excuse	last/persist
begin/start	fortune/wealth	late/tardy
below/under	fragile/delicate	leave/depart
bitter/tart	freedom/liberty	like/enjoy
brave/courageous	frequent/often	listen/hear
call/yell	giant/huge	little/small
car/vehicle	gift/present	make/build
change/swap	give/donate	mark/label
city/town	grab/take	mean/cruel
close/shut	grow/develop	mend/repair
continue/persist	guide/lead	messy/sloppy
dangerous/hazardous	happy/glad	mistake/error
decrease/lessen	hasten/hurry	model/example
delay/postpone	heal/cure	move/transport
demonstrate/show	high/tall	naughty/bad
different/diverse	hold/grasp	near/close
dislike/detest	huge/vast	neat/tidy
divide/split	idea/concept	need/require

new/fresh	relax/rest	untidy/messy
obey/follow	repeat/echo	uproar/noise
odor/smell	revise/change	use/apply
often/frequently	rule/law	usual/common
omit/delete	safe/secure	utter/talk
operate/use	say/tell	vacant/empty
overdue/late	scrape/scratch	vacation/break
own/have	scream/shout	value/worth
pack/fill	sharp/pointed	vanish/disappear
pain/ache	shove/push	vary/change
pair/couple	slam/bang	violent/rough
part/piece	sour/tart	vital/necessary
peak/summit	splash/spray	wag/wave
perform/act	spring/bounce	wail/cry
pick/choose	tear/rip	walk/stroll
praise/applaud	terrify/scare	warn/alert
quaint/odd	thin/slender	wash/clean
quake/shake	tiny/small	well/healthy
quick/fast	touch/feel	whack/hit
quiet/silent	trail/path	whole/entire
quit/stop	try/attempt	yank/pull
quiz/test	tug/pull	yell/shout
rage/fury	understand/know	yummy/tasty
rain/shower	undo/untie	zilch/nothing
raise/increase	unstable/wobbly	zoom/rush
record/write	untamed/wild	

Antonyms

above/below	birth/death	dirty/clean
absent/present	black/white	dry/wet
achieve/fail	blame/forgive	dull/bright
add/subtract	blunt/sharp	dwarf/giant
admire/dislike	boring/exciting	eager/lazy
admit/reject	bottom/top	early/late
adult/child	boy/girl	earn/spend
afraid/confident	break/fix	east/west
against/for	bright/dim	easy/difficult
alive/dead	buy/sell	effect/cause
all/none	cause/effect	empty/full
allow/forbid	cheap/expensive	ending/beginning
alone/together	clean/dirty	enemy/friend
always/never	cold/hot	enjoy/hate
ancient/modern	come/go	enter/exit
answer/question	cooked/raw	even/odd
appear/vanish	cool/warm	evening/morning
arrive/depart	coward/hero	evil/good
ask/tell	cruel/kind	exciting/boring
asked/told	cry/laugh	fact/fiction
asleep/awake	curved/straight	fail/pass
attack/defend	dangerous/safe	false/true
back/front	dark/light	fancy/plain
backward/forward	day/night	far/near
beautiful/ugly	deep/shallow	fast/slow
before/after	defend/attack	fat/thin
beginning/end	different/same	female/male
big/little	dim/bright	few/many

fiction/fact	hot/cold	messy/tidy
find/lose	icy/warm	morning/evening
finish/start	ill/healthy	most/least
first/last	illegal/legal	multiply/divide
flexible/rigid	imaginary/real	narrow/wide
float/sink	improve/damage	near/far
follow/lead	in/out	never/always
foolish/wise	increase/decrease	new/old
for/against	inside/outside	night/day
forget/remember	joy/grief	no/yes
forward/backward	kind/cruel	noisy/quiet
friend/stranger	large/small	north/south
from/to	last/first	nothing/everything
front/back	late/early	obey/command
frozen/melted	laugh/cry	odd/even
girl/boy	lead/follow	often/seldom
give/take	learn/teach	old/young
go/stop	left/right	on/off
good/bad	less/more	open/close
guilty/innocent	light/dark	over/under
happy/sad	long/short	pain/joy
hard/soft	loose/tight	pass/fail
harm/help	lose/find	plain/fancy
hate/love	lose/gain	pleasure/pain
heal/hurt	lose/win	poor/rich
hear/ignore	loud/soft	present/absent
heavy/light	love/hate	private/public
high/low	low/high	push/pull

question/answer	short/long	tall/short
quick/slow	shout/whisper	tame/wild
raise/lower	shut/open	thick/thin
real/imaginary	silly/serious	to/from
remain/change	simple/complex	top/bottom
repair/break	sit/stand	true/false
rich/poor	slow/fast	ugly/pretty
right/wrong	small/large	under/over
rough/smooth	smooth/rough	up/down
rude/polite	soft/hard	white/black
sad/funny	spend/earn	whole/part
sad/glad	start/finish	with/without
safe/dangerous	stop/start	work/play
same/different	sunrise/sunset	yes/no
shallow/deep	sweet/sour	young/old

Homographs

Homographs are words that are spelled the same but are different in meaning and origin. When they are pronounced differently, they are called heteronyms.

affect	content	gum	match	root
ball	contest	hatch	mean	row
band	contract	heel	minute	saw
bank	converse	hide	miss	school
bark	count	intern	mole	seal
bass	crow	invalid	object	second
bat	date	jam	palm	sewer
batter	desert	jumper	peaked	slip
bay	does	kind	peck	slug
bill	dove	lap	pen	sock
bit	down	last	pitcher	sow
bow	ear	lead	pool	story
bowl	entrance	left	pop	subject
box	excuse	lie	pound	tear
bridge	fair	light	present	tick
buffet	fan	like	primer	toll
can	file	line	pupils	top
close	fine	loaf	read	use
commune	fit	lock	record	well
compact	flat	long	refuse	wind
conduct	fly	mail	rest	wound
console	ground	mat	ring	yard

Portmanteau Words

Portmanteau words are made of two words that are blended into one.

autobus	automobile + bus	**skylab**	sky + laboratory
brunch	breakfast + lunch	**smash**	smack + mash
clash	clap + crash	**smog**	smoke + fog
hi-fi	high fidelity	**squiggle**	squirm + wiggle
o'clock	of the clock		

Eponyms

Eponyms are words made from the names of people and places.

America	Amerigo Vespucci
bikini	Bikini Atoll in the Pacific Ocean where atomic bombs were tested
bologna	city in northern Italy
bunsen burner	Robert Bunsen, German chemist
candy	French Prince Charles de Condé (con-Day)
cheddar	village in England where cheese was invented
Ferris wheel	George Washington Ferris, inventor
frankfurter	city in Germany: Frankfurt
Geiger Counter	German physicist, Hans Geiger
hamburgers	Hamburg, Germany
jeans	Italian city of Genoa, spelled GENE in middle English
Levi's	Levi Strauss, creator
marathon	a race named after the Greeks won the battle at Marathon in 490 B.C. and a messenger ran 26 miles to take news to Athens
sandwich	English Earl of Sandwich
teddy bear	President Theodore "Teddy" Roosevelt, who refused to shoot a small bear on a hunting trip
thug	gang of professional hoodlums who roamed northern India; comes from the word *thag*, which means *cheat* or *thief*

Spelling Demons

a lot	appearance	career	difficulty
about	appreciate	cemetery	dining
abrupt	arctic	certain	disappear
absence	are	chief	disappoint
accommodate	argument	choose	discipline
accumulate	arrangement	close	disease
accurate	athletic	clothes	dissatisfied
ache	audience	colonel	division
acquire	beautiful	color	doctor
across	because	column	does
address	been	come	doesn't
adequate	before	coming	don't
adjourn	beginning	committee	done
advice	believe	conscience	early
again	benefited	continuous	easy
all right	bicycle	correspondence	eighth
almost	blue	cough	embarrass
also	break	could	enough
always	breathe	country	environment
amateur	brilliant	courteous	equipped
among	built	criticism	especially
analysis	bulletin	curiosity	every
angle	business	cylinder	everybody
another	buy	dear	everyone
answer	by	decision	exaggerate
any	calendar	definitely	excellent
anyone	campaign	didn't	except
apologize	can't (cannot)	difference	excited
apparently	canceled	different	existence

experience	happily	into	lose
extremely	have	irrelevant	maintenance
familiar	having	it's (it is)	making
fascinate	he's	its	maneuver
favorite	hear	jealous	manufacture
February	heard	jewelry	many
field	height	journey	marriage
finally	here	judgment	mathematics
first	heroes	just	meant
foreign	hoarse	khaki	medicine
formally	hole	kindergarten	might
formerly	hoping	knead	mileage
forty	hour	knew	miniature
friend	humorous	know	minute
fulfill	hurriedly	knowledge	miscellaneous
fundamental	I'd	laboratory	misspell
getting	I'm	laid	mortgage
glimpse	illegible	laugh	much
gorgeous	illustrate	leisure	muscle
government	imaginary	let's	myself
governor	immediately	library	naturally
grammar	incidentally	license	necessary
groceries	independence	licorice	new
guarantee	indispensable	lightning	nickel
guard	instead	likely	niece
guess	intelligence	listen	ninety
guidance	interesting	livelihood	ninth
half	interpreted	loneliness	no
handsome	interrupt	loose	none

noticeable	piece	religious	strength
nuisance	pleasant	repetition	studying
o'clock	possession	restaurant	succeed
occasion	precede	rheumatism	sufficient
occur	privilege	rhubarb	sugar
occurred	probably	rhythm	sure
off	procedure	ridiculous	surprise
often	proceed	right	tear
omission	professor	safety	temperature
omitted	pronunciation	said	temporary
once	psychology	says	tendency
one	pumpkin	schedule	terrible
opinion	pursue	school	that's
opportunity	quantity	scissors	their
opposite	quarrel	seems	then
original	quite	seize	there
our	raise	separate	therefore
pamphlet	read	sergeant	they
parallel	ready	severely	they're
particular	realize	shoes	thorough
pastime	really	similar	though
peaceable	receive	since	thought
people	recognize	sizable	threw
performance	recommend	some	through
permanent	rehearse	something	tired
personal	relevant	sometimes	to
personnel	relief	souvenir	together
persuade	relieve	straight	tomorrow

tongue	usually	week	won
tonight	utensil	went	won't
too	vacancy	were	would
transferred	vacuum	what	wouldn't
trouble	vegetable	when	write
Tuesday	very	where	writing
two	vinegar	whether	wrote
typical	visible	which	yacht
unanimous	volume	who	yield
undoubtedly	want	who's	yolk
unique	was	whole	you're
unnecessary	we're	wholly	your
until	wear	whose	youth
upon	weather	with	zealous
used	Wednesday	women	

Shortened Words (Clipped Words)

These are the result of people shortening words for greater efficiency.

auto	automobile	**mart**	market
bike	bicycle	**math**	mathematics
burger	hamburger	**memo**	memorandum
cab	cabriolet	**mum**	chrysanthemum
champ	champion	**phone**	telephone
clerk	cleric	**photo**	photograph
cuke	cucumber	**plane**	airplane
doc	doctor	**ref**	referee
dorm	dormitory	**specs**	spectacles
exam	examination	**stereo**	stereophonic
fan	fanatic	**taxi**	taxicab
flu	influenza	**teen**	teenager
gas	gasoline	**tux**	tuxedo
grad	graduate	**typo**	typographical error
gym	gymnasium	**vet**	veterinarian
lab	laboratory	**zoo**	zoological gardens
limo	limousine		

25 Quick-and-Easy Phonics and Word Analysis Games

Many wonderful educational games and activities providing phonics practice are available from educational supply companies. However, countless simple and engaging activities requiring limited preparation and materials can also be used. Here are some of the easiest and best activities I've collected over the years.

Resource 4.20:
Word Card Template*

1 **Word-Building from English Roots** Provide students with a list of base words and a set of prefixes and suffixes. Have them combine the word parts to create and present new words.

2 **Word Webs with Latin and Greek Roots** On the board write a root word related to a social studies or science lesson in your curriculum. State the word's meaning and the language it comes from, then have students create a web of related words. Suggest that they search textbooks and dictionaries. Then have them provide definitions for the words on the web. Ask students to present their lists and display them in the classroom.

Resource 4.21:
Word Web Template*

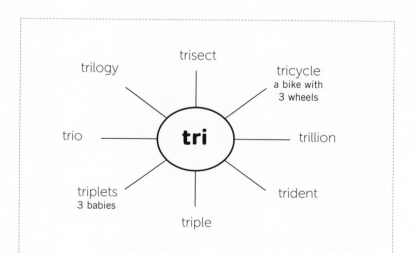

*Resources can be downloaded from www.scholastic.com/phonicsintermediate. See page 367 for details on how to access.

3 **Root Search** Write a common root on the board. Provide its meaning and the language it comes from. Have students brainstorm a list of words they think come from this root. Then have them check the dictionary to check their accuracy. Challenge students to find new words related to the root. Use the lists on pages 277–281 to create a Root-Word Dictionary.

4 **Beat the Clock** This is a timed word-recognition activity. Provide pairs of students with word lists and have the partners time each other on reading the lists. Have the children monitor and record times at the beginning and end of each week.

5 **Word Detective** List key words, syllable patterns, or roots for the week. Give students a point every time they see a words in print, or use one of the words (or another word containing the word, syllable pattern, or root) in speech or writing. Tally points at the end of the week and award prizes (e.g., select the book for oral reading for the week, earn extra recess time).

Resources 4.22 and 4.23 provide a sample Bingo game for consonant + *le* words.*

6 **Syllable Bingo** Make copies of a bingo game board and a set of picture cards whose names contain selected syllables. (Choose syllables from the lists on pages 204–218 and 230–235.) Put the syllables in a different order for each game board, and use each syllable at least twice per board. Place the picture cards in a bag. Syllable Bingo is played just like regular bingo. Before the game begins, give each player a game board and ample space markers. The caller (teacher) draws one picture card from the bag and displays it. If a player's game board contains the syllable in the picture's name, he or she places a marker over the space. The first player to get five markers in a row (vertically, horizontally, or diagonally), yells "Syllable Bingo!" The player then states aloud the syllable as the caller checks it against the picture cards drawn from the bag. If these match, the player wins. Players then clear their boards, the picture cards go back in the bag, and a new game begins.

7 Spin It! Cut out three spinners and dials. See example provided at right. On the outside edge of the first spinner, write the word parts *un* and *re*. On the outside edge of the second spinner, write the word parts *able*, *apply*, *cover*, *born*, *cap*, *check*, *cook*, *cut*, *fasten*, *fold*, *friend*, *load*, *mark*, *name*, *pack*, *paid*, *safe*, *sold*, *tie*, *wise*, and *wrap*. On the outside edge of the third spinner, write the word part *ed*. Paste the spinners in sequence on a piece of tag board or the inside of a folder. Using a brass fastener, attach the dials to the spinners. Then have each student spin all three spinners. If a word can be formed, the student writes it on a sheet of paper. Each word is worth one point. Students can continue until they have formed five words, or students can challenge one another to see who can form the most words.

Resource 4.24:
Spinner Templates*

8 Phonogram Families Create letter cards by writing a consonant, cluster, or digraph on a template such as the one in Resource 4.25. Make enough so that each student has three to five cards. Distribute cards to students. Then display a phonogram card; see phonogram lists on pages 126-191. Students who hold a card that, when combined with the phonogram card, forms a word come to the front of the classroom. They are "members" of this phonogram "family." Invite each student to place a card in front of the phonogram card and blend aloud the word formed.

Resource 4.25:
Letter Card Template*

9 Build It Draw a house or pyramid on a sheet of paper, or use the template in Resource 4.26; see image at right. Divide the house or pyramid into smaller segments, such as squares, rectangles, or triangles. Make a copy of the page and distribute one to each student. Then make a set of word-building cards. On each card write a consonant, cluster, digraph, vowel, or phonogram, depending on the phonics skills you are reviewing. Provide enough cards so that many words can be formed. Divide the class into small groups. Place a set of cards facedown on the table or floor

Resource 4.26:
Build It Graphic
Organizer*

*Resources can be downloaded from www.scholastic.com/phonicsintermediate.
See page 367 for details on how to access.

in front of each group. One at a time, each student in the group draws a set of five cards and builds as many words as possible, and each student writes his or her word in one segment of the house or pyramid, or colors in one segment. The student who builds (completes) the house or pyramid first wins.

10 **Syllable Checkers** On each square of an old checkerboard, write a word containing a syllable-spelling pattern that you want students to review. The game is played just like checkers, except players must read the word on each space they land on. If a player cannot read the word, he or she returns to the original space.

11 **Word Part Hunt** Assign each student a syllable, prefix, suffix, or root that you want to review. You might have students work with a partner or in small groups. Then have the students search for objects in the classroom whose names contain the word part. In addition, you might have them search through books, magazines, and newspapers for words that contain the word part. Provide time for students to share their findings.

12 **Environmental Print Boards** As you teach each syllable spelling pattern or root word, challenge students to find examples of the word parts in words on signs, cereal boxes, advertisements, junk mail, and other environmental print items. Have them bring these items to class (suggest that they take a photo or draw a picture if it's a large sign) and attach them to an environmental print bulletin board to refer to throughout the week.

13 **Graph It** Your students can create graphs that combine language arts with math concepts. For example, instruct students to search a passage for all the words with *-ble*, *-ple*, *-zle*, and *-tle* and list them. Have them use their list to create a bar graph showing the number of words found for each.

14 **Word Baseball** Divide the class into two teams. One at a time, each team member is "up at bat." Show the student a word card. If the player reads the word card, he or she can go to first base. As players reach home, their team gets a point. If a player can't accurately read the word, the team gets an "out." The team at bat continues until it has three outs. The team that earns more points after nine innings wins. (You might want to limit the game to fewer innings.) To make the game more exciting, level the word cards. Some words are worth a base hit, others are worth a double or triple, and a few are worth the treasured home run. In addition, you might ask the player at bat to read the word, and then state a related word or a word that contains the same syllable, prefix, suffix, or root.

15 **Concentration** This classic game can be played by 2–3 students to review almost any skill. Make a set of 12–20 playing cards. On each card write a word. For example, if you are reviewing compound words, you'll write words that, when combined, can form compound words. Place the cards facedown on the table or floor. Each player chooses two cards. If the cards form a compound word, the player keeps them. The player with the most cards at the end of the game wins. When reviewing vowel sounds, make a set of cards in which students can find rhyming word pairs.

16 **Password** This game is played by partners. Make a set of word cards with a multisyllabic word on each card; see word list on pages 235-236. One partner selects a card, then provides clues to his or her partner. For example, if a student draws the word card "sunflower," he or she might say: "My word is a compound word. The first syllable describes something very bright." The student continues providing clues until the partner figures out the word.

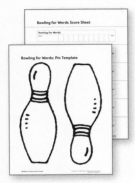

Resources 4.27
and 4.28 can be used
for Bowling for Words*.

17 **Bowling for Words** Make a bowling score sheet for each student (see Resource 4.27, shown at left). Then make a set of large paper or tagboard bowling pins using the template in Resource 4.28. On each pin write a word and a number from 1–10. The words with the highest numbers should be the most difficult to read. Divide the class into small teams. Place the bowling pins in a bag or box so that they cannot be seen. One player from each team reaches in and selects a bowling pin. If the player can correctly read the word, the score on the bowling pin is recorded on the score sheet. If the player can't read the word, she receives a "gutter ball," or a score of 0. The game ends when all ten frames of the bowling game have been played and the scores tallied. You might want to have the teams use calculators to tally their scores.

BOWLING FOR WORDS										TOTAL
Max	6	0	7	8	1	0	3	9	0 2	36

18 **Word Sort** Provide students with sets of word cards. First have the students sort the cards any way they choose (e.g., by common syllables or roots). Then suggest a specific way for the students to sort the words. Be sure that the words you include can be sorted in more than one way (e.g., multisyllabic words containing -le, -al, and -el).

19 **What's Missing?** Write a brief story or paragraph on a chart or board. Place self-sticking notes over every fifth or tenth word. Or, select words with target skills you want to review and cover those up. As an alternative, you might write the story or paragraph, leaving blanks for each word you want students to figure out. When you read the story and get to a missing word, have students guess it. Before telling the students whether or not they are correct, write the correct spelling for the first syllable and allow students to modify their guesses. (For example, you would write *ba* for the first syllable in the word *bagel*.) Continue in this fashion until the word is completely spelled.

20 **Unscramble It** Divide the class into teams of three to four students. Provide each team with a list of ten scrambled words. Give each team five minutes to unscramble as many words as possible. The team that unscrambles the most words wins. **Alternative:** Provide each team with scrambled sentences.

21 **Make a Match** Make word-part note cards—one for each student; see Resource 4.29, shown at right, for a sample. Be sure that all the cards can be combined with at least one other card to form a word. Distribute the cards. You might want to play music while the students circulate and search for their match—the student with another word part that can be combined with their card to form a word. When all the students find their match, provide time for them to share their words with the class. Continue with other word part cards, or challenge students to find another match.

Make a Match Word-Part Cards			
ap	ple	bat	tle
set	tle	bun	dle
fa	ble	no	ble
mar	ble	nee	dle
puz	zle	wig	gle

Resource 4.29:
Make a Match
Word-Part Cards*

22 **Word Card File** At the beginning of the year, have students bring in a card file box and blank index cards. Set aside time each week for students to write on one of their cards a word they are having trouble reading or spelling. Have them organize the cards in alphabetical order, and suggest that they add a sentence or picture clue to their cards to help them remember the words. Students should periodically review the cards in their card-file boxes. Point out times when looking at the file cards may help them with reading or writing.

23 **Syllable Race** Create a game board such as the one shown at right. Then make word cards, each containing a two-, three-, or four-syllable word. In turn, each player draws one card and reads the word aloud. If she reads it correctly, she moves forward on the game board as many spaces as there are syllables in the word. Consider writing this number under the word on each card for students to refer to. The game continues, until a player reaches the end.

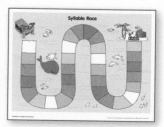

Resource 4.30: Syllable Race
Game Board*

*Resources can be downloaded from www.scholastic.com/phonicsintermediate.
See page 367 for details on how to access.

24 **Book Chat** Divide the class into small groups of four to five students. Ask each student to share a book he has recently read by talking briefly (a few sentences) about it. Students may also enjoy reading aloud a favorite paragraph or page of their book. If the book is fiction, remind students to avoid giving away the ending. Encourage students to read one of the books they heard about in their book chat. These chats honor students' accomplishments and remind them of the purpose of learning phonics—to read great books.

25 **Time It** Make one set of word cards using only base words and another using only prefixes and suffixes; see lists on pages 248–253 and 258–268. (See sample in Resource 4.31, shown at left.) Divide the class into small teams, then mix the cards and give an equal number to each group. Use a three-minute egg timer to time the game as the teams use their cards to form words. Designate one member of each team to record the words. At the end of the game, each team reads aloud the words they formed. The team with the most points (one per correctly formed word) wins.

Word-Part Cards: Time It

un	re	dis	in
do	quick	happy	solve
taste	big	use	side
play	freeze	ness	able
ly	y	er	ing

Resource 4.31 can be downloaded from www.scholastic.com/ phonicsintermediate. See page 367 for details on how to access.

Building Fluency

"Fluency...the neglected goal of reading instruction."

—Richard Allington

Recently, after several amazing trips to Israel, I began studying Hebrew. Since Hebrew doesn't employ the English alphabet, I was forced to learn a whole new set of symbols and sound-spelling correspondences. At first, these strange-looking squiggles and lines were meaningless to me. I tried everything I use with my students to learn them as quickly as possible. I wrote each letter as I said its sound. I created a set of flash cards and went over the cards several times a day. I even found a computer program that focused on learning the letters and contained mastery tests. After a couple of weeks, I felt ready to tackle my first simple Hebrew text. As I began to read, I struggled through every word, searched my mind for each letter-sound, blended the sounds together, then tried to recall the meaning of the word I had pronounced. Often, by the time I worked my way to the end of a sentence, I had forgotten what was at the beginning. My slow, labored, and inefficient reading was (and still is, unfortunately) characteristic of one who has not acquired reading fluency.

The Tale of Five Balloons by Miriam Roth

What Is Fluency?

Fluency is "the ability to read smoothly, easily, and readily with freedom from word recognition problems" (Harris & Hodges, 1995). Fluency is necessary for good comprehension and enjoyable reading (Nathan & Stanovich, 1991; Langenburg, 2000). A lack of fluency is characterized by a slow, halting pace; frequent mistakes; poor phrasing; and inadequate intonation (Samuels, 1979; Young & Rasinski, 2016)—all the result of weak word recognition skills.

Fluent reading is a major goal of reading instruction because decoding print accurately and effortlessly enables students to read for meaning. Fluency begins in Stage 2, the "Confirmation, Fluency, and Ungluing from Print" stage (see Chall's Stages of Reading Development, page 21), around grades 2 to 3 for many students. During this fluency stage, the reader becomes "unglued" from the print; that is, students can recognize many words quickly and accurately by sight and are skilled at sounding out those they don't recognize by sight. A fluent reader can:

- **read at a rapid rate** (pace—the speed at which oral or silent reading occurs)
- **automatically recognize words** (smoothness— efficient decoding skills)
- **phrase correctly** (prosody—the ability to read a text orally using appropriate pitch, stress, and phrasing)

Non-fluent readers read slowly and spend so much time trying to identify unfamiliar words that they have trouble comprehending what they're reading.

Automaticity theory, developed by LaBerge & Samuels (1974), helps explain how reading fluency develops. **Automaticity** refers to knowing how to do something so well you don't have to think about it. As tasks become easier, they require less attention and practice. Think of a child learning to play basketball; as initial attention is focused on how to dribble the ball, it's difficult for the child to think about guarding the ball from opponents, shooting a basket, or even running quickly down the court. However, over time, lots of practice makes dribbling almost second nature. The player is ready to concentrate on higher-level aspects of the game.

Three Signs of Automaticity

A student is reading fluently if he can:

1. read with expression
2. read aloud and then retell the story or content of the selection (decode and comprehend at the same time)
3. comprehend equally well a similar passage read if listened to

For reading, automaticity refers to the ability to recognize many words as whole units quickly and accurately. The advantage of recognizing a word as a whole unit is that words have meaning, and less memory is required for a meaningful word than for a meaningless letter. The average student needs between 4 and 14 exposures to a new word to recognize it automatically. However, students with reading difficulties need 40 or more exposures to a new word. Therefore, it's critical that students get a great deal of practice reading stories at their independent reading level to develop automaticity (Beck & Juel, 1995; Samuels, Shermer, & Reinking, 1992).

To commit words to memory, students need to decode many words sound by sound, and then progress to recognizing the larger word chunks. Now, instead of focusing on sounding out words sound by sound, the reader can read whole words, thereby focusing attention on decoding and comprehension simultaneously. In fact, the hallmark of fluent reading is the ability to decode and comprehend at the same time.

Evaluating Slow Readers

To find out why a student is reading slowly, ask her to read a passage from a book below her reading level. If she reads the passage slowly, her problem is probably poor fluency. If she can read the text easily, she's probably having trouble with decoding or comprehension. One way to determine whether the student's problem is with decoding or with comprehension is to have her read an on-level passage and then ask her a series of questions. If she accurately answers 75% or more of the questions, then the problem is one of weak decoding skills. To help this student with her decoding skills, have her read from material at a lower level, involve her in repeated reading or echo readings, and dictate stories to her for reading instruction and practice.

Another way to determine why a student is reading slowly is to give him a running list of the words he will encounter in a text. If he can't recognize 95% of the words, then decoding is likely the issue. If he does recognize 95% or more of the words but has difficulty reading, then comprehension or fluency is the issue. A major reason students experience reading difficulty is that too much is taught too fast. Go back to where they are successful and start again.

Richard Allington (1983) called fluency the "neglected goal" of reading instruction. In 2000, the National Reading Panel cited fluency as one of the "big 5" aspects of reading instruction, and a flood of fluency books and trainings followed. Fluency remains a key focus of reading instruction, and all aspects of learning need to be evaluated from a fluency perspective. However, many curricular materials, with their larger number of discrete skills covered each academic year, have an exposure focus to skills rather than a mastery focus. When teachers adopt a mastery focus, it changes the way they teach and assess (Blevins, 2016). There are many reasons why students fail to read fluently. Allington cites the following:

- **Lack of exposure.** Some children have never been exposed to fluent reading models. These children come from homes in which there are few books and little or no reading.
- **The good-reader syndrome.** In school, good readers are more likely to get positive feedback and more likely to be encouraged to read with expression and make meaning from text. Poor readers receive less positive feedback, and the focus of their instruction is often solely on figuring out words or attending to word parts.
- **Lack of practice time.** Good readers generally spend more time reading during instructional time and therefore become better readers. Good readers also engage in more silent reading. This additional practice stimulates their reading growth. Poor readers spend less time actually reading.
- **Frustration.** Good readers are exposed to more text at their independent reading level, whereas poor readers frequently encounter text at their frustration level. Consequently, poor readers tend to give up because they make so many errors.
- **Missing the "why" of reading.** Good readers tend to view reading as making meaning from text, whereas poor readers tend to view reading as trying to read words accurately.

Measuring Reading Rate

To determine a student's oral reading rate, take a one-minute, timed sampling of his oral reading of a passage at his reading level. Make a copy of the passage for the student and one for yourself so you can record his errors while he reads. As the student reads, follow along and mark on your copy any words he reads incorrectly. Use the guidelines below. For example, if a student stops or struggles with a word for 3 seconds, tell him the word and mark it as incorrect. Place a mark after the last word he reads. Then, tally the results and consult the chart on page 309, which shows national norms for oral reading rates of students in grades 2–8. Using these norms, you can determine how your students rate nationally and which students need more work in developing fluency.

Oral Reading Fluency–Test Scoring Guidelines

Words read correctly. These are words that the student pronounces correctly, given the reading context.

- Count self-corrections within 3 seconds as correct.
- Don't count repetitions as incorrect.

Words read incorrectly. Count the following types of errors as incorrect: (a) mispronunciations, (b) substitutions, and (c) omissions. Also, count words the student doesn't read within 3 seconds as incorrect.

- Mispronunciations are words that are misread: *bell* for *ball*.
- Substitutions are words that are substituted for the correct word; this is often inferred by a one-to-one correspondence between word orders: *dog* for *cat*.
- Omissions are words skipped or not read; if a student skips an entire line, each word is counted as an error.

3-second rule. If a student is struggling to pronounce a word or hesitates for 3 seconds, tell the student the word, and count it as an error.

Oral Reading Fluency Norms, Grades 2-8

(Hasbrouck & Tindal, 2006)

For additional details on the study used to create these norms, see "Oral Reading Fluency: 90 Years of Measurement" available at the University of Oregon's web site: brt.uoregon.edu/tech_reports.htm.

Grade	Percentile	WCPM Fall	WCPM Winter	WCPM Spring	Average Weekly Improvement
2	90	106	125	142	1.1
	75	79	100	117	1.2
	50	**51**	**72**	**89**	1.2
	25	25	42	61	1.1
	10	11	18	31	0.6
3	90	128	146	162	1.1
	75	99	120	137	1.2
	50	**71**	**92**	**107**	1.1
	25	44	62	78	1.1
	10	21	36	48	0.8
4	90	145	166	180	1.1
	75	119	139	152	1.0
	50	**94**	**112**	**123**	0.9
	25	68	87	98	0.9
	10	45	61	72	0.8
5	90	166	182	194	0.9
	75	139	156	168	0.9
	50	**110**	**127**	**139**	0.9
	25	85	99	109	0.8
	10	61	74	83	0.7
6	90	177	195	204	0.8
	75	153	167	177	0.8
	50	**127**	**140**	**150**	0.7
	25	98	111	122	0.8
	10	68	82	93	0.8
7	90	180	195	202	0.7
	75	156	165	177	0.7
	50	**128**	**136**	**150**	0.7
	25	102	109	123	0.7
	10	79	88	98	0.6
8	90	185	199	199	0.4
	75	161	177	177	0.5
	50	**133**	**151**	**151**	0.6
	25	106	124	124	0.6
	10	77	97	97	0.6

WCPM = Words Correct Per Minute

NOTE: Students who fall 10 or more words below the 50th percentile need a fluency-building program and/or additional instructional focus, including more frequent assessment to monitor progress.

Measuring Oral Reading Fluency

In order to help students develop fluency, you must first know their oral reading accuracy and rate. There are several measurement tools you can use to identify the accuracy and rate, and nationally normed averages exist. Many state standards now include these rates as benchmarks of students' reading progress. The combination of reading accuracy and rate is referred to as a student's oral reading fluency (ORF). It is expressed as "words correct per minute" (WCPM).

It is essential to measure both accuracy and rate. For example, if you measure only accuracy, you wouldn't know that it takes one student twice as long to read the same text as it does another student. Which student is fluent? Likewise, if you measure only rate, you wouldn't know that one student, who could read a text much more quickly than another student, makes significantly more mistakes. Which student is fluent?

Ways to Develop Fluency

There are many things you can do to develop your students' fluency. Rasinski (1989) has identified six ways to build fluency.

1 Model fluent reading

Students need many opportunities to hear texts read. This can include daily teacher read-alouds, books on tape, and books read by peers during book-sharing time. It's particularly critical for poorer readers who've been placed in a low reading group to hear text read correctly because they are likely to hear repeatedly the efforts of other poor readers in their group. They need proficient, fluent models; that is, they need to have a model voice in their heads to refer to as they monitor their own reading. While you read aloud to students, periodically highlight aspects of fluent reading. Point out that you are reading dialogue the way you think the character might have said it, or how you

Books on tape are great for developing a student's listening vocabulary.

speed up your reading when the text becomes more intense and exciting. Talk about fluency—how to achieve it, and why it's important. Continually remind students that with practice they can become fluent readers. An important benefit of daily read-alouds is that they expose students to a wider range of vocabulary.

2 Provide direct instruction and feedback

Direct instruction and feedback in fluency includes, but isn't limited to, independent reading practice, fluent reading modeling, and monitoring students' reading rates. Here are some ways to include lots of this needed instruction in your classroom.

Explicitly teach students the sound-spelling correspondences they struggle with, high-utility decoding and syllabication strategies, and a large core of sight words.

Have students practice reading new or difficult words prior to reading a text.

Occasionally time students' reading. Have students create charts to monitor their own progress. Encourage them to set new reading-rate goals.

Include oral recitation lessons (Hoffman, 1987; Hoffman & Crone, 1985). With this technique, the focus is on comprehension. Introduce a story and read it aloud. Discuss the content with the class and have the class create a story summary. Then discuss the prosodic (phrasing and intonation) elements of the text (e.g., reading dialogue as if it is spoken; reading all caps louder; the difference between question and statement voices; understanding a character's expressed emotion—anger, sadness, joy, or disgust; reading longer phrases with appropriate pauses). Then have students practice reading sections of the story both on their own and with your guidance. Finally, have individual students read sections of the story aloud for the class. Monitor each student's reading rate and word-recognition accuracy.

Teach students about "smooshing" the words together. Some poor readers mistakenly believe that they are supposed to read each word separately; consequently, they always sound like they are reading a list. Model fluent reading by reading a passage without pauses between words. Then read the passage using appropriate pauses and phrasing. Discuss the differences.

Explain the return-sweep eye movement. For some students, return sweeps are difficult. As a result, they lose their place as they read. A common technique to overcome this is to place a sheet of paper or bookmark under the line as one reads and move it down line by line. For many students this is disruptive because it halts the natural return-sweep motion, so some reading specialists suggest placing the bookmark above the line to avoid interfering with the return sweep. To illustrate for students how our eyes move as we read, poke a hole in a sheet of paper and hold it twelve inches away as you read a passage. Have the students comment on the jerkiness of your eyes (and your reading) as you move from word to word and line to line. This observation can result in an "aha moment" for some students.

Teach students about the eye-voice span. When we read aloud, there is a distinct and measurable distance between our eye placement and our voice. Our eyes are one to three words ahead of our oral reading. To illustrate this phenomenon, copy a story or passage onto a transparency. As you are about to finish a paragraph, turn off the transparency. Students will be amazed that you can still say a few words. They'll see how fluent readers phrase appropriate chunks.

Find alternatives to "round-robin" reading. Round-robin reading is one of the most harmful techniques for developing fluency. During round-robin reading, students read aloud only a small portion of the text. Although they are supposed to be following along with the other readers, often they don't. It is absolutely essential that students read a lot every day. When they're reading a new story, it is important that they read the entire story—often more than once. One way to avoid round-robin reading every day is to have students read the story silently a few pages at a time and then ask them questions or have them comment on strategies they used. Other appropriate techniques include partner reading, reading softly to themselves while you circulate and "listen in," and popcorn reading, in which students are called on frequently and randomly (often in the middle of a paragraph) to read aloud. If you use any technique in which students have not read the entire selection during their reading group, be sure that they read it in its entirety before or after the reading group.

Teach appropriate phrasing and intonation.
Guided oral reading practice and the study of punctuation and grammar can help. To teach appropriate phrasing, see page 318 (#5). For teaching intonation and punctuation, use some or all of the following. Have students:

- **recite the alphabet as a conversation.**
  ABCD? EFG! HI? JKL. MN? OPQ. RST! UVWX. YZ!
- **recite the same sentence using different punctuation.**
  Dogs bark? Dogs bark! Dogs bark.
- **practice placing the stress on different words in the same sentence.**
  I am tired. I <u>am</u> tired. I am <u>tired</u>.
- **practice reading sentences as if talking to a friend.**

Studying grammar fosters fluency because grammar alerts the reader to natural phrases in a sentence. For example, being able to identify the subject and the predicate of a sentence is one step in understanding phrase boundaries in text. Also, understanding the role of prepositions and conjunctions adds additional clues to phrase boundaries. Try providing students with short passages color-coded according to subject and predicate to assist them in practice reading.

- **Conduct two-minute drills to underline or locate a target word, syllable, or spelling pattern in an array or short passage** (Moats, 1998). This will help students rapidly recognize spelling patterns that are common to many words. And it's a lot of fun.
- **Motivate students to read using incentives, charting, and rewards.** You want to encourage students to practice reading for long enough periods of time to build accuracy and then automaticity in decoding.

3 Provide reader support (choral reading and reading-while-listening)

Readers need to practice reading both orally and silently. Research has shown that oral reading is very important for the developing reader, especially younger children. It appears that young children need to hear themselves read, and they benefit from adult feedback. As well as improving reading, this feedback shows students how highly we adults value the skill of reading. It is beneficial for intermediate grade students to continue to read orally on occasion to you, the teacher, to evaluate their fluency, and to partners during independent work time to assist each other in developing their reading skills. There are several ways to support students' oral reading without evoking the fear and humiliation struggling readers often feel when called on to read aloud. Here are the most popular techniques (always use text at the student's instructional level that models natural language patterns):

- **Reading simultaneously with a partner or small group.** With this technique, students can "float" in and out as appropriate without feeling singled out. For best results, have students practice reading the selection independently before reading it with the partner or group.

- **Echo reading.** As you read a phrase or sentence in the text, the student repeats it. This continues throughout the text. You can also use a tape recording of the text with pauses for the student to echo the reading.

- **Reader's theater.** Students choose a favorite part of a book, reading it aloud independently until they're confident, and then read it aloud to the class. This reading can be primarily for class enjoyment or it can be part of the student's oral book report.

- **Choral reading.** Reading together as a group is great for poetry and selections with a distinct pattern.

- **Paired repeated readings** (Koskinen & Blum, 1986). A student reads a short passage three times to a partner and gets feedback. Then the partners switch roles. To avoid frustration, it works best to pair above-level readers with on-level readers and on-level readers with below-level readers.

- **Books on tape.** Select and place appropriate books on tape in a classroom listening center. Have students follow along as the book is read, reading with the narrator where possible. An excellent books-on-tape collection is Read 180 Audiobooks (Houghton Mifflin Harcourt). These books contain audio models that periodically help students work through comprehension difficulties.

4 Repeated readings of one text

Repeated reading, a popular technique developed by Samuels (1979), has long been recognized as an excellent way to help students achieve fluency. It has been shown to increase reading rate and accuracy and to transfer to new texts. As a student reads a passage at his or her instructional level, the teacher times the reading. Afterwards, the teacher gives feedback on word-recognition errors and the number of words per minute the student read accurately, then records this data on a graph. The student should practice reading the same selection independently or with a partner. The process is repeated, and the student's progress plotted on the graph until the passage is mastered. This charting is effective because (1) students become focused on their own mastery of the task and competing with their own past performance, and (2) students have concrete evidence that they are making progress. In addition, repeating the words many times helps students build a large sight-word vocabulary.

Students who resist rereading selections need incentives. Besides simply telling the student that rereading is a part of the important practice one does to become a better reader, you might motivate her by having her:

- read to a friend, family member, or pet
- read to a student in a lower grade
- read into a tape player to record the session
- set a reading-rate goal for a given passage and try to exceed that goal in successive readings
- prepare to perform a reader's theater version of a selection.

Note: This technique is NOT recommended for students already reading fluently.

5 Cueing phrase boundaries in text

One of the characteristics of proficient (fluent) readers is the ability to group words together in meaningful units—syntactically appropriate phrases. "Proficient reading is characterized not only by fast and accurate word recognition, but also by readers' word chunking or phrasing behavior while reading connected discourse" (Rasinski, 1989). Students who are having trouble with comprehension may not be putting words together in meaningful phrases or chunks as they read. Their oral reading is characterized by a choppy, word-by-word delivery that impedes comprehension. These students need instruction in phrasing written text into appropriate segments.

One way to help students learn to recognize and use natural English phrase boundaries—and thus improve their phrasing, fluency, and comprehension—is **phrase-cued text** practice. Phrase-cued text is a short passage marked by a slash (or some other visual) at the end of each phrase break. The longer pause at the end of the sentence is marked by a double slash (//). The teacher models good oral reading, and students practice with the marked text. Later students apply their skills to the same text, unmarked. Have students practice the skill orally for 10 minutes daily.

Here's an example:

In the summer/I like/to swim/at the beach.//
Although it's very hot/I like the idea/
of being in the cool water
all day.// Summer truly is/
my favorite time/of the year.//

Phrase-Cued Text Practice Routine

Use the following routine for phrase-cued text practice sessions, which should take about 10 minutes a day, several times a week. Select passages on each student's instructional reading level. Make two copies of the passage. On one copy, mark the natural phrase boundaries; leave the other copy unmarked.

Day 1

1. Select, copy, and distribute a marked text passage (approximately 100–250 words) written at the students' reading level. Explain the format, and tell students that good phrasing will improve their comprehension. Assure them that, with practice, they will get used to reading from marked text.

2. Model reading the marked text aloud as students use their copies to follow along silently. Do this two or three times. Invite students to comment on what they observed about your phrasing and expression.

3. Have students use the marked text to read aloud chorally. They will have additional opportunities to practice throughout the week.

Day 2

1. Once again, model reading aloud the marked text.

2. Have students chorally read aloud from copies of their marked text two or three times. Encourage students to comment on their reading and give them your feedback. Also discuss the content of the passage.

3. Have students practice reading aloud the marked text in pairs or small groups. Encourage them to exchange constructive feedback.

Day 3

1. Have students use the marked text to read aloud chorally.

2. Follow up by having students practice reading aloud in pairs or small groups.

3. You may wish to have students tape record themselves so they can assess their own reading.

4. Encourage students to find opportunities during the day to practice reading their marked text.

Day 4

1. Distribute the unmarked version of the text.

2. Ask each student to read aloud the passage without the phrases marked. Give each reader feedback on his or her reading.

3. Have students practice reading the unmarked text in pairs. They may also tape record themselves and compare their various readings.

Day 5

1. Meet with each student individually. Ask him or her to read the unmarked version of the text. Note phrasing, appropriate pauses, expression, and reading rate. Give the student positive feedback.

2. Encourage students to take the passage home and read it to an adult.

6 Provide students with easy reading materials

Students need an enormous amount of individualized reading practice in materials that are not too difficult (Beck & Juel, 1995; Samuels, Shermer, & Reinking, 1992). I recommend at least 30 minutes of independent reading every day. Some should occur in school, and some can occur at home. Fluency develops through a great deal of practice reading stories in which students can use sound-spelling strategies (as opposed to contextual strategies) to figure out a majority of the unfamiliar words. In the early grades, there must be a match between instruction in phonics and reading practice—hence the need for practice stories that are decodable. This match encourages students to adopt sound-spelling strategies and at the same time, through extensive practice reading story after story after story, leads to fluent reading. This match should continue for students who struggle to read in the intermediate grades until they develop fluency with basic sound-spellings in context. It is critical that practice-reading materials not be at a student's frustration level. In other words, the student's reading accuracy (the proportion of words read correctly) should be above 90%. During individualized practice, students may be reading at different levels. They read aloud "quietly" to themselves as the teacher walks around listening to each student for a minute or so while still monitoring the group as a whole. Students need time to figure out unfamiliar words through phonic patterns. Expecting students to read fluently when they are not fluent only encourages guessing and memorization. For differentiated fluency instruction and practice techniques and routines, I recommend *Tiered Fluency Instruction: Supporting Diverse Learners in Grades 2–5* by Chase Young and Timothy Rasinski.

Meeting the Needs of Struggling Readers

❝Reading failure [is] a public health problem with major consequences and costs.❞

—Reid Lyon

What do Thomas Edison, Albert Einstein, Woodrow Wilson, Nelson Rockefeller, Hans Christian Andersen, George Patton, Galileo, Leonardo da Vinci, Michelangelo, Winston Churchill, and Tom Cruise have in common? These notable individuals were all dyslexic. Each struggled in his own way to master the art of reading.

One of the most difficult aspects of teaching is watching a child struggle with learning to read. During one of my early years of teaching, I was given a class of thirty grade 2 and 3 readers who were struggling. My class was designated a Chapter 1 classroom. Most of my students had serious reading difficulties, and a few received additional assistance from the Resource Room teacher. However, many received all their instruction from me and my teaching partner, a highly-skilled veteran instructor. The range of abilities in the class was broad. Matthew was a non-alphabetic reader with almost no sight-word knowledge. Bradley had severe motor-coordination problems that hampered his ability to form letters. Christon couldn't recall the alphabet. Brian had serious behavioral problems. Billy's learned helplessness and lack of motivation were a constant issue. Darlene could read on grade level but couldn't organize her thoughts and ideas logically. Jason had accurate but labored decoding skills. And the list went on.

This same situation exists in many classrooms across the country, but with only one full-time teacher in the room. By the time students enter the intermediate grades, the range of abilities is often extremely broad. Certainly, meeting the individual needs of each student in your classroom is perhaps the greatest challenge you will face.

State-of-Reading Statistics

Many sobering statistics regarding the state of reading instruction in this country circulate in the media each year. According to the 2015 National Assessment of Educational Progress, only 36% of fourth-graders read at or above the proficient level. This is a slight improvement from 1994, when 30% of students achieved proficient or above status. What was even more sobering back in 1994 (and little has changed) was that only 5% to 6% of these children can be classified as having severe learning disorders (Lyon, 1996). "The others are likely to be suffering the consequences of inappropriate teaching, low standards, and/or disadvantageous environmental circumstances for learning to read" (Moats, 2000). In addition, Miller (1993) cited the following:

- **Approximately 60 million U.S. citizens read below the eighth-grade reading level.**
- **About 85% of the juveniles appearing in juvenile court are functionally illiterate.**
- **Approximately 50 to 60% of U.S. prison inmates are functionally illiterate.**
- **About 75% of the unemployed adults are illiterate.**

It is evident that learning to read goes well beyond an educational issue; it is an extremely serious and important social issue. As the researchers at the National Institute of Child Health and Human Development report, "reading failure . . . constitutes not only an urgent challenge for our schools, but a public health problem with major consequences and costs" (Alexander & Entwisle, 1996; Lyon, 1995).

In a country with such tremendous wealth and resources, there is no excuse for the high numbers of children who leave our schools unable to meet the most basic reading demands of adult life. We must do all that we can to reverse these dispiriting statistics. Solutions often cited include improved teacher training, adequate instructional materials, smaller class sizes, family and community support, early preventive measures, and strong intervention programs. These are all important and could help. However, in today's classrooms you face today's reality—a reality that may not come close to these ideals. Who are these below-level readers, and how can you help them given the resources available?

Struggling Readers—They Have a Variety of Problems

We skilled readers read regularly for information and for pleasure. However, for many students reading is neither easy nor enjoyable. While some students seem to learn to read with relative ease, others experience great difficulties. Students with reading difficulties can possess a wide range of language deficits. Those with learning disabilities or who have dyslexia have normal or high intelligence and have no problems with vocabulary or understanding English syntax. However, they have trouble with sounds and print. Estimates reveal that 10% to 20% of the student population has this problem. Some estimates say the percentage is even higher. Recent statistics also reveal that as many girls as boys have difficulties learning to read.

Struggling readers might have problems with phonemic awareness, phonics, comprehension, or processing verbal information. They might also lack the auditory and visual skills needed for reading. Often, memory and concentration are a problem. The causes are many—educational, psychological, physiological, and social. Some educational factors that have been cited as causes of reading difficulties include: teaching reading skills too early, instruction that ignores a child's unique needs, inappropriately paced instruction, and large class size. A child's emotional reaction to these difficulties can compound the problems. Because of their lack of success, struggling readers often view themselves as incapable of learning to read. This "learned helplessness" may cause them to give up and resist making an effort. "Part of teaching children with reading problems is convincing them that they can learn to read, despite their experience to the contrary" (Stahl, 1997).

To help students with reading problems (see "Four Types of Struggling Readers" on the following page), it's critical to assess what they can and cannot do and then plan an intervention program to meet their unique instructional needs. What these students need may not be a different reading program or method, but rather adjustments to their existing program that include more time, more instructional support, and more practice reading connected text. All four types of struggling readers generally suffer from low motivation, low levels of practice, and low expectations. These have to be taken into consideration, too.

"Phonics must not be made to carry the whole burden of reading instruction, especially if students have difficulty with it. Although research and experience have demonstrated again and again that phonics knowledge and skill are essential for learning to read, and that they speed up learning to read, there is also considerable evidence that reading development depends on wide reading of connected text, the development of fluency, and the growth of vocabulary, knowledge and reasoning. Thus, it is wise for all students, even those having extreme difficulty with phonics, to read books they find interesting, learn the meanings of ever more difficult words, and continue to acquire knowledge."

—Chall & Popp, 1996

Four Types of Struggling Readers

Non-alphabetic: These children have difficulties during the first stage of reading development. They don't grasp the alphabetic principle. Since their word-recognition skills are extremely poor, in their efforts to read they try to depend on visual clues, such as a word's shape, length, or position on the page. These students need a great deal of phonological awareness training, and benefit most from explicit instruction in recognizing the alphabet and learning sound-spelling relationships.

Compensatory: These children have a limited grasp of the alphabetic principle and weak phonemic-awareness skills. Without a knowledge base of sound-spelling relationships, they have trouble decoding words. As a result, they compensate by relying on context clues and on their sight-word knowledge. These children do okay with easy material, but have serious difficulties when the reading demands increase.

Non-automatic: These readers can accurately sound out words, but with great effort. Since their word-recognition skills are not automatic, decoding requires much of their mental energies, and comprehension suffers. These children need practice and repetition to build fluency. They may also have motivational problems.

Delayed: These readers have automatic word-recognition skills, but acquired them much later than their peers. They lack comprehension skills because they were still concentrating on decoding when they were taught those skills. Therefore, when the reading materials became more complex—with many more multisyllabic words—they weren't ready for the increased comprehension demands. These children need a great deal of instruction on learning and using comprehension strategies. They might also benefit from further instruction in phonics and spelling.

Ways to Help Your Strugglers Succeed

When you note that a student has a reading problem, and have diagnosed it, it's time to intervene and turn things around. Effective interventions are generally characterized by the following:

- They are applied as early as possible (as soon as a problem is diagnosed).
- They involve well-trained, highly skilled teachers and specialists.
- They are intensive.
- They can close the reading gap for poor readers.
- They are short lived, lasting only as long as needed.
- They help children overcome "learned helplessness."
- They connect in terms of instructional strategies and content to the reading instruction occurring in the classroom with the "general student population."

In addition to these characteristics, the following techniques will support intervention instruction:

Prompting. While students read a passage, provide prompts that help them focus attention on reading strategies. For example, when a student encounters an unfamiliar word, use prompts such as, "What letter sounds do you know in the word?" or "Are there any word parts you know in the word?" You can also create and display Strategy Picture Cards or bookmarks for students to refer to when they're reading independently. These cards provide written and illustrated cues to help overcome reading stumbling blocks. For example, one card might remind students to "reread a confusing sentence or passage."

Assisted Reading. Give students a chance to read with assistance from you or with an audiocassette. Gradually decrease the assistance until the student is reading independently. Assisted readings are particularly helpful for text that is at a student's frustration level.

Supported Contextual Reading. This technique, developed by Stahl (1997), is designed to help students use their phonics knowledge. The assumption is that students with reading difficulties often do possess phonics knowledge, but are unable to use it effectively. First, read aloud to the student the text of some material one or two years above her instructional level and ask comprehension questions to make sure she understands the passage. This takes advantage of the student's oral listening skills and promotes concept development. Next, do an echo reading of the text with the student. Then send the text home with guidance for the family to help the student practice reading it. Finally, have the student reread the text multiple times in class until she has mastered the passage.

Cloze Passages. Select a passage that the student has previously read or that has been read to him. Leaving out every fifth or tenth word, write the passage on a chart. (You can insert blank lines in place of the words or cover them with self-sticking notes.) Now ask the student to use his background knowledge and understanding of English syntax to fill in the missing words. I like to provide the first letter or cluster of letters in each word to help the student use phonics cues, too.

Teacher Read-Alouds. Oral reading is critical for developing a student's listening and speaking vocabularies and world knowledge. Since students with reading difficulties are not developing these through their reading, they must be read to a lot.

Word-Family Construction. Building words belonging to the same word family can help students' reading and spelling by focusing their attention on common word parts. Use letter cards, pocket charts, apps such as Magnetic Alphabet, or any other type of manipulatives available. You might use the word families to create lists for a Word Wall in your classroom.

Read Aloud Tests. When I give content area tests, say in science or social studies, I read aloud the tests to my struggling readers. This enables me to assess more accurately their content knowledge rather than their ability to read the test.

Four Principles of Effective Intervention

As I reflect on my years of teaching and the mountain of reading research on intervention, many theories and guidelines emerge regarding meeting the individual needs of students. I will focus on four principles that I have found to be most useful.

Principle 1

Begin instruction at the level students need it most. Treat the cause, not just the symptoms of reading difficulties. This requires looking at deficits in prerequisite skills.

Principle 2

Assess, assess, assess. Effective diagnosis and ongoing assessment are critical.

Principle 3

Select the appropriate literature for instructional and independent uses. Be careful to avoid providing literature that is always at students' frustration level.

Principle 4

Maintain consistency. Using multiple instructional methods can confuse students. Use one clearly designed method of instruction, not a multitude of methods and techniques that may be at odds with one another.

Principle 1

Begin intervention at the level students need it most.

Sometimes we tend to treat the symptoms of reading difficulties, rather than the causes. For example, I recently encountered a teacher who was spending a lot of time reteaching sound-spelling relationships to one of her students. She commented that this didn't seem to be having much effect. When I asked her if the student had weak phonemic awareness skills, she didn't know. We did a phonemic awareness assessment and discovered that his skills were quite weak. He couldn't orally blend words effectively and had little knowledge of how words work. I suggested the student receive phonemic awareness training. It helped.

This anecdote illustrates the need to determine a student's lowest deficit skill and begin instruction there. To do otherwise is like building a house on sand. Without a strong foundation, the house is sure to collapse. Skills prerequisite for phonics instruction include phonemic awareness and alphabet recognition. I should point out that simply treating a lower-deficit skill isn't necessarily enough to correct the reading problem. It will indeed remove a reading road block, but more must be done. "The lowest level deficit should be identified and repaired, followed by a reevaluation of the reader for additional problems, and by further instructional intervention to repair newly identified problems" (Royer & Sinatra, 1994).

> "Provisions must be made for the student's continued conceptual and informational development while the reading issues are dealt with. If not, the reader will lose out on the knowledge, vocabulary, and concepts needed for further education and also as background information for reading in [later stages] and beyond" (Chall, 1996, pp. 119–120).

Although intervention techniques might not differ much from regular classroom instructional methods, once you determine where to start, be sure that you:

- begin your intervention right away.
- teach only one skill at a time and teach it until it is over-learned.
- adjust the pace at which you introduce skills. Allow students time to master each skill before moving on.
- continually review and reinforce learning.
- continually apply the learning to real reading and writing. Reading in context is critical.

Principle 2

Assess, assess, assess.

When students enter the intermediate grades, their phonic decoding abilities vary significantly. To provide effective and purposeful instruction, it's important to assess each student's phonics skills and develop differentiated instruction based on the results. A comprehensive diagnosis of each student is necessary. Both formal and informal assessments can assist you. Using your findings, frequently monitor the student's progress to determine the causes of reading difficulties and the success of your teaching strategies. I am constantly reminded of the old saying, "An ounce of prevention is worth a pound of cure." Certainly the best way to prevent reading difficulties is properly designed instruction and early detection of difficulties. However, even with these safeguards, some students will persist in struggling with decoding, and continual assessment will be necessary.

You can assess students in many ways, including the following:

- **Screening assessments** for phonics, phonemic awareness, and writing/spelling
- **Checklists** for phonics, phonemic awareness, and reading and writing attitudes
- **Miscue analysis (running records)** for assessing reading accuracy, identifying and analyzing consistent reading errors, and determining instructional and independent reading levels
- **Individual and group-administered tests** including formal assessments, basal reading program tests, and reading inventories

- **Portfolios** containing students' work throughout the year

Standardized diagnostic test batteries, with tests or subtests measuring word recognition, include the Stanford Diagnostic Reading Test (Karlsen, Madden, & Gardner, 1985), the Woodcock Reading Mastery Test–Revised (Woodcock, 1998), and DIBELS 6th Edition (University of Oregon, 2014). All have good reliability and validity. I have also provided the six quick assessments for you to use. See pages 333–334 for a descriptions of each, and access the assessments online; see page 367 for details.

In addition, many informal assessments such as observation and miscue analysis can provide you with enough vital information to guide instruction and determine what a student already knows. It's important to collect diagnostic information daily, weekly, and monthly.

Frequent and systematic observations of students' reading abilities will also help you in modifying instruction to meet individual needs. To be sure you observe your students regularly, establish a system or observation schedule. For example, you might choose one student to observe per school day, keeping the dated record and analysis in the students' files to monitor their progress during the year. Select a time when you can hear the student read without interruptions. Repeat observations more often for students for who need intervention.

Principle 3

Select the appropriate literature for instructional and independent uses.

Not only do students need to be reading successfully during formal reading instruction, they need to have successful independent reading opportunities each day. Students need to read text with which they have a sense of control and comfort. The relationship between silent reading (and out-of-school reading) and reading growth has been well documented (Rosenshine & Stevens, 1984). As Allington (1984b) pointed out, good first-grade readers read about

1,900 words a week, whereas their poor-reader counterparts read only about 16 words a week. By the middle grades, an average reader reads approximately 1,000,000 words a year, whereas a poor reader may read only 10,000 words. You can't become a skilled reader if you rarely read. The following guidelines highlight the differences among a student's independent, instructional, and frustration reading levels.

> "To encourage optimal progress with the use of any of these early reading materials, teachers need to be aware of the difficulty level of the text relative to a child's reading level. Regardless of how well a child already reads, high error rates are negatively correlated with growth; low error rates are positively linked with growth. A text that is too difficult, then, not only serves to undermine a child's confidence and will but also diminishes learning itself." (State Superintendent of Public Instruction and the State Board of Education in California, 1996, pp. 12–13)

To determine a student's independent, instructional, and frustration reading levels, use an individual reading inventory. During an individual reading inventory, a student is asked to read a passage or series of passages and then given sight-word tests, graded word lists, or comprehension questions. Many commercially produced reading inventories are currently available.

Levels of Reading

- **Independent or free reading level:** The level at which a student can read a text without the teacher's assistance. Comprehension should average 90% or better, and word recognition should average 95% or better.

- **Instructional reading level:** The level at which a student should receive reading instruction. The student reads with teacher guidance, and is challenged enough to continue reading growth. Comprehension should average 75% or better, and word recognition should average 90% or better.

- **Frustration reading level:** The level at which a student cannot read a text adequately. At this level, the student frequently shows signs of discomfort. Comprehension averages 50% or less, and word recognition averages less than 90%.

Six Quick Word–Recognition Tests

These assessments, Resources 6.1-6.6, can be downloaded from www.scholastic.com/phonicsintermediate. See page 367 for details on how to access.

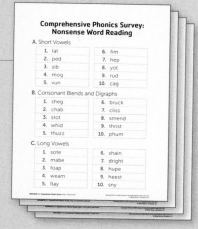

1 The **Comprehensive Phonics Survey** was developed so that students' sight-word knowledge wouldn't interfere with an assessment of their decoding abilities.

2 The **Names Test** (Cunningham, 1990) was developed for teachers who are less comfortable with nonsense-word assessments. Having the students read names (not sight words, but not nonsense words) has these advantages over other decoding tests:

- On other tests, some students are able to recognize words not because they can decode them, but because they know them as sight words. These tests tell you little about the students' phonics skills.
- Some students find reading nonsense words (an alternative to the above problem) confusing and attempt to make real words out of nonsense words.
- Name reading provides a context and purpose for reading isolated words.
- Most names are familiar and, therefore, in the student's listening vocabulary.

3 The **San Diego Quick Assessment** (Lapray & Ross, 1969) contains words common to children's reading materials at each of the grade levels included.

Six Quick Word–Recognition Tests *continued*

4 The **TOWRE** (Test of Word Reading Efficiency) was developed by Torgeson, Wagner, & Rashotte (1999) and is distributed by PRO-ED. These easily-administered tests take only 45 seconds each (I've included two parts of the test—one to measure phonemic decoding ability and one to measure sight-word ability). They test a student's ability to sound out words accurately and rapidly as well as recognize familiar sight words.

5 The **Sight Word Proficiency and Automaticity Assessment** checks a student's ability to accurately and effortlessly read the 150 most frequent words in English text. Reading these words proficiently is critical to fluent reading.

6 The **Phonological Awareness Assessment** identifies students who need phonological awareness training before they can benefit from phonics instruction.

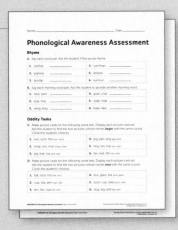

You can also use a readability formula such as the Spache, Dale-Chall, or Fry to determine reading levels. Another popular level assessment system is the Lexile system, developed by MetaMetrics Inc., which is currently being used to level trade books. Each book is assigned a level (for example, 100–400 = grade 1), and a student's scores on a reading inventory are used to help the teacher match a student to an appropriate text. The writers of the Common Core State Standards have assigned Lexile level bands to each grade as a guide to selecting appropriate reading materials for instruction of on-level students.

You can create your own informal reading inventories by selecting 100-word passages from various-level books (you might use the Lexile-system levels). Ask a student to read a passage at each level, count the errors, and ask a series of comprehension questions. Of course, matching students to text requires more than a readability formula or test. A student's background knowledge and experiences, as well as his or her interest in a particular topic, can affect the difficulty of a text.

Principle 4

Maintain consistency.

If a student's reading intervention is to be successful, there must be consistency among the many teachers and reading specialists instructing the student. In analyzing a student's total reading instruction, I frequently observe that each instructor is providing a unique and thorough program of instruction. However, the emphasis of methods they're using sometimes conflicts. For example, a student might be receiving explicit phonics instruction with practice reading controlled text in the Resource Room, yet is reading uncontrolled text in the regular classroom with an emphasis on using knowledge of sight words and context clues. The result is confusion that impedes the student's learning. Therefore, to maintain consistency among the methods or techniques being used to teach your students, coordinate with the other teachers who are part of their intervention.

"The paradox of children with reading problems is that they get more phonics instruction than children reading at expected levels, yet they have continued difficulties decoding words. . . . I recommend a two-pronged solution—first, providing a clear and consistent program of phonics instruction, and second, providing copious amounts of reading of connected text" (Stahl, 1997).

Standard English Learners

Students come to our classrooms with a wide range of literacy experiences, including great variation in the amount and form of English spoken at home. Standard English Learners (SELs) are native speakers of English who are ethnic minorities and use an ethnic-specific nonstandard dialect of English, such as African American English or Chicano English. That is, the home language of these students differs from the language of schools. (White students who live in impoverished communities can also be categorized as Standard English Learners.)

African American English (AAE) and Chicano English (CE) are language systems with well-informed rules for sounds, grammar, and meanings. They show the influence of other languages, such as sounds, words, and sentence patterns in languages from Mexico (Náhuatl) or West Africa. Over years, these dialects have developed into consistent rule-based forms of English common to a particular community. They reflect how the people in these communities hear and "feel" language.

African American English and Chicano English serve as a way for many students to identify with their specific community and are often a source of pride. In schools, it is important to take an additive approach to language learning for all our students. That is, we use the language students come to school with and add on the rules of standard English and the contexts in which both (standard English and AAE or CE) are most appropriately used. Students who can successfully code switch between the two forms of English increase their chances of success in academic and workplace settings. This is the goal of our instruction.

How Can I Help SELs?

Throughout the year you will help students speaking African American English and Chicano English to learn standard English by focusing on those places where AAE and CE differ from standard English and on those patterns that will have the most immediate impact on the students' reading, writing, and speaking development.

These students will need help in understanding that what is appropriate in one setting is not appropriate in another so they can shift easily and competently between varieties in different social contexts. Instruction will be more effective if it identifies nonstandard varieties of English as different, rather than inferior. All students should be taught standard English in a way that respects their home language.

The charts on pages 340–343 focus only on phonics and phonemic awareness differences associated with African American English and Chicano English. These are a small subset of the many differences prevalent in these forms of English, most of which deal with grammatical issues. When focusing on phonics and phonemic awareness, provide students with clear enunciation examples during lessons targeting difficult sounds. Additional practice can be provided during small group phonics and spelling lessons.

Instructional Routines and Activities

Contrastive Analysis Drills

Instructional activities that compare and emphasize the differences in standard English versus African American English and Chicano English in terms of usage and situational appropriateness are the most effective. These include a wide variety of Discrimination Drills and Translation Drills.

Translation Drills In Translation Drills, students are given a sentence in African American English or Chicano English and asked to restate it orally or rewrite it in standard English (or vice versa). Sentences can be created by you based on a specific instructional focus for the week or drawn from students' writing and speech. It is helpful for teachers of SELs to keep a notebook where they record these sample sentences throughout the week for use in these drills.

Discrimination Drills In Discrimination Drills, students hear or see two words or sentences and are asked if they are the same or different. For example, the teacher might say "help" and "hep" or "I help my sister" and "I hep my sister." A discussion of the difference (e.g., sounds in a specific word) provides articulation and spelling support. There are many different types of Discrimination Drills. These include Word Discrimination Drills (focusing on pronunciation of specific sounds in words), Sentence Discrimination Drills (focusing on pronunciation of words in context), and Home-School Discrimination Drills (focusing on the difference between home dialect and standard English).

On-the-Spot Recasting

Recasting, or restating student speech to address grammar or pronunciation issues, is best done one-on-one or during small group lessons in which the focus is on speaking using standard English. We never want to create a classroom environment in which students are intimidated to talk for fear of being wrong or constantly criticized. However, you are the best model of standard English for your students and should take available opportunities to provide these explicit models.

Since pronunciations can greatly affect students' spelling of words, use oral segmentation exercises for target sounds. For example, distribute sound boxes to students (see below). Say a word, such as *sand* (ending in a consonant blend, which breaks the phonological rules of AAE and CE). Clearly state and stretch the sounds. Have students repeat. Then have them write one letter in each box for each sound they hear. This guided spelling practice (dictation) will assist students in remembering the standard English pronunciation and correct spelling.

Sample Sound Box

Additional Resources

The California Department of Education provides additional resources for Standard English Learner professional development.

- The California Adoption Framework, Chapter 9, provides background information on Standard English Learners and designing culturally and linguistically responsive teaching. Go to http://www.cde.ca.gov/ci/rl/cf/elaeldfrmwrksbeadopted.asp.
- For more information on African American English, go to https://www.sdcity.edu/Portals/0/CollegeServices/StudentServices/LearningCommunities/Af.Amer.CRR.PDF.
- For more information on Chicano English, go to http://achieve.lausd.net/cms/lib08/CA01000043/Centricity/Domain/217/MEXICAN%20AMERICAN_TEACHER%20GUIDE.PDF.

African American English (AAE) Phonics Differences

English/Language Arts Skill	Linguistic Differences and Instructional Modifications
Digraph *th* as in *bathroom*	For many speakers of African American English, the initial /th/ sound in function words like *this* and *then* is often produced as a /d/ sound. In some words, such as *thing* and *through*, the /th/ sound is produced as a /t/ sound. At the ends of words and syllables, such as *bathroom*, *teeth*, *mouth*, and *death*, the /th/ sound is replaced by the /f/ sound. In the word *south*, it is replaced by the /t/ sound (*sout'*). This will affect students' spelling and speaking. Students will need articulation support prior to spelling these words.
Final Consonant *r*	Many speakers of African American English drop the /r/ sound in words. For example, these students will say *sto'* for *store* or *do'* for *door*. They might also replace it with the "uh" sound as in *sista* for *sister*. Clearly pronounce these words, emphasizing the /r/ sound. Have students repeat several times, exaggerating the sound before spelling these words.
***r*-Blends**	Many speakers of African American English drop the /r/ sound in words with *r*-Blends. For example, these students will say *th'ow* for *throw*. Clearly pronounce these words in the lesson, emphasizing the sounds of the *r*-Blend. Have students repeat several times, exaggerating the sound.
Final Consonant *l* and Final *l*-Blends	Many speakers of African American English drop the /l/ sound in words, particularly in words with *-ool* and *-oal* spelling patterns, such as *cool* and *coal*, and when the letter *l* precedes the consonants *p*, *t*, or *k*, as in *help*, *belt*, and *milk*. The /l/ sound might also be dropped when it precedes /w/, /j/, /r/ (*a'ready/already*); /u/, /o/, /aw/ (*poo/pool*), or in contractions with *will* (*he'/he'll*). These students will drop the *l* when spelling these words, as well. Provide additional articulation support prior to reading and spelling these words.
Final Consonant Blends (when both are voiced as in *ld* or voiceless as in *sk*)	Many speakers of African American English drop the final letter in a consonant blend (e.g., *mp*, *nd*, *nt*, *nk*, *kt*, *pt*, *ld*, *lt*, *lk*, *sk*, *st*, *sp*) or consonant blend sounds formed when adding *-ed* (e.g., /st/ as in *missed* or /pt/ as in *stopped*). For example, they will say *des'* for *desk*. Clearly pronounce the final sounds in these words and have students repeat several times, exaggerating the sounds.

African American English (AAE) Phonics Differences *continued*	
English/Language Arts Skill	**Linguistic Differences and Instructional Modifications**
Other Final Consonants	Many speakers of African American English drop the final consonant in a word when the consonant blend precedes a consonant, as in *bes'kind* for *best kind*. They also drop the final consonant sound in words ending in *-ed*, as in *rub* for *rubbed*. Provide additional articulation support prior to reading and spelling these words.
Plurals	When the letter *-s* is added to a word ending in a consonant blend, such as *test* (*tests*), many speakers of African American English will drop the final sound. This is due to the phonological (pronunciation) rules of AAE that restricts final consonant blends. Therefore they will say *tes'* or *tesses*. These students will need additional articulation support.
Contractions	Many speakers of African American English drop the /t/ sound when pronouncing the common words *it's*, *that's*, and *what's*. These words will sound more like *i's*, *tha's*, and *wha's*. These students will need additional articulation support in order to pronounce and spell these words.
Short Vowels *i* and *e*	When the /i/ and /e/ sounds appear before the consonants *m* or *n* in words, such as *pen/pin* and *him/hem*, many speakers of African American English won't pronounce or hear the difference. Focus on articulation, such as mouth position for each vowel sound, during lessons.
Inflectional Ending *-ing*	Many speakers of African American English will pronounce words with *-ing* as /ang/. For example, they will say *thang* for *thing*. Emphasize the /i/ sound in these words to help students correctly spell and pronounce them.
Stress Patterns	Many speakers of African American English place the stress on the first syllable in two syllable words instead of the second syllable (more common in standard English). For example, they will say *po'lice* instead of *police*. These students will need additional articulation support in order to pronounce these words.
Homophones	Due to the phonological rules of AAE, many words that are not homophones in standard English become homophones in African American English. This will affect students' spelling and understanding of these words. Some examples include *find/fine*, *run/rung*, *mask/mass*, *pin/pen*, *coal/cold*, *mold/mole*. Focus on articulation, such as mouth position, and differences in meaning for each word pair during lessons.

Chicano/a English (CE) Phonics Differences

English/Language Arts Skill	Linguistic Differences and Instructional Modifications
Final Consonants	Many speakers of Chicano English will drop sounds in words or syllables that end with multiple final consonants, thereby reducing the consonant cluster sound to one consonant sound. For example, they will say "mine" instead of "mind" or "harware" for "hardware." This occurs when consonant clusters are voiced and unvoiced as in *prized/price, worst/worse,* and *strict/strick.* Other consonant clusters that are problematic include *ft, sk, sp,* and *pt.* This will affect students' spelling and speaking. Students will need articulation support prior to spelling these words. Clearly pronounce these words. Have students repeat several times, exaggerating the final consonant sounds before spelling these words.
Digraphs /ch/ and /sh/	Many speakers of Chicano English will switch (or merge) the /ch/ and /sh/ sounds. This is more common in Tejanos (Chicanos from Texas) than Californianos. Some examples include *teacher/teasher, watch/wash, chop/shop, chair/share, shake/chake, shy/chy, shame/chame, shop/chop, share/chair.* Provide articulation support. Exaggerate the sound and have students repeat.
Consonants /z/ and /v/	Many speakers of Chicano English will replace the /z/ sound with /s/ and the /v/ sound with /f/. Examples include *prized/price, fuzz/fuss, raise/*race, (*When I don't race my hand the teasher makes a fuzz*) and *lives/lifes, save/safe* (*The hero safe many lifes*). Articulation support connected to word meanings will be beneficial.
Homophones	Because of the unique phonological rules of Chicano English, many words that are not homophones in standard English will sound like homophones. For example, "fine" will be used for both *fine* and *find*, "tin" will be used for both *tin* and *ten*, and "pen" will be used for both *pen* and *pin*. Clearly pronounce these words and focus on mouth position during articulation. Have students repeat several times, exaggerating the sound before spelling these words.
Stress Patterns	In Chicano English, stress is placed on one syllable prefixes as well as roots. The stress is also often elongated. For example, speakers of Chicano English will say *tooday* for "today," *deecide* for "decide," and *reepeat* for "repeat." Articulation work will be needed.

Chicano/a English (CE) Phonics Differences *continued*	
English/Language Arts Skill	**Linguistic Differences and Instructional Modifications**
Intonation	Many speakers of Chicano English will exhibit a pattern of intonation that is different from standard English. This pattern, derived from the Náhuatl language, involves a rise and sustain (or rise and fall) at the end of a phrase or sentence. For example, these speakers will say "Doont be baaad." Provide articulation support. Recast students' sentences to emphasize intonation when working with students one-on-one.
Consonant /w/	Many speakers of Chicano English will pronounce the /w/ sound with an added breath so that is sounds more like /wh/. As a result, words like *with* sound like *whith* and *will* like *whill*. This might also affect students' spelling. Contrast words beginning with *w* and *wh* and have students keep lists in their writing notebooks.
Pronouncing "the"	The word *the* is pronounced in standard English with a schwa sound (*thuh*) before a word beginning with a consonant, and a long *e* sound (*thee*) before a word beginning with a vowel. Many speakers of Chicano English will use the schwa pronunciation for all words. Point out the distinction and usage of each.

What About Commercial Intervention Programs?

The number of quality intervention programs is small, but increasing. Several print programs have been available for many years, and there is an increasing number of new computer programs. Computer programs can assist students during independent reading and skills practice. Today's best offer features that allow students to highlight and hear confusing words read aloud and provide corrective feedback. Computer programs can be highly motivational for struggling readers. Here are exemplary print and computer programs.

Language! (Available from Sopris West) This program, designed for the middle grades, contains a comprehensive language curriculum. Each unit includes: phoneme awareness; decoding and encoding isolated words; varieties of word structures; reading sentences, paragraphs, and passages for meaning; understanding and using figurative language; applying principles of composition; pragmatic language use; abstract language interpretation; the grammatical structures of English and their interrelationships; the idioms and collocations of English; punctuation, capitalization, and mechanics in writing; morphology; vocabulary expansion; and expository and narrative writing. A series of readers accompanies the program.

The Wilson Reading System (Available from Wilson Language Training) Designed for older students with significant reading problems, this program is based on the Orton-Gillingham instructional principles. It teaches basic reading skills using multisensory, cumulative techniques. The program emphasizes the syllable unit of words and includes decodable text.

Lindamoods' Auditory Discrimination in Depth and Visualizing and Verbalizing (Available from Lindamood-Bell Learning Processes) *Auditory Discrimination in Depth* teaches the ability to identify speech sounds in words. *Visualizing and Verbalizing* teaches concept imagery to improve reading comprehension.

Read 180 (Available from Houghton Mifflin Harcourt)
This state-of-the art computer and print program, directed toward grades 4 through 8, features highly-motivating videos linked to decodable computer passages, computer-assisted learning, books for independent reading, audiobooks, practice books, and teacher support materials. Students receive instruction from the teacher and guided practice from the computer. The program is designed to provide students the level and amount of practice needed to achieve mastery of basic reading and spelling skills.

McGraw-Hill *Reading Wonders* Adaptive Learning
This program, one of many adaptive phonics programs currently being offered by major educational publishers, offers an individualize learning path for students at all levels of phonics learning. It is ideal for students at the intermediate grades who are struggling in their mastery of basic phonics skills, but the scope of the software extends through word study skills (including syllabication).

A Word About Adaptive Technology

The burden of creating and maintaining a phonics scope and sequence that meets the daily needs of all your students is greatly lessened with the use of an adaptive technology phonics and word study program. Adaptive technology holds the promise of future instruction. Companies are beginning to create phonics adaptive programs that can be used as stand-alone supports for classroom instruction (especially in the area of differentiation with ease) or with digital teaching and learning platforms. Although these programs have yet to meet their full promise, they are improving each year and hopefully will become a mainstay of phonics instruction in classrooms within the next 5-10 years. It is an area of instruction with which I have great interest, having designed a couple adaptive systems for publishers. Why? These programs create an individualized learning pathway for students based on their strengths and weaknesses. Also, the stronger programs provide graduated levels of support based on student responses as they complete the individual activities.

Students receive just what they need when they need it—no more and no less. Plus, the better programs have loads of practice activities and built-in review to ensure mastery. It is a tool that can greatly assist you in providing all your students the differentiated support they need.

A Final Note

I encourage you to continue your professional development. Consult or join professional organizations, attend local and national conferences, and read professional books and magazines of interest. In addition, continue to take graduate courses and share your expertise with fellow teachers. As I travel around the country, I am struck by the wealth of untapped talent among the teaching staffs in our nation's schools. I constantly remind teachers that their best resources for professional growth are their colleagues.

I wish you all much success!

Glossary of Phonics Terms

affix: a collective term for prefixes and suffixes.

affricative: a subgroup of the fricatives. An affricative is a consonant sound produced by the sequence of a stop immediately followed by a fricative. (For example, /ch/.)

alliteration: the repetition of the same sound at the beginning of a series of words. (For example, Bob busts big balloons.)

allograph: one of the graphic forms of a letter. (*F* and *f*, for example, are allographs.)

allophone: a slightly different version of a phoneme (sound). A sound can have more than one allophone, depending on its position in a word. The difference in sound among allophones is slight and not great enough to affect meaning. (For example, the /l/ sound in *like* and pill.)

alphabet books: picture books that present, in order, the letters of the alphabet.

alphabetic principle: the assumption underlying any alphabetic writing system that each speech phoneme (sound) is represented by a unique graphic symbol or symbols (spelling).

alveolar: refers to consonant sounds in which the tongue either touches or comes close to the alveolar ridge when the sound is produced. (For example, /t/, /d/, /l/, /n/)

alveolar ridge: the roof of mouth just behind the upper teeth. The alveolar ridge is also called the tooth ridge.

analytic phonics: one of two major instructional approaches used to teach sound-spelling relationships. This approach is also known as implicit phonics or the discovery method. In this approach, readers are expected to learn a spelling-sound relationship by thinking about a sound that is common to a series of words. For example, readers are to deduce from the words *sat, send,* and *sun* that the letter s stands for the /s/ sound. The sound is not produced in isolation.

articulation, manner of: the way in which the flow of air is obstructed or altered when a sound is produced.

articulation, place of: the location in which the flow of air is obstructed when a sound is produced.

articulators: the movable parts of the mouth such as the bottom lip, bottom teeth, tongue, and jaw that are used to produce sounds.

aspiration: a burst of air that accompanies a voiceless stop consonant sound such as /p/, /t/, and /k/ when it is produced.

assonance: refers to the repetition of a vowel sound in a series of words. (For example: The green team is mean.)

automaticity: refers to decoding that is rapid, accurate, and effortless. Automaticity develops through extensive practice in decoding words.

basal reader: a book or series of books designed for a specific grade level that are used during reading instruction.

bilabial: refers to consonant sounds in which both lips are used to produce the sound. (For example, /p/, /b/, and /m/).

blending: a procedure used to teach students how to combine the sounds that comprise a word in order to decode and pronounce it. The two most effective blending procedures are successive blending and final blending.

breve: a diacritical mark (˘) used to represent a short-vowel sound.

choral reading: the simultaneous oral reading of a passage by two or more students.

closed syllable: a syllable that ends in a consonant phoneme (sound). (For example, both syllables in the word *pumpkin*—pump/kin.)

cloze passage: a reading passage of approximately 250 words in which, beginning after the twenty-fifth word, every fifth word is omitted. Learners are asked to read the passage and fill in the missing words. A student's independent, instructional, and frustration reading levels can be determined based on the percentage of correct words filled in.

compound word: a word made up of two smaller words. Often the meaning of a compound word can be derived from the meaning of the two smaller words that comprise it. (For example, *pancake*.)

comprehension: the understanding of, or meaning gained from, a written passage when read or an oral passage when heard.

concepts of print: the understanding of the elements of a book (print tells the story, cover, title, author, beginning and ending, left to right and top to bottom sequence), sentences (meaning of a sentence, beginning and ending, role of capital letters and punctuation), words, and letters. Concepts of print is also known as print awareness.

consonant: a phoneme (sound) produced by an obstruction or altering of the air flow through the speech cavities. Consonants can be described as plosives, fricatives, nasals, laterals, and semivowels.

consonant letter: a letter used to represent a consonant phoneme (sound).

consonant blends: the sounds that a consonant cluster stands for.

consonant clusters: two or more consonants that appear together in a word, each consonant retaining its own sound. (For example, the letters *cl* in the word *clown*.)

consonant digraphs: two consonants that appear together in a word and stand for one sound that is different from either sound of each individual consonant. (For example, *sh*, *ch*, *wh*, *th*, *ph*.)

context clues: clues to the meaning and/or pronunciation of an unfamiliar word derived from the words appearing before and/or following the word.

continuous sounds: sounds that can be prolonged or sustained without distortion. (For example, /f/, /l/, /m/, /n/, /r/, /s/, /v/, /z/.)

controlled text: text that is written with specific constraints. One type of controlled text is decodable text.

cueing systems: the three cues readers use. These include semantic cues (using knowledge of the meaning of the surrounding context to identify a word), syntactic cues (using knowledge of the grammatical structure of sentences to predict what a word might be), and graphophonic cues (using knowledge of sound-spelling relationships).

cursive handwriting: the style of writing in which letters are connected. For example:

cursive

decodable text: text in which all or most of the words are decodable based on the sound-spelling relationships previously taught. This type of text is sometimes used in early reading instruction.

decoding: refers to the process of taking printed words and changing them to spoken words. This generally occurs when the reader maps a sound onto each letter or spelling pattern in the words. It can also occur when the reader applies sight-word recognition, structural analysis, and context clues.

descender: the part of a letter that extends below the base line.

diacritical marks: special markings that aid in representing sounds in written form. Some common diacritical marks include the macron (‾), breve (˘), dieresis (¨), and circumflex (^). Diacriticals are used in dictionaries to aid in the pronunciation of words.

diagnosis: refers to the careful investigation of a problem, such as a reading difficulty, done to determine the amount and type of remediation needed by a student.

dialect: one form of a given language. In English, different dialects are spoken in certain areas or geographical regions, or by specific racial or social groups. A dialect is characterized by the different pronunciations of words from other dialects. However, a dialect is not sufficiently different from other dialects to be regarded as a distinct language. Any region can have at least two dialects—the standard and nonstandard speech of the region.

digraph: a combination of two letters that stand for a single sound. There are consonant digraphs and vowel digraphs.

(For example, the letters *sh* in the word *shop* and the letters *oa* in the word *boat*.)

diphthong: refers to a speech sound in which the position of the mouth changes or "glides" from one place to another as the sound is produced. (For example, /oi/ and /ou/.)

direct instruction: a teaching approach that is focused, sequential, and structured. The teacher presents information to the students and monitors the pacing and learning of the material.

echo reading: a technique used for improving fluency. The teacher reads aloud a passage. The student then tries to duplicate the passage using the same phrasing and intonation.

e-marker: refers to the letter e when it occurs at the end of a word such as *rope*. In these words, the letter *e* is a part of the vowel grapheme (spelling) and, although not voiced, signals that the vowel spelling stands for a long-vowel sound.

encode: to spell a word. Encoding is the opposite of decoding.

final blending: a form of blending in which each new spelling in a word is sounded out along with the previous sound-spellings. A word is not completely pronounced until the last sound-spelling is reached. For example, the word *sat* is blended in this sequence: /s/. . . /sa/. . . /sat/.

fluency: the ability to recognize words accurately, rapidly, and automatically. Fluency is a term often used synonymously with the term efficiency skills.

fricative: a consonant sound formed by a partial obstruction of the flow of air. (For example, /s/ and /f/). Fricatives can be prolonged or sustained.

function words: words other than verbs, adverbs, nouns, or adjectives. Function words are also known as marker words or structure words. In the following sentence the function words are in italics. (For example, *Where* are *the* horses and cows *in the* barn?)

geminate: a pair of identical letters appearing together in a word, such as the letters *pp* in the word *happy*.

generalizations: sometimes referred to as rules, generalizations are predictable and fairly reliable sound-spelling relationships.

glide: a sound formed much like a vowel. Glides are sometimes referred to as semivowels. (For example, /w/ and /y/.)

glottal stop: a sound produced by a blockage of the air flow at the glottis.

glottis: an opening between the vocal cords.

grapheme: the written representation of a phoneme (sound). Graphemes can be single letters as in the letter *s* for the /s/ sound, or multiple letters as in the letters *sh* for the /sh/ sound.

hard palate: the part of the roof of the mouth located just behind the tooth ridge.

high-frequency words: the words that appear most often in text and speech. A small number of these words accounts for a relatively large percentage of all the words spoken or read.

homophones: words that sound the same but have different meanings and spellings.

hybrid text: a form of controlled text for the early grades that combines decodable words and high-frequency words, all of which are covered in the instruction prior to the reading of the text.

informal reading inventory: a procedure used to evaluate a student's oral reading. Omissions, mispronunciations, substitutions, additions, and repetitions of words are counted. A reader's inattention to punctuation is also recorded. The scores obtained are used to determine a reader's frustration, instructional, and independent reading levels.

International Phonetic Alphabet: the set of standardized graphic symbols used to represent the sounds for every language in the world.

kinesthetic method: the use of touch, hearing, sight, and muscle movement to teach letters or words.

labiodental: refers to sounds produced by an obstruction of the airflow occurring when the top teeth touch the lower lip. (For example, /f/ and /v/.)

Language Experience Approach (LEA): an approach to reading instruction in which the student's own words are written down and used for instruction in reading, writing, spelling, listening, and speaking. Students' oral language is used to develop their reading skills. This approach is regarded as more personalized and motivating, but less systematic or sequential than other approaches.

lateral phoneme: refers to a sound produced when the airflow passes out of the mouth over the sides of the tongue. (For example, /l/.)

letter knowledge: refers to the ability to discriminate, recognize, and name the letters of the alphabet.

letter-sound correspondence: see sound-spelling relationship.

levels of reading:

Independent or free reading level: The level at which a student can read a text without the teacher's assistance. Comprehension should average 90% or better, and word recognition should average 95% or better.

Instructional reading level: The level at which a student should receive reading instruction. The student reads the text with teacher guidance, and is challenged enough to stimulate reading growth. Comprehension should average 75% or better, and word recognition should average 90% or better.

Frustration reading level: The level at which a student cannot read a text adequately. At this level, the student often shows signs of discomfort. Comprehension averages 50% or less, and word recognition averages 90% or less.

linguistics: the formal study of language and how it works.

liquid: a sound produced by only slightly interrupting the airflow. No friction results, and the air passes through the mouth in a relatively fluid manner. (For example, /r/ and /l/.)

long vowels: the phonemes (sounds) /ā/, /ē/, /ī/, /ō/, and /yōō/. The /ī/ and /yōō/ sounds are sometimes referred to as diphthongs. Long-vowel sounds are also referred to as glided sounds.

macron: a diacritical mark (—) used to represent long-vowel sounds.

manuscript handwriting: the style of writing in which letters are not connected. For example:

manuscript

metacognition: the knowledge of one's own thought processes while reading. This knowledge enables a reader to select appropriate strategies while reading to help comprehend the text.

minimal pairs: pairs of words that differ in only one sound. In minimal pairs, the differing sound occurs in the same position in each member of the pair, such as *sat/cat*.

miscues: refers to the deviations from a text that a reader makes when reading aloud a passage. Miscues is a term used in place of "reading errors" to indicate that the misreading of a word can be used to glean information about the kinds of cues and strategies the learner is using when reading. This information can be used to modify instructional support.

monosyllabic words: words that have one syllable.

morpheme: the smallest unit of meaning in our language. There are two primary types of morphemes—bound (*un-*, *-ly*, *-ing*) and free (*happy, run, cat*).

morphology: the study of morphemes.

nasal: a consonant sound produced when the mouth is closed forcing the air through the nose. (For example, /m/, /n/, and /ng/.)

onset: refers to the part of the syllable that comes before the vowel. An onset can be a single consonant, a consonant cluster, or a consonant digraph. (For example, the letter *c* in *cat*, the letters *pl* in *plate*, and the letters *ch* in *chair*.)

open syllable: a syllable that ends in a vowel phoneme (sound).

oral blending: the process of combining individual phonemes orally. For example, /s/ + /u/ + /n/ = sun. Oral blending is an important phonemic awareness task. Oral blending is necessary for sounding out words.

oral segmentation: the process of separating a word into its individual phonemes. Oral segmentation is an important phonemic awareness task and is necessary for spelling.

orthography: another name for the spelling system of a language. Orthography is sometimes referred to as the study of spelling.

patterned/predictable text: text written with a predictable plot structure due to the regular repetition of phrases or sentences.

phoneme: the smallest unit of speech sound that distinguishes one word from another in a language.

phonemic awareness: the understanding or insight that a word is made up of a series of discrete sounds. This awareness includes the ability to pick out and manipulate sounds in spoken words.

phonemic manipulation: a phonemic awareness task in which a sound or sounds are deleted, added, or substituted in a word.

phonemics: the study of the phonemes or speech sounds of a particular language.

phonetics: the study of speech sounds.

phonic analysis: the use of phonic information to decode words.

phonic blending: the process of sounding out a word in which a sound is mapped onto each letter or spelling in a word and strung together to pronounce the word. Phonic blending is different from oral blending in which no print is involved.

phonic elements: consonants, consonant digraphs, consonant clusters, vowels, vowel digraphs, and other letter combinations that are the focus of phonics instruction.

phonics: refers to the relationship between sounds and the spelling patterns that are used to represent them in print. The study of these sound-spelling (phoneme-grapheme) relationships is generally included in beginning reading instruction.

phonics generalization: a sound-spelling relationship that occurs as a predictable spelling pattern.

phonogram: a series of letters that stands for a sound, syllable, or series of sounds without reference to meaning. Also known as word families.

phonological awareness: a global term that includes an awareness of words within sentences, rhyming units within words, beginning and ending sounds within words, syllables within words, phonemes within words (phonemic awareness), and features of individual phonemes such as how the mouth, tongue, vocal cords, and teeth are used to produce the sound.

plosive: a sound produced by closing or blocking off the air flow, and then exploding a puff of air. A plosive is also known as a stop sound. (For example, /p/, /b/, /t/, /d/, /k/, /g/.)

polysyllabic words: words that have more than one syllable. Polysyllabic words are also known as multisyllabic words.

prefix: a group of letters that appears at the front of a word. (For example, the letters *un* in the word *unhappy*.)

***r*-controlled vowels:** a vowel that comes before the letter *r* in a word. The letter *r* changes and thereby "controls" the sound of the preceding vowel. (For example, *ar, er, ir, or, ur*.)

rime: a vowel and any consonants that follow it in a syllable. (For example, the letters *at* in the word *cat*.)

schwa: a vowel phoneme (sound) that is less accented than other vowels. The schwa is usually heard in polysyllabic words and appears in unstressed syllables. The schwa sound is written as /ə/.

scope and sequence: refers to the skills taught in a reading program and the order in which they are taught.

semantics: the study of the connotations and denotations (meanings) of words.

semivowel: a sound made with a wide opening in the mouth and little disruption of the airflow, such as /w/ and /y/. A semivowel can be either a vowel or a consonant depending of where it is heard in a word.

sequential redundancy: the likelihood that if a certain letter appears in a syllable or word, only certain letters will follow. (For example, the letter *q* is almost always followed by the letter *u*.)

short vowels: the phonemes (sounds) /a/, /e/, /i/, /o/, and /u/.

sight word: any word that a reader is able to recognize instantly. This is often the result of repeated opportunities to decode the word in text. The term "sight word" is sometimes confused with the term "high-frequency word." High-frequency words are the words that appear most often in printed English. Sight words can be high-frequency words, but can be other words as well.

silent letters: letters that appear in a word but are not vocalized. (For example, the letter *k* in the word *knot*.)

silent speech: the subvocalization, or inner speech, one makes when reading. Skilled, mature readers use less silent speech in reading than do beginning or poor readers.

soft palate: the back part of the roof of the mouth. The soft palate is also called the velum.

sound-spelling relationship: the relationship between a phoneme (sound) and the grapheme (letter or spelling) that represents it in writing. Some of these relationships are said to be predictable (reliable/dependable) spellings; others are not. (For example, the letter *s* stands for the /s/ sound.)

stop consonant: a consonant sound produced by the blockage of the airflow. (For example, /p/ and /b/.)

stress: the emphasis on a particular syllable in a word, or a particular word in a sentence. This involves making the vowel sound longer, louder, and higher in pitch.

structural analysis: reading words, specifically polysyllabic words, according to their structural units such as root words, prefixes, suffixes, and possessives.

successive blending: a form of blending in which each letter or spelling in a word is mapped onto a sound and the sounds are strung together as the word is pronounced. For example, the word *sat* is pronounced as *ssssaaaat*.

suffix: a letter or group of letters that is added to the end of a root, or base, word. (For example, the letters *-ly* in the word *quickly*.)

syllabication: refers to strategies used to figure out polysyllabic words.

syllable: a unit of pronunciation. A syllable also refers to the unit into which a word is divided. A syllable usually consists of a vowel and one or more consonant(s) before and/or after it.

synthetic phonics: one of two major instructional approaches used to teach sound-spelling relationships. This approach is also known as explicit phonics. In this approach, learners are taught to say the sounds of individual spellings, which are then combined to form words (part-to-whole). The sounds are produced in isolation.

systematic, explicit instruction: refers to a type of direct instruction. The term systematic means that instruction is sequenced and sounds are introduced at a relatively slow pace but continually reviewed and applied to reading and writing. The term explicit means that relationships are explicitly pointed out and taught rather than implicitly referred to or discovered on one's own.

tactile: having to do with the sense of touch.

trade books: a book published for sale to the general public. The term often refers to commercial books, other than basal readers, that are used for instruction.

unvoiced (voiceless) phoneme: a sound produced with no vibration of the vocal cords. (For example, /t/ and /s/.)

velar: refers to sounds that, when produced, involve the back of the tongue and the soft palate or velum. (For example, /k/, /g/, and /ng/.)

velum: the back part of the roof of the mouth. The velum is also called the soft palate.

virgules: slashes [//] used in the transcription of sounds. (For example, /s/.)

visual perception skills: the ability to see and identify the characteristics of things such as shape, color, size, and distance.

vocal cords: two folds of ligament and elastic membrane found at the top of the windpipe (in the larynx).

voiced phoneme: a sound produced with a vibration of the vocal cords. (For example, /g/ and /z/.)

vowel: a phoneme produced with an unobstructed passage of air through the mouth. Vowel phonemes have greater prominence than consonant phonemes.

vowel digraphs: refers to pairs of vowels appearing together in a word. Some vowel digraphs stand for the sound of a long vowel (*ai, ay, ee, ea, igh, oa*); others do not (*oo, oi, oy, ou, ow, au, aw*).

vowel letters: letters used to represent vowel phonemes.

word-analysis skills: skills a reader must use to determine how to pronounce a word when it is not recognized instantly. These include phonics, structural analysis, and context clues. Word-analysis skills are sometimes referred to as word-attack skills.

word identification: refers to the ability to give the name of a word after seeing it in print. Word identification is sometimes referred to as "word recognition," "word attack," or "decoding." Word identification can involve the use of graphophonic cues (phonics), semantic and syntactic context cues, and structural analysis.

For additional definitions of phonics-related terms see *The Literacy Dictionary: The Vocabulary of Reading and Writing* by T. Harris and R. Hodges (editors), Newark, DE: International Reading Association, 1995.

Bibliography

Adams, M. J. (1990). *Beginning to read: Thinking and learning about print*. Cambridge: Massachusetts Institute of Technology.

Adams, M. J., Treiman, R., & Pressley, M. (1996). Reading, writing, and literacy. In I. Sigel & A. Renninger (Eds.), *Handbook of child psychology*, 4, child psychology in practice. New York: Wiley.

Alexander, K., & Entwisle. D. (1996). Schools and children at risk. In A. Booth & J. Dunn (Eds.) *Family-School Links: How Do They Affect Educational Outcomes?* (67–88) Hillsdale, NJ: Erlbaum.

Allington, R. L. (1983). Fluency: The neglected reading goal. *The Reading Teacher, 36*, 556–561.

Allington, R. L. (1984a). Content coverage and contextual reading in reading groups. *Journal of Reading Behavior, 26*, 85–96.

Allington, R. L. (1984b). Oral reading. In D. D. Pearson (Ed.), *Handbook of reading research*. New York: Longman.

American Federation of Teachers. (2013). AFT Poll of 800 teachers finds strong support for Common Core standards and a moratorium for new assessments until everything is aligned. Retrieved from: http://www.aft.org/press-release/aft-poll-800-teachers-finds-strong-support-common-core-standards-and

Anderson, R. C., Hiebert, E. H., Scott, J. A., & Wilkinson, I. A. G. (1985). *Becoming a nation of readers: The report of the commission on reading*. Champaign, IL: The Center for the Study of Reading and The National Academy of Education.

Anderson, R. C., Wilson, P., & Fielding, L. (1998). Growth in reading and how children spend their time outside of school. *Reading Research Quarterly, 23*, 285–303.

Bear, D. R., Templeton, S., Invernizzi, M., & Johnston, F. (1996). *Words their way: Word study for phonics, vocabulary, and spelling instruction*. Englewood Cliffs, NJ: Merrill/Prentice-Hall.

Bear, D. R., Templeton, S., Invernizzi, M., & Johnston, F. (2016). *Words their way: Word study for phonics, vocabulary, and spelling instruction* (6th ed.). Upper Saddle River, NJ: Pearson.

Beck, I., & Beck, M. E. (2013). *Making sense of phonics: The hows and whys* (2nd ed.). New York: Guilford Press.

Beck, I., & Juel, C. (1995, Summer). The role of decoding in learning to read. *American Educator*.

Beck, I., & McCaslin, E. (1978). An analysis of dimensions that affect the development of code-breaking ability in eight beginning reading programs. LRDC Report No. 1978/6. Pittsburgh, PA: University of Pittsburgh Learning Research and Development Center.

Biemiller, A. (1970a). The development of the use of graphic and contextual information as children learn to read. *Reading Research Quarterly, 6*.

Biemiller, A. (1970b). Relationships between oral reading rates for letters, words, and simple text in the development of reading achievement. *Reading Research Quarterly, 13*.

Biemiller, A. (2009). *Words worth teaching: Closing the vocabulary gap*. New York: SRA/McGraw-Hill.

Blevins, W. (1997). *Phonemic awareness activities for early reading success*. New York: Scholastic.

Blevins, W. (2011). *Week-by-week phonics and word study activities for the intermediate grades*. New York: Scholastic.

Blevins, W. (2016). *A fresh look at phonics: Common causes of failure and 7 ingredients for success*. Thousand Oaks, CA: Corwin Literacy.

Blevins, W. (2017). *Phonics from a to z: A practical guide*. (3rd ed.) New York: Scholastic.

Bruck, M., & Treiman, R. (1990a). Phonological awareness and spelling in normal children and dyslexics: The case of initial consonant clusters. *Journal of Experimental Child Psychology, 50.*

Bruck, M., & Treiman, R. (1990b). Phonological awareness and spelling in normal children and dyslexics: The case of initial consonant clusters. *Journal of Experimental Psychology, 28*(5).

Bryson, B. (1990) *The mother tongue: English and how it got that way.* New York: Avon Books.

Burmeister, L. E. (1971). Content of a phonics program based on particularly useful generalizations. In N. B. Smith (Ed.), *Reading methods and teacher improvement.* Newark, DE: International Reading Association.

Burmeister, L. E. (1968a). Usefulness of phonic generalizations. *The Reading Teacher, 21.*

Burmeister, L. E. (1968b). Vowel Pairs. *The Reading Teacher, 21.*

California Department of Education. (1996, Summer). *Teaching reading: A balanced, comprehensive approach to teaching reading in prekindergarten through grade three.* Sacramento, CA.

Carnine, L., Carnine, D., & Gersten, R. (1984). Analysis of oral reading errors made by economically disadvantaged students taught with a synthetic-phonics approach. *Reading Research Quarterly, 19.*

Carreker, S. (1999). Teaching reading: Accurate decoding and fluency. In J.R. Birsh (Ed.), *Multisensory teaching of basic language skills.* Baltimore, MD: P.H. Brookes.

Carreker, S. (2011) Teaching reading: Accurate decoding and fluency. In J. R. Birsh (Ed.), *Multisensory teaching of basic language skills* (3rd ed.) Baltimore, MD: Paul H. Brookes Publishing Co.

Carroll, J. B. (1990, May). Thoughts on reading and phonics. Paper presented at the National Conference on Research in English. Atlanta, Georgia.

Carroll, J. B., Davies, P., & Richman, B. (1971). *Word frequency book.* Boston: Houghton Mifflin.

Chall, J. S. (1967). *Learning to read: The great debate.* New York: McGraw-Hill.

Chall, J. S. (1983). *Stages of reading development.* New York: McGraw-Hill.

Chall, J. S. (1996). *Stages of reading development.* San Diego, CA: Harcourt Brace & Company.

Chall, J. S., & Popp, H. (1996). *Teaching and assessing phonics: Why, what, when, how.* Cambridge, MA: Educators Publishing Service, Inc.

Clymer, T. (1963). Utility of phonics generalizations in the primary grades. *The Reading Teacher, 16.*

CORE (Consortium On Reading Excellence). (2000). Novato, CA : Arena Press.

Coxhead, A. J. (1998). *An academic word list* (English Language Institute Occasional Publication No. 18). Wellington, New Zealand: Victoria University of Wellington.

Cunningham, A. E., & Stanovich, K. E. (1991). Tracking the unique effects of print exposure in children: Associations with vocabulary, general knowledge, and spelling. *Journal of Educational Psychology, 83.*

Cunningham, P. M. (1975-76). Investigating a synthesized theory of mediated word identification. *Reading Research Quarterly, 11.*

Cunningham, P. M. (1990). The names test: A quick assessment of decoding ability. *The Reading Teacher, 44.*

Cunningham, P. M. (1995). *Phonics they use: Words for reading and writing.* New York: HarperCollins College Publishers.

Durkin, D. (1993). *Teaching them to read.* Boston, MA: Allyn and Bacon.

Durrell, D. (1963). *Phonograms in primary grade words.* Boston, MA: Boston University.

Ehri, L. C. (1987). Learning to read and spell words. *Journal of Reading Behavior, 19.*

Ehri, L. C. (1992). Reconceptualizing the development of sight word reading and its relationship to recoding. In P. Gough, L. Ehri, & R. Treiman (Eds.), *Reading Acquisition*. Hillsdale, NJ: Erlbaum.

Ehri, L. C. (1995). Phases of development in reading words. *Journal of Research in Reading, 18*.

Eldredge, J. L. (1995). *Teaching decoding in holistic classrooms*. Englewood Cliffs, NJ: Merrill Publishing Co.

Evans, M. A., & Carr, T. H. (1985). Cognitive abilities, conditions of learning, and the early development of reading skill. *Reading Research Quarterly, 20*.

Foorman, B. (1998). The role of instruction in learning to read: Preventing reading failure in at-risk children. *Journal of Educational Psychology, 90*(1), 37–55.

Fox, B. J. (1996). *Strategies for word identification: Phonics from a new perspective*. Englewood Cliffs, NJ: Prentice-Hall.

Freedman, S. W., & Calfee, R. C. (1984). Understanding and comprehending. *Written Communication, 1*, 459-490.

Fry, E. B., Fountoukidis, D. L., & Polk, J. K. (1985). *The new reading teacher's book of lists*. Englewood Cliffs, NJ: Prentice-Hall.

Fry, E., Sakiey, E., Goss, A., & Loigman, B. (1980). A syllable frequency count. *Visible Language, 14*(2), 137–150.

Gaskins, I., Downer, M., Anderson, R. C., Cunningham, P. M., Gaskins, R., Schommer, M., & the Teachers of Benchmark School. (1988). A metacognitive approach to phonics: Using what you know to decode what you don't know. *Remedial and Special Education, 9*(1).

Gaskins, I., Ehri, L., Cress, C., O'Hara, C., & Donnelly, K. (1996, Dec/1997, Jan). Procedures for word learning: Making discoveries about words. *The Reading Teacher, 50*(4).

Gillingham, A., & Stillman, B. W. (1997). *The Gillingham manual: Remedial training for children with specific disability in reading, spelling, and penmanship*. (8th ed.). Cambridge, MA: Educators Publishing Service.

Golinkoff, R. M. (1978). Phonemic awareness skills and reading achievement. In F. B. Murray & J. H. Pikulski (Eds.), *The acquisition of reading: Cognitive, linguistic, and perceptual prerequisites*. Baltimore, MD: University Park.

Gough, P. B., & Juel C. (1991). The first stages of word recognition. In L. Rieben & C. A. Perfetti (Eds.), *Learning to read: Basic research and its implications*. Hillsdale, NJ: Erlbaum.

Gough, P. B., Juel, C., & Roper-Schneider, D. (1983). A two-stage model of initial reading acquisition. In J. A. Niles & L. A. Harris (Eds.) *Searches for meaning in reading/language processing and instruction*. Rochester, NY: National Reading Conference.

Gough, P. B., Alford, Jr., J. A., & Holley-Wilcox, P. (1981). Words and context. In O. J. L. Tzeng & H. Singer (Eds.), *Perception of print*. Hillsdale, NJ: Erlbaum.

Gough, P. B., & Walsh, M. A. (1991). Chinese, Phoenicians, and the orthographic cipher of English. In S. A. Brady & D. P. Shankweiler (Eds.), *Phonological process in literacy: A tribute to Isabelle Y. Liberman*. Hillsdale, NJ: Erlbaum.

Groff, P. (1977). *Phonics: Why and how*. Morristown, NJ: General Learning Press.

Haddock, M. (1976). Effects of an auditory and a visual method of blending instruction on the ability of prereaders to decode synthetic words. *Journal of Educational Psychology, 68*.

Hall, S. L., & Moats, L. C. (1999). *Straight talk about reading*. Chicago, IL: Contemporary Books.

Hanna, P. R., Hodges, R. E., Hanna, J. L., & Rudolph, E. H. (1966). *Phoneme-grapheme correspondences as cues to spelling improvement*. Washington, DC: U. S. Office of Education.

Hasbrouck, J., & Tindal, G. (2006). Oral reading fluency norms: A valuable assessment tool for reading teachers. *The Reading Teacher, 59*(7), 636–644.

Harris, A. J., & Jacobson, M. D. (1972). *Basic elementary reading vocabularies*. New York: Macmillan.

Harris, T., & Hodges, R. (Eds.). (1995). *The literacy dictionary: The vocabulary of reading and writing*. Newark, DE: International Reading Association.

Hattie, J. (2012). *Visible learning for teachers: Maximizing impact on learning*. New York, NY: Routledge.

Henderson, E. (1967). *Phonics in learning to read: A handbook for teachers*. New York: Exposition Press.

Henry, M. (1997). The decoding/spelling continuum: Integrated decoding and spelling instruction from pre-school to early secondary school. *Dyslexia, 3*.

Henry, M. K. (1988). Beyond phonics: Integrated decoding and spelling instruction based on word origin and structure. *Annals of Dyslexia, 38*, 258–275.

Hoffman, J. V. (1987). Rethinking the role of oral reading in basal instruction. *Elementary School Journal, 87*, 367–373.

Hoffman J. V., & Crone, S. (1985). The oral recitation lesson: A research derived strategy for reading in basal texts. In J. A. Niles & R .A. Lalik (Eds.), *Issues in literacy: A research perspective*. Thirty-fourth yearbook of the national reading conference. Rochester, New York: National Reading Conference.

Honig, B. (1995). *How should we teach our children to read?* Center for Systemic School Reform, San Francisco State University.

Honig, B. (1996). *Teaching our children to read: The role of skills in a comprehensive reading program*. Thousand Oaks, CA: Corwin Press.

Johns, J. L. (1980). First graders' concepts about print. *Reading Research Quarterly, 15*.

Johnson, D., & Bauman, J. (1984). Word identification. In P. D. Pearson, R. Barr, M. L. Kamil, & P. Mosenthal (Eds.), *Handbook of reading research*. NY: Longman.

Juel, C. (1991). Beginning reading. In R. Barr, M. L. Kamil, P. Mosenthal, & P. D. Pearson (Eds.). *Handbook of reading research, 2*. New York: Longman.

Juel, C. (1988). Learning to read and write: A longitudinal study of fifty-four children from first through fourth grades. *Journal of Educational Psychology, 80*.

Juel, C., & Roper-Schneider, D. (1985). The influence of basal readers on first-grade reading. Reading Research Quarterly, 20.

Just, M.A., & Carpenter, P. A. (1987). *The psychology of reading and language comprehension*. Boston, MA: Allyn and Bacon.

Karlsen, B., Madden, R., & Gardner, E. F. (1984). *Stanford Diagnostic Reading Test* (3rd Ed.). San Antonio, TX: The Psychological Corporation, Harcourt Brace Jovanovich.

Kahneman, D. (1973). *Attention and effort*. Englewood Cliffs, NJ: Prentice-Hall.

Koskinen, P., & Blum, I. (1986). Paired repeated reading: A classroom strategy for developing fluent reading. *The Reading Teacher, 40*, 70–75.

LaBerge, D., & Samuels, S. J. (1974). Toward a theory of automatic information processing in reading. *Cognitive Psychology, 6*(2).

Langenburg, D. (April 13, 2000). Testimony before the U.S. Senate Appropriations Committee's Subcommittee on Labor, Health & Human Services, and Education. National Reading Panel, National Institute of Child Health and Human Development.

LaPray, M., & Ross, R. (1969). The graded word list: Quick gauge of reading ability. *Journal of Reading, 12*(4).

Lesgold, A. M. & Curtis, M. E. (1981). Learning to read words efficiently. In A. M. Lesgold & C. A. Perfetti (Eds.) *Interactive processes in reading*. Hillsdale, NJ: Erlbaum.

Lesgold, A. M., & Resnick, L. B. (1982). How reading disabilities develop: Perspectives from a longitudinal study. In J. P. Das., R. Mulcahy, & A. E. Walls (Eds.), *Theory and research in learning disability*. New York: Plenum.

Lindamood, C. H., & Lindamood, P. C. (1979). *Auditory discrimination in depth*. Hingham, MA: Teaching Resources Corporation.

Lovett, M. W. (1987). A developmental approach to reading disability: Accuracy and speed criteria of normal and deficient reading skill. *Child Development, 58*.

Lundberg, I. (1984, August). *Learning to read*. School Research Newsletter. Sweden: National Board of Education.

Lyon, G. R. (1995, January). Research initiatives in learning disabilities: Contributions from scientists supported by the national institutes of child health and human development. *Journal of Child Neurology, 10*(1S), s120-s126.

Lyon, G. R. (1996). Learning disabilities. *The future of children: Special education for students with disabilities, 6*(1).

Lyon, G. R. (July 19, 1997). Hearing on Literacy: Why Kids Can't Read. Child Development and Behavior Branch, National Institute of Child Health and Human Development Committee on Education and the Workforce, U.S. House of Representatives, Washington, DC.

Manguel, A. (1996). A History of Reading. New York: Viking.

Mazurkiewicz, A. (1976). Teaching about phonics. New York: St. Martin's Press.

McConkie, G. W., & Zola, D. (1987). Two examples of computer-based research on reading: Eye movement monitoring and computer-aided reading. In D. Reinking (Ed.), *Reading and computers: Issues for theory and practice*. New York: Teachers College Press.

Miller, W. (1993). *Complete reading disabilities handbook*. West Nyack, NY: The Center for Applied Research in Education.

Moats, L. (1998). Reading, spelling, and writing disabilities in the middle grades. In B. Y. L. Wong (Ed.), *Learning about learning disabilities* (2nd ed.). San Diego, CA: Academic Press.

Moats, L. C. (1995a). *The missing foundation in teacher education*. American Federation of Teachers (Summer).

Moats, L. C. (1995b). *Spelling: Development, disabilities, and instruction*. Timonium, MD: York Press, Inc.

Moats, L. C. (1998). Teaching decoding. American Educator, 22(1 & 2), 42–29, 95–96. In *Reading all about It*. California State Board of Education, 1999.

Moats, L. C. (2000). *Speech to print: Language essentials for teachers*. Baltimore, MD: Brookes.

Moats, L. C. (2010). *Speech to print: Language essentials for teachers* (2nd ed.). Baltimore, MD: Brookes.

Murphy, H. A. (1957). The spontaneous speaking vocabulary of children in primary grades. *Journal of Education, 140*.

Nagy, W. E., & Anderson, R. C. (1984). How many words are there in printed school English? *Reading Research Quarterly, 19*, 304–330.

Nathan, R. G., & Stanovich, K. E. (1991). The causes and consequences of differences in reading fluency. *Theory into Practice, 30*, 176–184.

Nicholson, T. (1992). Historical and current perspectives on reading. In C. J. Gordon, G. D. Lahercano, & W. R. McEacharn (Eds.), *Elementary reading: Process and practice*. Needham, MA: Ginn.

Pinnell, G. S. (1994). Children's early literacy learning. Scholastic Literacy Research Paper. New York.

Rasinski, T. V. (1989). Adult readers' sensitivity to phrase boundaries in texts. *Journal of Experimental Education, 58*.

Rasinski, T. V. (2005). *Daily word ladders: Grades 4–6*. New York: Scholastic.

Read, C. (1986). *Children's creative spelling*. London: Routledge and Kegan Paul.

Resnick, L., & Beck, I. (1976). Designing instruction in reading: Initial reading. In A. J. Harris & E. R. Sipay (Eds.), Readings on reading instruction. New York: Longman.

Rinsland, H. D. (1945). A basic vocabulary of elementary school children. New York: Macmillan.

Rosenshine, B., & Stevens, R. (1984). Classroom instruction in reading. In P. D. Pearson, R. Barr, M. L. Kamil, & P. Mosenthal (Eds.), *Handbook of reading research*. New York: Longman.

Royer, J., & Sinatra, G. (1994). A cognitive theoretical approach to reading diagnostics. *Educational Psychology Review, 6*(2).

Samuels, J. (1979). The method of repeated readings. *The Reading Teacher, 32*, 403–408.

Samuels, S. J., Shermer, N., & Reinking, D. (1992). Reading fluency: Techniques for making decoding automatic. In S. J. Samuels & A. E. Farstrup (Eds.), *What research has to say about reading instruction*. Newark, DE: International Reading Association.

Scholastic, Inc. (2014). Kids & family reading report, 5th ed. New York: NY.

Share, D. (1995). Phonological recoding and self-teaching: Sine qua non of reading acquisition. *Cognition, 55*(2), 151-218.

Shefelbine, J. (1990). A syllabic-unit approach to teaching decoding of polysyllabic words to fourth- and sixth-grade disabled readers. In J. Zutell, S. McCormick, M. Connolly, & P. O'Keefe (Eds.), *Literacy theory and research: Analyses from multiple paradigms*. Chicago, IL: National Reading Conference.

Shefelbine, J., Lipscomb, L., & Hern, A. (1989). Variables associated with second-, fourth-, and sixth-grade students' ability to identify polysyllabic words. In S. McCormick, J. Zutell, P. Scharer, & P. O'Keefe (Eds.), *Cognitive and social perspectives for literacy research and instruction*. Chicago, IL: National Reading Conference.

Stahl, S. (1992). Saying the 'p' word: Nine guidelines for exemplary phonics instruction. *The Reading Teacher, 45*(8).

Stahl, S. (1997). Teaching children with reading problems to recognize words. In L. Putnam (Ed.), *Readings on language & literacy: Essays in honor of Jeanne S. Chall*. Cambridge, MA: Brookline Books.

Stahl, S., & Miller, P. D. (1989). Whole language and language experience approaches for beginning reading: A quantitative research synthesis. *Review of Editorial Research, 59*.

Stahl, S., Osborn, J., & Pearson, P. D. (1992). The effects of beginning reading instruction: Six teachers in six classrooms. Unpublished paper. University of Illinois at Urbana-Champaign.

Stanbach, M. L. (1992). Syllable and rime patterns for teaching reading: Analysis of a frequency-based vocabulary of 17,602 words. *Annals of Dyslexia, 42*, 196–221.

Stanovich, K. E. (1980). Toward an interactive compensatory model of individual differences in the development of reading fluency. *Reading Research Quarterly, 21*.

Stanovich, K. E. (1984). Toward an interactive-compensatory model of reading: A confluence of developmental, experimental, and educational psychology. Remedial and *Special Education, 5*(3), 11–19.

Stanovich, K. E. (1986). Matthew effects in reading: Some consequences of individual differences in the acquisition of literacy. *Reading Research Quarterly, 21.*

Stanovich, K. E. (1992). Speculations on the causes and consequences of individual differences in early reading acquisition. In P. B. Gough, L. C. Ehri, & R. Treiman (Eds.), *Reading acquisition.* Hillsdale, NJ: Erlbaum.

Stanovich, K. E., & West, R. F. (1989). Exposure to print and orthographic processing. *Reading Research Quarterly, 24*(4), 402–433.

State Superintendent of Public Instruction and the State Board of Education in California. (1996). State call for reading programs.

Sulzby, E. (1985). Children's emergent reading of favorite storybooks: A developmental study. *Reading Research Quarterly, 20*(4).

Treiman, R., & Baron, J. (1981). Segmental analysis ability: Development and relation to reading ability. In G. E. MacKinnon & T. G. Waller (Eds.), *Reading research: Advances in theory and practice, 3.* New York: Academic Press.

Tyler A., & Nagy, W. (1989). The acquisition of English derivational morphology. *Journal of Memory and Language, 28,* 649–667.

Vacca, J., Vacca, R., & Gove, M. (1995). *Reading and learning to read.* New York: HarperCollins College Publishers.

Velluntino, F. R., & Scanlon, D. M. (1987). Phonological coding, phonological awareness, and reading ability: Evidence from a longitudinal and experimental study. *Merrill-Palmer Quarterly, 33.*

Wagstaff, J. (1994). *Phonics that work!* New York: Scholastic.

Whaley, W. J., & Kirby, M. W. (1980). Word synthesis and beginning reading achievement. *The Journal of Educational Research, 73.*

White, T., Power, M., & White, S. (1989). Morphological analysis: Implications for teaching and understanding vocabulary growth. Reading *Research Quarterly, 24,* 283–304.

White, T. G., Sowell, J., & Yanagihara, A. (1989). Teaching elementary students to use word-part clues. *The Reading Teacher.*

Wilde, S. (1997). *What's a schwa sound anyway? A holistic guide to phonetics, phonics, and spelling.* Portsmouth, NH: Heinemann.

Wong, M. (2015, May 29). Brain wave study shows how different teaching methods affect reading development. Medical Xpress. Retrieved from http://medicalxpress.com/news/2015-05-brain-methods-affect.html

Wylie, R., & Durrell, D. (1970). Teaching vowels through phonograms. *Elementary Education, 47.*

Wysocki, K., & Jenkins, J. (1987). Deriving word meanings through morphological generalization. *Reading Research Quarterly, 22,* 66–81.

Yoncheva, Y. N., Wise, J., & McCandliss, B. (2015, June-July). Hemispheric specialization for visual words is shaped by attention to sublexical units during initial learning. *Brain and Language, 145–146,* 22–33.

Young, C., & Rasinski, T. (2016). *Tiered fluency instruction: Supporting diverse learners in grades 2–5.* North Mankato, MN: Maupin House.

How to Access Downloadable Resources

Go to www.scholastic.com/phonicsintermediate and enter your email address and this code: **SC811348**.

PAGE	RESOURCE
50	RESOURCE 3.1: **Evaluation Checklist**
65	RESOURCE 3.2: **Word Ladder Template**
68	RESOURCE 3.3: **Sample High-Frequency Word Speed Drill**
68	RESOURCE 3.4: **High-Frequency Word Speed Drill Template**
69	RESOURCE 3.5: **The Most Frequent Words: Word Cards**
221	RESOURCE 4.1: **Decoding Big Words Strategy Reference Sheet**
223	RESOURCE 4.2: **Decoding Big Words Strategy Practice Sheet**
226	RESOURCE 4.3: **Sample Syllable Speed Drill**
226	RESOURCE 4.4: **Sample Consonant + *le* Words Speed Drill**
226	RESOURCE 4.5: **Closed Syllables: What's My Word?**
226	RESOURCE 4.6: **Consonant + *le* Syllables: What's My Word?**
227	RESOURCE 4.7: **Closed Syllables: Unscramble It!**
237	RESOURCE 4.8: **Sample High-Frequency Syllable Fluency Sheet (Syllables 1-10)**
237	RESOURCE 4.9: **High-Frequency Syllable Fluency Sheet Template**
237	RESOURCE 4.10: **High-Frequency Syllable Fluency Activity Sheet**
246	RESOURCE 4.11: **Prefix or Pretender?**
246	RESOURCE 4.12: **Prefixes: Connect-a-Word**
256	RESOURCE 4.13: **Suffixes: Build-a-Word**
274	RESOURCE 4.14: **Sample Greek Roots: Word Web**
274	RESOURCE 4.15: **Greek Roots: Word Web Template**